The Mayan Prophecies

Adrian G Gilbert, widely known from the BBC documentary *The Great Pyramid—Gateway to the Stars*, is co-author of the bestseller *The Orion Mystery* and has also written and published a number of other books.

Maurice M Cotterell is an internationally acclaimed writer, engineer, and independent scientist who has appeared on television and in the press both nationally and internationally.

The Mayan Prophecies

UNLOCKING THE SECRETS
OF A LOST CIVILIZATION

Adrian Gilbert
and
Maurice Cotterell

ELEMENT
Shaftesbury, Dorset ● Rockport, Massachusetts
Brisbane, Queensland

© Adrian Gilbert and Maurice Cotterell 1995

First published in Great Britain in 1995 by
Element Books Limited
Shaftesbury, Dorset SP7 8BP

Published in the USA in 1995 by
Element Books, Inc.
PO Box 830, Rockport, MA 01966

Published in Australia in 1995 by
Element Books Limited
for Jacaranda Wiley Limited
33 Park Road, Milton, Brisbane 4064

Cover illustration by Mark Topham
Cover design by Bridgewater Book Company
Text design by Roger Lightfoot
Illustrations by Countryside Illustrations and David Woodroffe

Typeset by WestKey Limited, Falmouth, Cornwall
Printed and bound in the U.S.A. by
Edwards Brothers, Inc.

British Library Cataloguing in Publication
data available

Library of Congress Cataloging in Publication
data available

ISBN 1–85230–692–0

To the people of Mexico

Past
Present
and To come

Picture credits

Thanks must go to the sources below for permission to reproduce the following illustrations:

2, 3, 4 Karl Taube, *Aztec and Maya Myths*, British Museum Press, 1993; 5, 6 B Harrison, *Mysterious Regions*, ABC; 7, 8, 9 Sylvanus Griswold Morley, *An Introduction to Maya Hieroglyphs*, Dover Publications, NY; 10 Sandy Huff, *The Mayan Calendar Made Easy*, 1984; 11 Jeff Mayo and Hans Eysenck, London Institute of Psychiatry; 13 Moore (ed) *The Atlas of the Solar System*, Mitchell Beazley; 14 Maurice Cotterell, *Astrogenetics*; 15 Iain Nicholson, *The Sun*, Mitchell Beazley; 16, 18 Moore (ed), *The Atlas of the Solar System*, Mitchell Beazley; 19 Moore (ed), *The Atlas of the Solar System*, Mitchell Beazley; 20 © John Baldock; 35 John L Stephens, *Incidents of Travel in Yucatan*, Dover Publications; 42, 43 José Diaz Bolio, *Why the Rattlesnake in Mayan Civilization*;.48, 49, 50, 51, 52 Adrian Gilbert; 54 Pearson, *Climate and Evolution*, The Academic Press, 1978; 55, 56 Maurice Cotterell; 57 Iain Nicholson, *The Sun*, Mitchell Beazley; 58, 59 Ronald Pearson, *Climate and Evolution*, The Academic Press, 1978; 61 John White, *Pole Shift*, ARE Press; 62 Adrian Gilbert

Plates 2, 5, 9, 10, 11, 12, 16, 17, 18, 19, 27, 28, 29, 32, 38, 39, 40 © Deirdre Gilbert; 37 © Jim Henderson; 20, 21, 22, 22a, 23, 24 © Maurice Cotterell

Appendix illustrations: 1, 2, 3, 4, 6, 7, 8, 10, 11, 12, 13, 14, 15, 16, 17, 19, 20, 21, 22, 26, 27, 28, 29, 30, 35, 36, 37, 38, 39, 40, 41, 42, 43, 44, 49, 58, 59, 60, 61, 62, 63, 64, 65, 66, 68, 71, 74, 76, 77, 78, 79, 80, 81, 82, 83, 84, 85, 86 © Maurice Cotterell; 9 Richard Knox, *The Book of Time*, David and Charles; 18 *The Sun* op. cit.; 24, 25 Price, Glickstein, Horton, Bailey, *The Principles of Psychology*, Rheinhart Winston, 1982; 32, 33 *The Atlas of the Solar System* op. cit.; 45 *Philips Universal Atlas*, Philip and Son; 46 *The Sun* op. cit.; 55, 56, 57 *An Introduction to Mayan Hieroglyphs* op. cit.; 67 after Hartung, Evan Hadingham, *Early Man and the Cosmos*, Heinemann; 47, 48, 69, 70, 80 Ronald Pearson, *Climate and Evolution*, The Academic Press, 1978; 70 H H Lamb, *Climate, Past, Present and Future*, Methuen & Co.; 72, 73 *Pole Shift* op. cit.

Appendix plates: 1, 2 after Hartung, Evan Hadingham, *Early Man and the Cosmos*, Heinemann; 3, 4, 5, 6, 7, 8, 9 © Maurice Cotterell

While every effort has been made to secure permissions, if there are any errors or oversights regarding copyright material, we apologize and will make suitable acknowledgement in any future edition.

Contents

Acknowledgements

... Thanks to Michael Mann, Chairman of Element Books, who proposed we get together to write the book; to John Baldock, who seems to have grasped the essence of *The Mayan Prophecies* in a remarkably short time and seamlessly edited it; and to everyone else at Element, without whose contribution this book would never have come into print. Finally, thanks to my wife, Dee Gilbert, who offered enormous encouragement and support, and who took many of the photographs.

Adrian Gilbert

By way of acknowledgement let me thank all those who paved the way for this remarkable story, among them, Jeff Mayo and Dr Hans Eysenck for their early work on astrological dispersion and personality observations; James Van Allen and fellow engineers and scientists at NASA who in 1962 engineered the *Mariner II* spacecraft, which in turn detected the sectored structure of the solar wind; to astronomer Iain Nicolson for his behavioural observations of solar wind interaction with the Earth; to Dr A R Lieboff of Oakland University USA for his work on magnetic fields and mutations in cells; and to Dr Ross Adey, White House Medical Advisor USA, for his dedication and work on the effects of magnetic fields on living organisms. Finally, special thanks to my wife, Ann Cotterell, for her hard work, encouragement and support.

Maurice Cotterell

Prologue

On the morning of 12 September 1993 I was sitting in the kitchen of my colleague, Robert Bauval, discussing final changes to our forthcoming book *The Orion Mystery*. We had been working closely together on this project for nearly a year and had just attended a conference with all of our publishers' sales staff. Elated by the reception we had received and yet exhausted by lack of sleep, we were doing our best to unwind over the Sunday papers. As I flicked through one or other of them, my eye was almost immediately caught by an article written by a Michael Robotham. Over pictures of a crumbling palace, a pyramid and a horrifying sculpture of a bat god 'HE HAS SOLVED A CENTURIES-OLD MYSTERY' was written in capitals. Below the palace and above another picture, this one showing a man like Indiana Jones emerging from the jungle and holding a stone slab towards the camera, was a banner headline: 'THE MAN WHO BROKE THE CODE OF MAYA CARVING'. By now not a little intrigued as to what this was all about, I pulled up a chair and settled down to read the article.

It turned out that the palace and pyramid shown in the pictures are located in a remote area of southwest Mexico at a place called Palenque. This was one of a number of cities built by the Maya, a highly gifted people yet one whose civilization suddenly collapsed at some time in the 9th century AD. Though their descendants continue to farm the hills further to the north, Palenque and their other low-lying cities were abandoned to the jungle, to be lost under a canopy of fast-growing climbers and trees. The man in the picture, the one who had apparently broken the 'Maya code', was a certain Maurice Cotterell and the stone slab he was holding out in front of him was a replica of a tomb lid found in the pyramid. I had heard before of this mysterious slab, the so-called 'Lid of Palenque', mainly connected with theories of gods from outer space. I was therefore somewhat surprised to discover that Cotterell was not putting forward any such wild speculations. His decoding of the lid seemed to be based on a much more scientific approach, analysing the lid in terms of Mayan mythology and certain ideas concerned with solar cycles. In the article he put forward a plausible case for why he thought the Mayan civilization had suddenly collapsed. This is something that is still a mystery, and his ideas seemed to be breaking new ground.

Reading the article I realized how little I knew about the Maya or indeed any of the pre-conquest civilizations of America. Like many other people I had, of course, seen documentaries concerning such mysteries as the Nazca lines of Peru but I did not have an overall picture of the succession of civilizations in Central America in the same way that I had for, say, Europe, Egypt or Mesopotamia. I had also not realized just how sophisticated the pyramids and temples of Mexico are. Having been to Egypt and visited the Great Pyramid, I tended to think of pyramids as either very large, geometrically simple buildings or collapsed rubble heaps. The pyramids of Mexico were different, more like Babylonian ziggurats or even Chinese pagodas than Egyptian pyramids. Yet like those of Egypt they were connected with a cult of the dead, and it now also seemed that they had some sort of symbolic significance linking them with a sky religion. This last connection I found particularly intriguing. Robert Bauval and I were on the point of publishing *The Orion Mystery*, presenting a new stellar theory for Egyptian pyramids. I was now keen to know if this man Cotterell could find similar connections with the Mexican pyramids. The newspaper article didn't go as far as to say this, but before putting down the paper I made a mental note to look into the matter when I had more time.

It was some months later, in May 1994, that I found myself driving down to Cornwall to meet Maurice Cotterell face to face for the first time. *The Orion Mystery* had been published the previous February accompanied by a BBC documentary entitled

The Great Pyramid—Gateway to the Stars featuring Robert Bauval and myself. Overnight the book had become a bestseller, in spite of strong opposition from some senior Egyptologists who were dismayed that we had effectively bypassed the slow-lane of academia. I had all but forgotten about the Lid of Palenque in the excitement surrounding both the launch of the book and the making of the documentary, when a mutual acquaintance showed me a digest of Cotterell's work. I was amazed at how wide-ranging and original his work was; he seemed to have researched not only Mexico and the Maya but many other subjects as well. I now had his telephone number and I decided to call him up. He was reluctant to say very much over the phone, but we arranged that I should come down for the weekend and spend as much time as needed to quietly go through this vast corpus of work. After driving down some narrow, winding, tree-lined lanes and passing through a narrow gate at right-angles to the steeply gradiented approach, I found myself standing before a quaint 18th-century farmhouse overlooking the River Tamar. I didn't have to knock, for Cotterell had heard my approach and opened the gate. It simply remained for us to introduce ourselves and to go inside for a cup of tea.

Maurice Cotterell is about 40 years old, though he looks somewhat younger. Lightly built and quick in speech and movements, his temperament is clearly mercurial. Clasping our cups of tea in our hands we immediately went upstairs to his office and, with the aid of a whiteboard and felt-tip pens, he set about explaining his theories to me. For some six hours he talked non-stop, occasionally rolling out a computer printout of a graph or demonstrating a point using a child's spinning top as a three-dimensional model. Yet as the hours rolled by it seemed like no time at all, so interesting and so novel were the facts he was presenting. Like a viewer engrossed in a movie plot, I wanted to hear more and yet was impatient to get to the end. At times our conversation would become deeply technical and I would be scratching my head trying to remember what I had learnt 25 years before concerning partial differentiation and wave mechanics. At other times we would be playing with acetate copies of the Lid of Palenque, laying them one on top of the other to produce bizarre images of gods and dragons. His work had two sides to it—the one rational and 'scientific', the other intuitive and 'artistic'—yet the two blended together and had definite points of reference one to the other. The patterns revealed on the acetates were not without their own logic and neither was the science without its own strange beauty. The two aspects of his work were like the faces of a coin or the hemispheres of the brain; they were two, yet one and the same. Even though they appeared different, at the centre of both series of studies was the same overwhelming and somewhat frightening subject: humanity's total dependence on sun cycles. The subject is overwhelming in the sense that just as one cannot look directly into the sun without going blind, so the more one studies the subject of solar cycles the more one realizes how blind we are on planet Earth to the realities governing our existence. It is frightening simply because of our ignorance.

My head spinning like a top, we emerged from his office to eat the very fine supper of local salmon prepared by his wife Ann. Over wine and dessert we confirmed what we had already decided, that we would write a book together making these ideas available to as wide an audience as possible. Having co-authored *The Orion Mystery* I was well aware of how difficult it is to get a proper airing for radically different ideas that challenge the scientific orthodoxies of archaeology. It is all too easy for a professor to use his authority to silence all academic debate over theories with which he disagrees. I was therefore not surprised to hear that Cotterell, like Bauval with whom I had also worked, had run into a brick wall of opposition with the academic world. His ideas on sunspot cycles alone deserved proper attention, yet responsible academic journals refused to publish his articles largely, one suspects, because he isn't an acknowledged 'expert' in their narrow sense. Yet, looked at in a different way, as the originator of these theories and the only person who as far as we know has studied the subject in this way, he is the world expert. Who, one asks, is the scientist? Is it the professor with strings of letters after his name who actually does nothing but sit behind his desk, or the outsider who actually comes up with original ideas?

Cotterell's ideas are radical and they are bound to be controversial. Yet they have a coherency of their own. His studies of the Lid of Palenque and sunspot cycles point to the need for a radical rethink not just about the history of Central America but our own possible fate. Today there is much fear over the thinning of the ozone layer, global warming, pollution, overpopulation and the exhausting of resources. But underneath this fear there is still a strong current of belief in the ability of modern civilization to ride the storm and overcome any temporary setbacks. Even those who believe such faith is unfounded and that we should do all we can to get back to a simpler lifestyle without the trappings of technological society have a view of humanity as somehow self-determined and self-determining. All our utopias presume that it is at least theoretically possible for humanity to live peacefully and in harmony with the planet—even if in practice we don't. Yet what if this is a fallacy? What if there are cosmic factors over which we do not have even a possibility of control? What if the rise and fall of civilization itself is governed, as Cotterell suggests, by the sun? Should we scoff, bury our heads in the sand or try to understand more about these influences?

The Maya were in possession of a complex and extremely accurate calendar. We are now able to decode at least some of their hieroglyphs, many of which turn out to be dates. What was of the greatest concern to the Maya was the sun and their belief in an apocalyptic future for humanity. It is easy to dismiss their concerns as simple superstitions but what if (as Cotterell's work would seem to suggest) they knew more about this subject than we do? We owe it both to ourselves and our children to do the best we can to resurrect this knowledge. At least then we may be prepared for global changes even if we cannot control them. This surely must be the responsible attitude of all true scientists, and I for one—though I take no credit for Maurice Cotterell's discoveries—want to know. We can but trust that you, the reader, feel the same way.

Adrian Gilbert

1

THE MYSTERIOUS MAYA

Lost in the jungles of Central America are the remains of a most mysterious people; the Maya. Who were they? Where did they come from? What message, if any, did they leave for our own times? These are some of the questions that have taxed explorers, scholars and writers for over 200 years since the ruins of their most famous city, Palenque,[1] were rediscovered in 1773. This amazing city, which is still not fully excavated and is constantly threatened by the encroaching jungle, is one of the wonders of the New World. Made out of resplendent white limestone and built with a perfection that would have done justice to Renaissance masons, its pyramids, temples and palaces continue to amaze all who see them. Yet it is only since the later part of the 20th century, as we have slowly deciphered the inscriptions that cover the walls of many of its most important buildings, that we have truly been able to appreciate this jewel.

The pattern that is emerging is of a people very different from ourselves. Unlike us the Maya had few personal possessions other than the bare necessities of life. They cultivated the earth using the simplest of tools to grow maize and a few other staples. Meanwhile their gorgeously attired rulers performed strange and painful rituals on themselves to ensure the fertility of the land. It was a stratified society, in which both rulers and peasants knew their place, but there was one great difference between it and the sort of Dark Age societies that were their contemporaries in Europe at the time: they were expert astronomers. They believed that they were living in the fifth age of the sun: that prior to the creation of modern men there had been four previous races and four previous ages. These had all been destroyed in great cataclysms, leaving few survivors to tell the tale. According to Mayan chronology, the present age started on 12 August 3114 BC and is to end on AD 22 December 2012. At that time the Earth as we know it is again to be destroyed by catastrophic earthquakes.

Many books have been published about the Maya, yet nobody has, until this time, been able to explain their remarkable calendar or what led them to these particular dates. Whereas a great deal has been written about the mechanics of their calendar (as dealt with in detail in later chapters), their reasons for developing such complex systems of marking time as the 'Long Count' have until now remained obscure. It is only now, as their alarm-clock is about to ring, that we are at last able to see what it was that drove them. We are beginning to understand that they had knowledge vital not only for their own time but for the very survival of the human race in our own.

Their civilization may have been primitive by our standards—they had no running water but the babbling brooks, no cars or roads and certainly no electronic computers—but they were richly endowed in other respects. Recent researches show that they developed their psychic faculties in ways that we have not even suspected are possible.[2] Like the Aborigines of Australia they made active use of dreaming as a way of foretelling the future and of understanding the present. They also followed the planets and stars with uncanny accuracy even though they had no telescopes or modern instruments. Above all they were deeply religious, believing, like many mediaeval Christians, in the need for mortification of the flesh and self-sacrifice if they were to gain entry into heaven.[3]

From their early beginnings at the dawn of time, through a brief golden age between around AD 600–800, to a post-Classic period lasting a few centuries more, they produced some of the world's greatest art. Then, as mysteriously as they had entered them, they disappeared from the pages of history. Because of some event, the nature of which is still unknown, their civilization collapsed and they abandoned their cities. A large part of the area where they had once lived, studied the stars and built fabulous pyramids, returned to jungle. As the Toltecs and later the Aztecs rose to power in the more northerly provinces surrounding present-day Mexico City, the surviving Maya retreated either to the hills in the south or to the plains of the Yucatan Peninsula in the north. The central area, which had been the site of their greatest flowering, was abandoned forever.

In 1511[4] the first of several Spanish expeditions landed in the Yucatan, trying without much success to find a source of gold. But by then even this peninsula, the last outpost of a hybrid Toltec-Mayan culture, had sunk into decadence. Though they were to abandon the conquest of Yucatan for the time being, the Spanish did learn of a much larger and better prey further to the north and west: the flourishing empire of the Aztecs. It would be a long time before anyone would again pay much attention to the lost knowledge of the Maya.

The Empire of Montezuma

The Aztecs were a warrior nation who arrived in the valley of Mexico during the 13th century AD (*see* Figure 1). Tradition states that they came from a place called Aztlan, believed to be in northern Mexico and from which the name Aztec is derived, though they called themselves Mexica. According to legends, which they related to later Spanish chroniclers, the Mexica were led to the valley of Mexico by a seer called Tenoch. He had been told in a dream that he and his people must continue their wandering until they came to a place that he would recognize when he saw an eagle fighting with a serpent. When they finally arrived in the Valley of Mexico, which at that time was still largely filled by a great lake, they discovered the surrounding land was already occupied by five other tribes. These peoples were naturally

4   The Mayan Prophecies

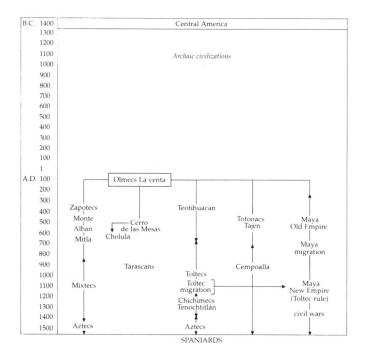

Figure 1   Accepted chronological table of the Indian empires of Central America

apprehensive at meeting the new arrivals and were not at all keen to give up their land. Conferring together they arrived at a solution to the problem: they would offer the Aztecs an uninhabited island in the middle of the lake, on which they could settle if they so pleased.

The offer of the island was a barbed gift, for the natives of the area knew that it was infested with poisonous snakes, which they hoped would take care of their Aztec problem for them. They were to be disappointed. When Tenoch and his followers went out to the island they saw the sign for which they had been seeking: a great eagle, grappling with a serpent in its beak, settled on a cactus. Delighted, he declared that this was the place that he had been told to look for in his dream. Nor were the Aztecs put off by the snakes, for where they came from these were considered to be a great delicacy. Thanking the natives for providing them with not only a home but a well-stocked larder too, they there and then accepted the offer of the island and began building a new city, called Tenochtitlan after its founder.

Within a very short time the Aztecs became the dominant tribe in the Valley of Mexico, uniting with their neighbours to form a powerful nation with Tenochtitlan as its capital. They in turn were assimilated by the peoples of the Valley of Mexico, who taught them much about local religious beliefs, customs and attitudes. In the main these ideas derived from the earlier Toltecs, another warlike people who centuries earlier had ruled over much of Mexico and even parts of the Yucatan.

The Toltecs, whose capital had been at a place called Tula, 25 kilometres to the northwest of Tenochtitlan, were a bloodthirsty race. As part of their solar religion they carried out human sacrifices on a regular basis. Using obsidian[5] knives, they cut open their victims' chests and tore out their still-beating hearts as an offering to the sun god. They believed that by doing this they were feeding it with its favourite food, human life-force, which would ensure that the sun would keep on rising.

The Aztecs—to what would have been the horror of Tenoch had he lived to see it—adopted these superstitious beliefs and customs, and took them to absurd limits. Human sacrifice, and especially the removal of hearts, became the central mystery of their religion. It is estimated that, for the consecration of Tenochtitlan's main temple alone, some 20,000 victims were sacrificed. At least 50,000 unfortunates would perish in this way every year. To supply the voracious appetite of the sun for human hearts there was a whole warrior caste, organized into regiments, whose task it was to keep the priests supplied with fresh victims. The Aztecs encouraged rebellion amongst the subjects of their far-flung empire, for this gave them the excuse to send in their army and take prisoners.

Needless to say they were greatly feared and hated by all the neighbouring peoples of Mexico, who seethed with resentment and longed for the overthrow of the hated Aztecs. Their one hope lay in a half-forgotten legend that one day a god-king, a white man with a beard named Quetzalcoatl, would return from across the

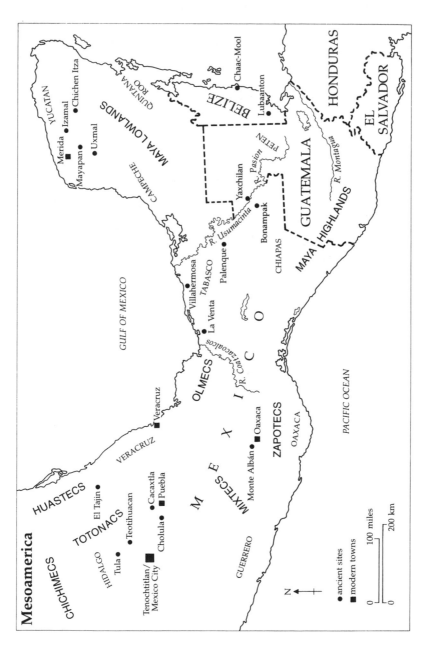

Figure 2   The territory of the Maya and neighbouring peoples

sea to free his people and reclaim his kingdom. Sword in hand, he would end Aztec dominance and usher in a new age of peace, prosperity and justice. As it had long ago been prophesied that Quetzalcoatl would return in a year named 1 Reed, it was with some trepidation that Montezuma II, King of the Aztecs, heard that men with beards and white faces had arrived in his kingdom in this very year.

The Conquest of Mexico

On 4 March 1519 Hernan Cortes, with 11 ships, 600 foot soldiers, 16 horses and some artillery landed on the coast of Mexico and immediately took possession of the town of Tabasco. Before going inland, he founded a new Spanish colony called Vera Cruz, promoted himself to the rank of Captain-General and then, so that there could be no possibility of retreat, burnt his ships. Hungry for gold and with new allies gathered from the native republic of Tlaxcala, he set out for the Aztec capital of Tenochtitlan. Thus began one of the most extraordinary adventures in the whole history of the world: for the Conquistadores were to destroy an empire of whose might they can have had little inkling when they first landed.

At first it was believed by both the Aztecs and their native enemies that the Spanish invader Cortes was indeed the god Quetzalcoatl,[6] whose return from the east had long been prophesied. God or not, Cortes came with a sword in his hand, and in a campaign lasting little more than two years he completely destroyed the Aztec empire. By 13 August 1521 Tenochtitlan was in his hands, Montezuma II was dead, and his successor, Cuahtemoc the last Emperor of the Aztecs, was his hostage.[7] Thus it was that one of the richest countries in the world, which had up until that time been totally unknown to Europeans, became a province of Spain.

When Cortes arrived in Tenochtitlan he was both amazed and appalled by what he saw. It was a large and vibrant metropolis with a culture all of its own. The city was built on the original island in the middle of the lake, and surrounding it was a network of canals giving access to a myriad of other artificial islands. On these, crops were grown: mainly the maize, chilli peppers and beans that are still the staples of Mexico today.

The city was huge in comparison with those Cortes had left behind in Europe, by some estimates having a population of 200,000. Though most of the houses were made of wattle-and-daub, the nobility and priests lived in magnificent palaces of stone. There were also open areas of the city in which markets were held. Here, as in any other civilized habitation, the people traded goods and services in exchange for food. At the centre of the city was a temple complex including buildings shaped like step-pyramids.[8] These were covered with brightly coloured stucco and at first glance must have been quite resplendent. However, an appalling stench lingered over these towering monuments, for it was here that the priests carried out the bloody rituals that were part and parcel of the Aztec religion. After the still-beating hearts of victims had been torn out and offered to the sun, the dead bodies were hurled down the steps of the pyramid. It was reported by the Spanish—though this may be a calumny—that the Aztecs were cannibals, and that at least some of the victims of these barbarous rituals ended up in the cooking-pot.

Whatever the truth of this last report, there can be no doubting that the Spaniards were deeply shocked by these rituals and hardened their hearts against both the city and its people. As far as the Spanish were concerned, all Indians were devil worshippers and needed to be converted to Christianity—forcibly, if necessary. Having defeated the Aztecs and taken Cuahtemoc captive, Cortes ordered the wholesale destruction of their capital so that the memory of its Satanic past would be erased. Tenochtitlan was razed to the ground, its palaces and temples dynamited so that the stone could be used to build new churches and villas for the conquerors. Meanwhile the natives were reduced to serfdom and put to the arduous task of reconstruction. In a short time the population was decimated through overwork, disease and casual slaughter. Under threat of death, the people of Mexico were forced to convert to Catholicism and to give up their old gods. They were forbidden to write in their own language, and had now to learn Spanish. All written records from the old days that could be found were destroyed. Idols and other large objects that could not easily be broken up, burnt or melted down were buried to remove their evil influence. Of the unspeakable acts of cruelty carried out by the Inquisition in the name of Christianity probably the less said the better. For rather like the Chinese who, following Mao's invasion of Tibet, set about robbing that country not only of its gold, silver and other precious metals but more importantly of its culture, so also did the Spaniards in Mexico. Fortunately there were one or two more enlightened individuals in the Church who did their best to record at least some of the native traditions before they perished completely.

Foremost among these was the Franciscan friar Bernardino de Sahagun. In 1529 he sailed to Mexico in the company of several Indians, who were being repatriated after having been paraded in Spain for the amusement of the court. From them he was able to learn Nahuatl,[9] their native language. He subsequently travelled throughout Mexico and during his long life acquired a vast store of folklore, which he recorded in 12 volumes. Seeking out the most learned of the surviving Indians and asking them to narrate the legends of their people as best they could remember, Sahagun was able to record much of their recent history prior to the conquest.

During the Spanish occupation, both Church and state actively discouraged scholars from publishing anything that might indicate that Mexico prior to the invasion of Cortes had any sort of civilization or history worth the title. It was Sahagun who discovered from his Indian friends that, on the contrary, prior to the Aztecs there had been an earlier race ruling the Valley of Mexico whom they referred to simply as 'Toltecs',[10] a name meaning 'artist' or 'builder', and which referred to their amazing skills in this respect. Their capital had been a fabled city called Tollan where, under the guidance of a divinely inspired leader called Quetzalcoatl,[11] they had developed their arts and crafts to a very high level. As I was later to discover, Quetzalcoatl was more than a folk-hero: he personified the goal and purposes of a very high and peaceable religion that at one time—long before the coming of the Spanish—held sway over most of Central America. Apparently the Toltecs were also skilled in astronomy, counting the days and keeping careful track of the movements of the planets. This golden age ended when in around AD 950 Quetzalcoatl was obliged to move on eastwards after a feud. Thereafter the valley had been invaded by a succession of less civilized tribes from the north, the last of which were the Aztecs themselves.[12] The Aztecs had preserved some of the knowledge of the earlier Toltecs, but much had been lost including, it seemed, the city of Tollan itself.

Sahagun believed that there must indeed have been a great civilization in Mexico before the Aztecs, and that it must have been centred, prior to the building of Tollan, on the abandoned city of Teotihuacan. This site, some 40 miles to the north of Mexico City, contains the impressive pyramids of the Sun and Moon, at that time hidden under mountains of earth. The Aztecs had inherited the belief from the Toltecs that Quetzalcoatl, who was revered as a god, would one day return to rule his people. They also believed that it was at Teotihuacan that Quetzalcoatl had sacrificed certain gods in order to make the sun move through the sky. Their seers and prophets told them that he would return to this, his ancestral city, and overthrow the Aztec empire.

Curiously enough it was on the site of Teotihuacan that Cortes and his men fought a crucial battle against the hordes of Montezuma. As in the rest of America, native weapons proved no match for the firearms and armour of the Europeans. Even so, the Spaniards were heavily outnumbered and should have been overwhelmed. Surrounded by many thousands of spear-wielding Indians, the Spaniards made a desperate attack and killed their opponents' military commander, 'Snake Woman'. At this evil omen many of the natives panicked and fled the field, thereby enabling Cortes and his remaining men to escape to fight another day. A year later he returned with a much larger army and captured the Aztec capital of Tenochtitlan.

Out of the ashes of this destruction was to rise Mexico City, capital of New Spain, the richest of all the King of Spain's possessions. Soon it was attracting immigrants by the thousand, nearly all male and mainly adventurers, missionaries and merchants. Mexico City was rebuilt as a glittering capital in the European style. Other cities, such as Guadalajara, Veracruz and Acapulco were built, initiating a new world of prosperity for the immigrants—though not for the indigenous Indians, who were treated very badly.

Sahagun researched deeply into this period of history and was shocked by the stories he heard. In his writings he toned down much of what the natives told him about the atrocities that followed the invasion, but even so he was not allowed to publish his work openly. His books were kept out of sight by an establishment that was trying to promote a positive image of the conquest. However, though his work was suppressed and eventually lost in its entirety, an incomplete copy of the manuscript did surface during the French invasion of Spain in 1808. This was eventually published in 1840.[13]

Travellers' tales

Very few foreigners, ie non-Spaniards, were allowed to enter Mexico prior to its gaining independence, and those who did get in were watched carefully. One of those who succeeded was a Neapolitan called Giovanni Careri. He arrived in Acapulco on the west coast in 1697 having endured a gruelling five-month cruise from Manila in the Philippines (then also a part of New Spain). Travelling extensively through the country, he was shocked to discover just how much of its wealth was in the hands of the Church. He did, however, make friends with a priest called Don Carlos de Sigüenza y Gongora, who had been expelled from the Jesuit order. He, having cultivated the friendship of the Indians, was in possession of a priceless collection of manuscripts and paintings that had escaped the mass burnings 150 years earlier. One of his friends was Don Juan de Alva, the son of a certain Fernando de Alva Cortes Ixtlilxochitl and a direct descendant of the kings of Texcoco. This Ixtlilxochitl was an educated man and had written the first-ever history of Mexico in Spanish. Sigüenza showed this to Careri, who was amazed to see that it spoke of an ancient Mexican calendar that had vanished at the time of the conquest. With the help of this calendar the Aztec priests had, so it was said, been able to keep an accurate chronology over very long periods of time. It was apparently based upon 52- and

104-year cycles, but also recorded solstices, equinoxes and the movements of the planet Venus.

Sigüenza had himself done much research into the chronology of ancient Mexico. As Professor of Mathematics at the University of Mexico and a keen astronomer, he was well qualified to carry out this research. Using the rare documents in his possession and making careful calculations for eclipses of the sun and moon as well as the movement of comets and other celestial bodies, he was able to reconstruct an Indian chronology. So accurate was this that he was even able to pin down specific dates, including the beginning of the Aztec empire and the founding of Tenochtitlan in 1325. He also concluded that before the rule of the legendary Toltecs there had been another race, the Olmecs[14] or 'rubber people', so called because they lived in the region of Mexico where rubber trees are indigenous. Sigüenza believed they had come from the mythical island of Atlantis, and that they were the race responsible for building the pyramids at Teotihuacan. He initiated Careri into this strange knowledge and the latter dutifully included the Atlantis theory as well as the material on the calendar in his own book, *Giro del Mondo*, which he wrote when he returned to Europe. It was just as well that Careri put pen to paper, for following Sigüenza's death the same year his priceless archive was either dispersed or destroyed by the Inquisition. His own manuscripts were acquired by the Jesuits, but these also were lost (they may still be buried in some library) when that order was itself thrown out of Mexico in 1767.

Because most Europeans were of the opinion that prior to the conquest the Mexican Indians were mere savages and hardly able to count to ten on their own fingers, Careri's report on the Aztec calendar in *Giro del Mondo* met with derision. His case was not helped by the fact that he was himself a poor mathematician and had not represented Sigüenza's arguments very well. However, he had at least recorded the idea of an Aztec Calendar Stone for posterity. Soon another explorer, who had read Careri, would arrive from Europe and more of Mexico's past would come to light.

Baron Friedrich Heinrich Alexander von Humboldt was a well-known figure in European literary and political circles, and a friend of Goethe, Schiller and Metternich. He had narrowly missed going to Egypt with Napoleon and his *savants* because the ship on which he was to have travelled had sunk in a storm. Instead he went to America to see what adventures fortune might bring him there. In 1803 he and several friends arrived in Acapulco from Equador with many of the latest scientific instruments, including surveying equipment and telescopes. After carrying out various surveys of the locale, they set out for Mexico City, passing through the silver-mining region of Taxco on the way. Although a Protestant, Humboldt was well received by the viceroy who unexpectedly gave him access to the country's classified archives. After going through these, he turned his attention to whatever remaining antiquities the city had to offer. One of these was a huge stone sun-wheel which had been unearthed only some 12 years earlier. This had been carefully examined by a historian called Leon y Gama who had spent a lifetime studying ancient Mexican documents and who, like Sigüenza, was fluent in Nahuatl, the native language. He recognized the stone as the legendary Aztec calendar mentioned by Ixtlilxochitl and Sigüenza. However, when he published a pamphlet on his findings to this effect he was ridiculed by the Spanish clergy who insisted the stone was a sacrificial altar, its intricate design simply decorative (*see* Figure 3).

Figure 3 The Aztec Calendar Stone

Humboldt, seeing the stone still propped up against the west wall of the cathedral near to where it had been found, agreed with Leon y Gama. As an astronomer it was clear to him that the stone had a calendrical meaning. To his trained eye the stone was evidence that the Aztecs did indeed have advanced knowledge of astronomy and must have had a quite sophisticated system of mathematics. He not only confirmed Leon y Gama's opinion that the eight radiating triangles from the centre represented divisions of the day, but also saw that many of the symbols used by the Aztecs to denote their 18-day months were the same as those used in East Asia. He concluded that the two zodiacs must have had a common source.

Travelling on to New York, where he visited a brother Mason, Thomas Jefferson, Humboldt set about the task of producing several large folios on his travels through the Americas. These, when they were published, were to amaze his European contemporaries. It seemed that at last a respectable figure, a man of science and standing, was challenging the accepted consensus that, prior to the conquest, the Mexicans were out-and-out savages.

As well as exploiting the country's mineral wealth, the Europeans were keen to develop it agriculturally. Because most of the land was unfit for arable farming, cattle rearing was the most profitable method of making use of it. However, this meant dispossessing the Indians of their traditional small-holdings. The consequent growth of large ranches added further discomfort to the already impoverished rural Indians. There was plenty of cause for discontent, and the French Revolution of 1789, with its clarion call for Liberty, Equality and Fraternity, was indirectly to act as a catalyst for change in Mexico as well as France. When Napoleon deposed the King of Spain and placed his own brother on the throne, it led many to question the legality of Spain's continued hold over Mexico. To the north the Mexicans already had the example of the United States to show them that a colony could throw off its European masters, so it was not long before they too were in open revolt. The Spanish were thrown out, and a long period of strife—the stuff of a thousand spaghetti Westerns that was to last for over a century—began.

One side-effect of Mexican independence was that it became much easier for foreigners other than Spaniards to enter the country. As a result, a number of intrepid explorers, including an Englishman, William Bullock, paid the country a visit. He sailed for Veracruz from Liverpool in 1822, retracing Humboldt's footsteps back to Mexico City. Like Humboldt he was greatly impressed by the Aztec Calendar Stone, which he believed must once have been part of the roof of the great temple of Tenochtitlan, rather like the famous Egyptian Zodiac of Denderah, then only recently removed to the Bibliothèque Nationale in Paris.[15] Having taken plaster-casts of the stone, he turned his attention to another antiquity which had been dug up by Humboldt and then hastily reburied by the authorities as too horrible to look at.

This was a massive, nine-foot-high, twelve-ton statue of Coatlicue, the mother goddess of the Nahuatl pantheon (*see* Figure 4). Bullock was to record: 'I had the pleasure of seeing the resurrection of this horrible deity, before whom tens of thousands of human victims had been sacrificed in the religious and sanguinary fervour of its infatuated worshippers.' Hewn out of a single block of basalt, and vaguely human in shape, the idol was frightening in the extreme. Its head comprised two serpents' heads facing one another; its arms likewise were serpents, as was its writhing drapery, entwined with the wings of a vulture. Its feet were those of a jaguar, claws extended as though ready to seize its prey. Hanging above its huge, deformed breasts was a sculpted necklace consisting of skulls, hearts, and severed hands all held together by entrails. Strange and terrifying as it was, this image of the goddess of life and death, with its strange echoes of the Hindu deity Kali, was wonderfully crafted. Whoever executed this extraordinary piece of art was clearly a master of sculpture on a par with the best of ancient Egypt, Europe or the Far East. Bullock realized that there was a strange dichotomy here, for how could a society at the level of sophistication needed to have produced such a superb piece as this have been so incredibly savage? Why on earth would civilized people have wanted to sacrifice human beings by the thousand to satisfy the bloodlust of a lifeless piece of stone, however wonderfully carved? The Mexican authorities of the early 19th century had no answers to these questions, and

Figure 4   Coatlicue, the earth goddess

so, rather than be constantly reminded of such uncomfortable
contradictions, they had the statue hastily reburied.

Bullock went on to visit Teotihuacan before returning to
London with an exotic collection of flora and fauna to add to his
plaster-casts of Coatlicue and the Calendar Stone, his models of
the pyramids of Sun and Moon, and other trophies. These were

put on display in his redesigned 'Egyptian Room' in Piccadilly, the Calendar Stone being nicknamed 'Montezuma's watch' by the ever-inventive British press. Apart from a few rare manuscripts and Humboldt's expensive illustrated folios, these were the first Mexican antiquities to be brought back to Europe to be appreciated for what they were, and not just their silver or gold content. Bullock, a jeweller and merchant, had other motives, however, that were not entirely philanthropic. He used the money raised by his London exhibition to purchase a silver mine in Mexico.

Discovery of the Maya

Surprisingly, for over two centuries after Cortes' invasion neither intellectuals nor adventurers paid much attention to the south of the country. Perhaps because of the hot, pestilential climate but more likely because of its lack of obvious mineral resources, they preferred to go north, pressing up into Florida, Texas, New Mexico and California—all of which were colonized by the Spanish before being ceded to the emergent United States. As a result southern Mexico remains to this day more purely Indian than any other part of the country, retaining many of its traditions and having separatist tendencies. As recently as 1994 there was a rebellion in Chiapas State against the central government of Mexico. The city of San Cristobal de las Casas was occupied by 'Zapatista' guerrillas, so named after the Mexican hero and freedom fighter Emiliano Zapata. Many people died and it was with some difficulty that the insurrection was put down by the army, the whole event proving extremely embarrassing to a government anxious to impress the World Bank that Mexico is a safe place in which to invest.

The people who carried out this rebellion were Cholan Maya,[16] descendants of a nation that had once produced the greatest of all the pre-Columbian civilizations in America. Little was known of this amazing past until in 1773 a canon of the cathedral town of Ciudad Real in Chiapas, Friar Ordoñez, got wind of a rumour that hidden in the jungle was a whole abandoned city of amazing proportions. In true colonial spirit, he had his parishioners carry him in a palanquin for nearly 70 miles to the presumed location of this lost city. There, completely overgrown with jungle vegetation, was a most astonishing sight, Palenque.

Overlooking the green floodplain of Usumacinta, this abandoned city with its pyramids, temples and palaces made of white limestone stands at the foot of a chain of low hills all covered in rain forest. Here brightly-coloured macaws and parrots fly over the treetops and the howl of monkeys can be heard in the distance. In this magnificent setting the Maya built their most impressive city, one which to this day contains many secrets and puzzles for archaeologists and historians alike. Father Ordoñez wrote of his findings in a monograph entitled *A History of the Creation of Heaven and Earth*. He attempted to explain the ruins, which he called the Great City of Serpents, in terms of local myths. He claimed that Palenque had been built by people who came from the Atlantic led by a man called Votan, whose symbol was the serpent.

This story of Votan had been contained in a Quiché Maya book burnt by the bishop of Chiapas, Nuñes de la Vega, in 1691. Fortunately the bishop had copied part of the book before committing it to the flames, and it was from this copy that Friar Ordoñez had obtained his story. According to the book, Votan had arrived in the Americas with a retinue of followers dressed in long robes. The natives had been friendly and submitted to his rule, the strangers marrying their daughters. Though he had burnt the original book, Bishop Nuñes was sufficiently interested in the story to take seriously a report in it that Votan had placed a secret treasure in a dark, subterranean house. Searching his whole diocese for this treasure he eventually found what he presumed was it, ordering its guardians to surrender what turned out to be no more than a few lidded clay jars, some green stones (probably jade) and some manuscripts. These last he promptly burnt in the marketplace along with Votan's book.

According to the copy that came into the hands of Friar Ordoñez, Votan made four trips backwards and forwards across the Atlantic to his old home called Valum Chivim. This the friar identified as the city of Tripoli in Phoenicia. The implication, then, was that Votan was a Phoenician sailor who had discovered the Americas perhaps two millennia or more before Columbus.

According to the legend, on at least one of his voyages back home Votan visited a great city where a temple was under construction that would reach to heaven, though it would be doomed to lead to a confusion of languages. Bishop Nuñes, writing in his own book *Constitutiones Diocesianos de Chiapas*, was sure that the city Votan must have visited was Babylon with its famous tower, given that the real tower of Babel was a ziggurat and that Babylon was the greatest city on Earth at the time of the sea-faring Phoenicians, this was a tempting idea. The ziggurats of Mesopotamia were stepped pyramids with crowning temples, and were very similar in design to the pyramids at Palenque, so this was not as fanciful a suggestion as it sounds.

Following Ordoñez's discovery, an official survey of the ruins was ordered and a captain of artillery, Don Antonio del Rio, was ordered to carry it out. He set teams of natives to work cutting back the jungle with machetes to reveal one extraordinary building after another. One of his assistants made drawings of the buildings and casts of the stucco reliefs, which were exceptionally beautiful. Del Rio thought the buildings might have been the work of the Romans and quoted other authorities who claimed that in ancient times North America had been visited by Egyptians, Greeks, Britons and others.

The report, sent back to Madrid, met with clerical opposition and was quietly buried in the archives. All was not quite lost, though, for a copy of it had been made and lodged in Guatemala City. This was edited by an Italian, Dr Paul Felix Cabrera, who in his own foreword concluded that Carthaginians must have gone to America before the First Punic War (264 BC) and interbred with native girls to produce the race of Olmecs. This amended version of del Rio's report eventually found its way to London and into the hands of a bookseller, Henry Berthoud. He had it translated and published it under the title *Description of the Ancient City Discovered Near Palenque*. This was the first published report on the ruins of Palenque, and as usual it took an outsider to get it into print.

In the years that followed, various other European adventurers made their way to Palenque to investigate the fabled ruins for themselves. Maximilien Waldeck, a former pupil of Jacques

David,[17] made fine engravings of the buildings. An American, John Stephens, and his English friend Frederick Catherwood, who had previously made sketches of rare antiquities in the Near East, set about measuring the temples and pyramids of Palenque. Working under the most appalling conditions, sick with malaria and under constant attack from ticks and flies, they made the first proper survey of the site. They were eventually to publish their findings along with many excellent illustrations in what was to become a bestseller of its time, *Incidents of Travel in Central America, Chiapas and Yucatan.*

Though Stephens and Catherwood had done much to bring Palenque and other ancient Mayan cities such as Copan, Quiché and Uxmal to the attention of the general public, without an understanding of the language of the Maya either written or spoken, their work could go only so far. What was needed was a scholar with the intellectual equipment to crack the code of the Maya language in the same way that Champollion had deciphered the Egyptian hieroglyphs.

Such a man was the Abbé Brasseur de Bourbourg. A Frenchman like Champollion, he set out for America in 1845, going first to New York before embarking for Mexico. There, through the influence of powerful friends, he was able to gain access to the archives of the viceroy and read for himself the history of the Aztecs by Ixtlilxochitl. He also made friends with a descendant of one of Montezuma's brothers, who taught him Nahuatl. Travelling all over the country in search of ancient texts, he was able to rescue a number of precious manuscripts then languishing in convents and libraries. Among these was the *Popol Vuh*, which he translated after first learning the local Mayan dialects of Cakchiquel and Quiché. This turned out to be one of the great epics of the world, a poetic Creation myth. Returning to Paris, he published it and then set to work on a much larger opus, his *Histoire des Nations Civilisées du Méxique et de l'Amérique Centrale.* By now he was well in with the Spanish authorities who allowed him access to their archives in Madrid. Here he found bishop Diego de Landa's original manuscript *Rélacion de las Cosas de Yucatan.* Because it contained drawings of the Mayan hieroglyphs relating to their calendar, he was able to decipher their language, at least in part.

Still in Madrid, he met up with a descendant of Hernan Cortes himself, a professor called Jean de Tro y Ortalano, who had in his possession a document (known as the *Troano Codex*) which had been in his family for generations. This 70-page document, later reunited with its other half, the 42-page *Cortesianus Codex*, and renamed the *Madrid Codex*, makes up the largest known surviving Mayan manuscript in the world. Perhaps naively Brasseur found support in this Mayan document for Atlantean myths that were talked of by the natives of Mesoamerica. He believed that a great island continent, Atlantis, had once extended from the Gulf of Mexico to the Canary Islands. The Maya, so he thought, were descended from survivors of a great cataclysm, or rather a series of cataclysms, which had engulfed that continent. He also put forward the revolutionary theory that civilization had begun in Atlantis and not in the Middle East as was generally supposed; that it was survivors of Atlantis who brought culture to Egypt as well as to Central America. These ideas were and still are not taken seriously by academics, but they did at least offer some explanation for certain puzzling similarities between Mayan and ancient Egyptian alphabets.

Other precious Mexican documents were copied and incorporated into nine oversized and lavishly illustrated volumes by another Englishman, Lord Kingsborough. He was convinced that the Maya were descended from the Lost Tribes of Israel,[18] and wrote long commentaries to this effect in his mammoth work. Interestingly, he produced an illustration from the *Codex Borgia* showing how the 20 day signs of the Mayan calendar (*see* Figure 3) corresponded to different parts of the human body, rather like mediaeval depictions of the 12 signs of the zodiac and their attributions. Commenting on this in his own book *Mysteries of the Mexican Pyramids* and for no apparent reason, Peter Tomkins[19] suggests this picture is connected with a theory that life-energy from the sun is diffused through the various planets to the glands in the human body over which they have control.

The first photographs of Mexican pyramids were taken by a Frenchman, Claude Charnay, working under the auspices of Napoleon III's Minister for Fine Arts, Viollet-le-Duc. Charnay later carried out excavations at Teotihuacan and made

papier-mâché mouldings of the reliefs at Palenque; these last were
sent back to Paris. He had a rival in the field in the form of an
Englishman employed by the colonial service, Alfred Maudsley.
Maudsley's meticulous survey of Maya ruins and their hieroglyphic texts was eventually published in a 20-volume edition
between 1889 and 1902.[20] With great difficulty he made plaster-of-
Paris moulds of the Mayan stelae, which he sent back to England,
where they were consigned to the basement of the Victoria and
Albert Museum, South Kensington, London. Presumably they
have been decaying there ever since.

The Lid of Palenque

As the 19th century gave way to the 20th, so the adventurers and
travellers who had till then had the field to themselves were
gradually superseded by a new breed of professional archaeologists. Though New World archaeology was, and still remains, a
poor relation of the European and Middle Eastern science, the veil
was slowly lifting from the cities of the Maya. Much of the jungle
around Palenque was cut back, fully revealing its monuments for
the first time since they had been abandoned more than a millennium before. The discovery of remains belonging to a culture
earlier than the Mayans', and most especially of huge basalt
heads, gave substance to the legend of the Olmecs as the earliest
civilized race in Central America. Modern excavation techniques
and a breakthrough in understanding of the Mayan calendar
made it possible to date monuments with precision so that by the
1950s there was a recognized chronology for the rise and fall of
Central American civilizations.

By that time various well-stocked tombs had been found by
archaeologists at Palenque, sometimes intruded into temple platforms and even palaces. However, these were as nothing compared to the discovery made by a Mexican archaeologist, Alberto
Ruz, in 1952.

Among the ruins at Palenque is a remarkable building known
as the Temple of Inscriptions (*see* Plates 1 and 2). This building,
which stands on top of a 65-metre-high stepped pyramid, has a

floor made out of large stone slabs. Ruz' attention was drawn to this floor when he noticed that one of these slabs had a double row of holes in its surface with removable stone stoppers. He decided these had been put there so that the stone could be lifted, which he then proceeded to do. On taking up the stone he discovered that underneath it was a rubble-filled staircase (*see* Plate 8). It took him four field seasons to clear this staircase, which changed direction halfway down, but at the bottom, at about the same level as the base of the pyramid, he found a chamber. Lying on the floor of this, underneath the rubble, were the skeletons of six young adults—almost certainly human sacrifices. At its far end was a passage, blocked by a large triangular slab (*see* Plate 7). On pulling this back the archaeologists were amazed to discover an intact tomb (*see* Plate 6).

The tomb chamber turned out to be quite large: 9 metres long and 7 metres high. Around its walls were stucco relief figures of men in very archaic costume that are now thought to represent the Nine Lords of the Night of Mayan theology. Lying on the floor were various objects, which seemed to have been placed there with a purpose: two jade figures and two beautifully moulded heads. However, what was of most immediate interest was the tomb itself. This was covered by a huge rectangular lid, intricately carved with highly stylized reliefs. Hauling back the lid, the researchers were stunned by what they found inside—a veritable treasure trove of Mayan artefacts. Covering the face of the now decayed corpse was an exquisite, mosaic jade mask (*see* Plate 3). The man in the tomb had jade and mother-of-pearl ear-spools, several necklaces of tubular jade beads, and jade rings on his fingers. A large jade was placed in each hand and another in his mouth—a very Chinese practice as well as Mayan and Aztec. Splendid as this treasure was—and the jade mask itself is the finest yet found—the more puzzling discovery was the lid of the coffin (*see* Plate 20).

The Lid of Palenque weighs some 5 tons and is too large to be removed from the tomb, where it resides to this day. It has received a great deal of attention from students and scholars anxious to interpret its mysterious designs. The most famous of these was the Swiss writer and extraterrestrialist, Erich von

Däniken. In his book *Chariots of the Gods* he put forward the hypothesis that the enigmatic figure in the centre of the lid represented a spaceman at the controls of his ship. Needless to say such a suggestion met with derision on the part of archaeologists working in the field. Though they were able to identify the man in the tomb as a highly respected king of Palenque called Sun Lord Pacal, who had died in AD 683 at the age of 80, there was nothing to suggest that he or anyone else in Mexico at that time had ever seen, still less controlled, a space ship! Like earlier theories linking the Mayans with Atlantis, ancient Egypt and the Lost Tribes of Israel, the god-is-a-Mayan-spaceman theories of von Däniken were consigned to the refuse-tip of fringe speculation. However, unwelcome as his ideas were to mainstream academia, they were in tune with the mood of the 1960s and his book became an international bestseller. Like it or not, Mexican archaeologists were faced with a public that was only too willing to go along with von Däniken's theories, and the Lid of Palenque became a totem representing all that he stood for. Little wonder then that they were on their guard when Maurice Cotterell was to come forward with another new yet controversial theory for the Lid on his visit to Mexico in 1992.

There is a great mystery surrounding the Maya and it is still unsolved. Where did they come from? Why did they build their monuments? How was it that they suddenly disappeared, leaving their fabulous cities to be consumed by the jungle? These are the pressing questions that have perplexed generations of explorers and visitors to Palenque and other Mayan cities. Archaeology has given us some of the answers, particularly in decoding the ancient Mayan calendar, but it has so far failed to explain the real motives of the Maya. In this it seems that the Lid is an important clue—and at last it seems that we are breaking its code.

2

MAYAN CONCEPTS OF TIME

Recovering the Mayan Calendar

That the wholesale destruction of ancient Mexico has done irrep-
arable damage cannot be doubted. So many archives, monuments
and even languages were lost during the early years of Spanish
rule that there is probably much that we will never know about
the culture of the ancient Maya. Even so, great strides have been
taken over the last couple of centuries, and a great deal has been
recovered from the ashes of history. The exploration and recording of Mayan ruins by dedicated amateurs such as Stephens,
Maudsley and Charnay was only part of it. Of equal interest and
of just as much importance has been the steady work of decipherment of the Mayan texts by other scholars. The first, and in many
ways the most important of these was the colourful character,
Charles Étienne Brasseur de Bourbourg. Now scorned by academics as something of a crank because of his belief in the former
existence of Atlantis, he was in fact extremely clever. In his own
time he was highly thought of in the best circles of European
society, and was even employed by the French government of
Napoleon III to write the text of a book on Yucatan. The engravings

to accompany Brasseur's text were to be supplied by Count Jean-Frederick Waldeck, who is also considered extremely suspect today on account of his 'diffusionist' opinions. He believed that the civilization of the Maya was not all home-grown, that knowledge had been brought to them from other lands by Chaldeans, Phoenicians and Hindus.

Waldeck must have been hardy for he spent a year studying and drawing the ruins at Palenque, including a period of four months living on site in a building still known as the House of the Count. There is no doubting that he was different: at the age of 100 he married a 17-year-old girl, attributing both his virility and longevity to a preparation of horse-radish that he consumed for six weeks every spring. He is also said to have died from a stroke after a pretty girl caught his eye as she walked down the street opposite the Paris café where he was sitting.

Though these stories continue to amuse his more starchy detractors, his published lithographs attract nothing but opprobrium for their obvious inaccuracies. His original working drawings, now contained in the Ayer Collection of the Newberry Library, Chicago, are of the highest quality, so it would seem more than likely that he embellished the finished lithographs to make them more appealing to a public that wanted the sort of romantic images contained in the famous *Description d'Egypte.*[1] He was not to know that later Mayanists would need scientifically accurate drawings to aid them in their attempts at deciphering Mayan texts. Even if he had, he would probably have replied that science was not his concern, he was an artist and more interested in capturing the spirit of what he saw.

Brasseur himself was born in France in 1814. He made an early career out of writing trashy novels before realizing, sometime in his late twenties, that if he was going to get anywhere in life he needed better connections. He accordingly entered the Church, not it seems out of any great religious feeling but rather as a method of self-advancement. In the 19th century an intelligent gentleman could, without too much difficulty, become an Abbé. This was a title which often had little to do with practising any kind of ministry yet still carried with it a certain religious cachet. It was especially suitable for men who wanted either to act as tutors to the children of the nobility or, like Brasseur, to ferret around in church archives. As we have seen, he was particularly adept at this, and not only discovered the *Popol Vuh* but in 1862 brought to light both an edited edition of Bishop Landa's *Rélacion de las Cosas de Yucatan* and the important Mayan Codices then called the *Troano* and *Cortesianus* now joined together as the *Madrid Codex*. The third great Mayan codex, the *Dresden*, was available to him in the form of the massive Kingsborough edition which had been published between 1831 and 1838.

Using the information concerning the Maya contained in the *Rélacion* Brasseur set about decoding all three Codices. Prior to his recovery of Landa's book, the greatest barrier to interpreting authentic Maya writings was that nobody had a clue as to what their peculiar hieroglyphs meant. It was assumed that because the Maya and other Indians were 'primitives', they were incapable of expressing complex ideas in the form of writing. However, Landa's work was to turn out to be the Rosetta Stone[2] of Mayan archaeology—and one can just imagine Brasseur's excitement when he realized that this might be so. It was still only 41 years since another Frenchman, Jean François Champollion, had published his first decipherment of Egyptian hieroglyphs by analysing the Rosetta Stone and Brasseur must have been hopeful that he could make a similar coup. It was by this time well known that

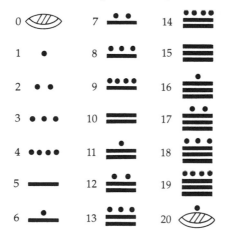

Figure 5 Mayan numbers

the Aztecs and Maya used two calendars, the first a repeating cycle of 260 days, called a *tzolkin*, and the second a 'vague year' of 365 days. Brasseur now found that in the *Rélacion* there was a table giving the names of the days in the *tzolkin*, of which there were 20, as well as those of the nineteen months in the vague year. However, there was more information than that, for alongside each name, written in Spanish, was the appropriate Mayan glyph. With excitement Brasseur realized that what he had before him was a calendrical lexicon, the key to Mayan time-keeping. He was now able to apply this to the texts contained in the Codices.

His first discovery—although unknown to him this had already been found out by another researcher, Constantine Rafinesque—was the way that the Maya used lines and dots to represent numbers. Individual digits up to 4 were represented by dots, and 5s were shown by lines. The number 6 was thus shown as a line with a dot, and 13 as two lines with three dots (*see* Figure 5).

2-MANIK, 67th day of the 260-day cycle which begins I-IMIX

Figure 6   Calculating the 260-day cycle

The workings of the two calendars and their interactions are actually quite simple once a few basic concepts have been grasped. The use of the *tzolkin* is of very great antiquity and seems to go back to at least the time of the Olmecs[3]; it is still used for magical purposes by some of the more remote Mayan tribes even today. Based on the counting together of 20 day names with the numbers 1 to 13, the calculation is not done in the same sequential manner

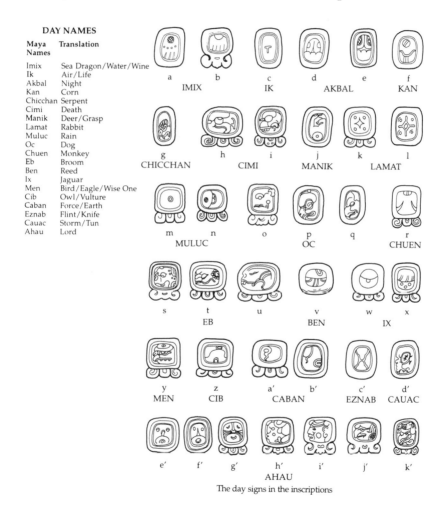

DAY NAMES

Maya Names	Translation
Imix	Sea Dragon/Water/Wine
Ik	Air/Life
Akbal	Night
Kan	Corn
Chicchan	Serpent
Cimi	Death
Manik	Deer/Grasp
Lamat	Rabbit
Muluc	Rain
Oc	Dog
Chuen	Monkey
Eb	Broom
Ben	Reed
Ix	Jaguar
Men	Bird/Eagle/Wise One
Cib	Owl/Vulture
Caban	Force/Earth
Eznab	Flint/Knife
Cauac	Storm/Tun
Ahau	Lord

a b c d e f
IMIX   IK   AKBAL   KAN

g h i j k l
CHICCHAN   CIMI   MANIK   LAMAT

m n o p q r
MULUC   OC   CHUEN

s t u v w x
EB   BEN   IX

y z a' b' c' d'
MEN CIB CABAN EZNAB CAUAC

e' f' g' h' i' j' k'
AHAU

The day signs in the inscriptions

Figure 7   Day names and symbols

as we count our Gregorian calendar with 30- or 31-day months, however, but by an entirely different method. An easy way to understand this is to imagine counting the number cycle against the names of our own months. We would begin 1 January as usual, but then instead of going on to 2 January, the next date would be 2 February. This would be followed by 3 March and so on up until 12 December, and then 13 January. The full cycle would be 156 days (12 × 13) and then we would be back to 1 January again (*see* Figure 6).

The names of the days were depicted with special hieroglyphs

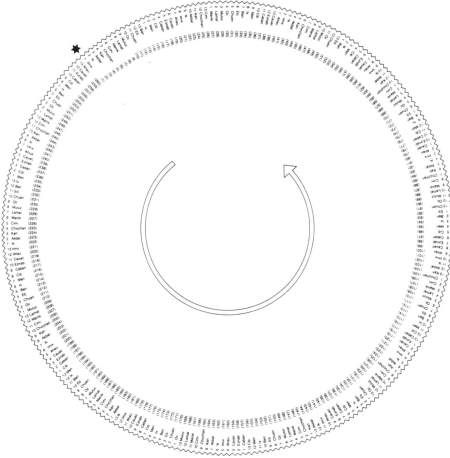

Figure 8   The 260-day Tzolkin *cycle*

(*see* Figure 7). Thus the cycle would go 1 Imix, 2 Ik, 3 Akbal ... 13 Ben, 1 Ix, 2 Men ... etc. The last day in the 260 count would be 13 Ahau, which would be followed by 1 Imix in the next count.

The entire cycle makes a wheel of its own (*see* Figure 8).

As has already been pointed out, the Maya also used a vague year, or *Haab*, of 365 days (ignoring the extra quarter day that gives rise to our leap years).[4] This year was composed of 360 days divided up into 18 months of 20 days' duration plus a short 'month' of 5 extra, and much dreaded, intercalary days.

The 20-day months and the short 5-day month also had their own name signs (*see* Figure 9). The last of these, Uayeb, was the short, intercalary month of only 5 days. The 20 days of these months were counted from zero (called the 'seating' of the month) to 19, and were numbered sequentially : Seating of Pop, 1 Pop, 2 Pop, 3 Pop ... 3 Uayeb, 4 Uayeb, and back to Seating of Pop.

The effect of having the two cycles, the *tzolkin* and the vague year, meant that each day had two names—one for each cycle, eg 3 Akbal 4 Cumhu. Because the two cycles were of different lengths, any specific dual combination of day names did not recur for 52 vague years or 73 *tzolkins* ($52 \times 365 = 18,980 = 73 \times 260$). This period of time is often referred to as the Aztec Century[5] or Calendar Round.

Now for most day-to-day purposes this way of recording dates is obviously fine. In any case, the principle concern of the Aztec priests—who continued to operate this calendar right up until the Spanish invasion—was magical. Certain days, particularly the five intercalary days of Uayeb, were considered unlucky. A person's date of birth also had enormous significance: it determined the course of the rest of his or her life, including name and career. But whereas the Calendar Round was quite adequate for recording dates in the recent past, it had obvious limitations. The Maya got round this by developing a second way of recording time called the 'Long Count'.[6]

The Mayan Long Count

One of the unique achievements of the Maya, which differentiates them from the later Aztecs, was their ability to manage their highly

HAAB

The 365-day year, or *haab.* was composed of 18 months (*uinals*) of 20 days each, to make a year of 360 days (18 x 20 = 360). Five 'unlucky' days, called Uayeb, were added to bring the year to 365 days.

The month names were:

1	Pop	11	Zac
2	Uo	12	Ceh
3	Zip	13	Mac
4	Zotz	14	Kankin
5	Tzec	15	Muan
6	Xul	16	Pax
7	Yaxkin	17	Kayab
8	Mol	18	Cumhu
9	Chen	19	Uayeb (5 days)
10	Yax		

Each had 20 days except the last which had only 5.

The month signs in the inscriptions

Figure 9   The Haab *or 365-day cycle*

sophisticated calendar. Today in the West we make use of the Gregorian Calendar (an updated version of the Julian) and all our dates are pegged to a specific event, the birth of Christ, in the notional year AD 0. All dates before this are BC and all dates after AD. Using our calendar we are able to give dates to any period or epoch in history, and to look forward to future epochs. So much a part of our daily lives has the Gregorian Calendar become that we tend to forget that it is neither the only one currently used in the world, nor was it used in the distant past. In Mesoamerica before the arrival of the Spaniards the Christian calendar was unknown. For them the beginning of the calendar was not the birth of Christ but another event far back in antiquity, the Birth of Venus. This had nothing to do with the beautiful goddess of European mythology but rather the 'first' rising (or Birth) of the planet Venus. The Maya were great astronomers and, as we shall see, the movements of Venus were followed closely, forming the basis of a complex calendrical system that stretched over thousands of years.

The breaking of the code of the Mayan Long Count calendar owes much to the work of a German librarian by the name of Ernst Förstemann. He was a native of Danzig who by 1867 was working in the library of Dresden. Nothing very unusual in this, one might think, but it just happened that the library was in possession of the most important of all Mayan documents—the *Dresden Codex*. In 1880 he started studying the Codex in earnest, beginning by making an extremely accurate facsimile. He only issued 60 sets of these, but it is just as well that he went to such trouble for the original was to be severely damaged by water when it was stored in a wine cellar during the Second World War.

Already in 1882 an American named Cyrus Thomas had adduced from a close study of a photograph of a partial inscription that Mayan numbers were to be read from left to right and top to bottom. Working with the *Dresden* and a copy of Landa's *Rélacion*, Förstemann was able to take this work further and fully elucidate the workings of the Mayan calendar. He discovered that they used a base-20 (vigesimal) system instead of a decimal one such as our own, and that they had recorded dates in the form of a Long Count which had as its inception a Calendar Round date of 4 Ahau 8 Cumhu thousands of years earlier.

To understand this—and it is important for what follows later in the book—it is necessary to grasp a few more simple concepts of Mayan time-keeping. As well as making use of the *tzolkin* of 260 days, the vague year of 365 days and the Calendar Round of 52 years, the Maya counted and added up individual days. With only a slight variation they used a vigesimal or base-20 system to do this, counting in units called uinals (pronounced *wee-nals*), tuns, baktuns and so on. At first sight this looks to be a very cumbersome system but really it isn't, once the idea of counting in 20s is grasped. The whole system worked like this:

20 kins (days) = 1 uinal   (20-day 'month')
18 uinals   = 1 tun   (360-day 'year')
20 tuns   = 1 katun   (7,200 days)
20 katuns   = 1 baktun (144,000 days)

On monuments such as stelae, Maya dates are inscribed in the form of a double column of hieroglyphs. These are read from left to right and top to bottom. The series starts with an introductory glyph and often ends with data referring to lunar cycles and to which of the Nine Lords of the Night was ruling at the time in question. In between these there is the date, expressed as the number of baktuns, katuns, tuns etc., plus the date according to the *tzolkin* (260-day count) and *Haab* (365-day year). Figure 10 shows a typical Long Count date as recorded on the so-called Leyden Plate. The full date reads: introductory glyph, 8 baktuns, 14 katuns, 3 tuns, 1 uinal, 12 kins; 1 Eb 0 Yaxkin.

In addition to rediscovering the Long Count system, Förstemann made other discoveries in the course of his researches on the *Dresden Codex*. He was able to show how it contained a Venus Table for calculating the movements of that planet in its cycle of approximately 584 days, and also lunar tables for calculating possible eclipses. In all he was able to demonstrate that what had appeared to be no more than a brightly painted relic of mere historical interest was in fact a work of genius. Little wonder then that the Indians had wailed pitifully when ignorant bishops consigned their writings to the bonfire. In doing so they were

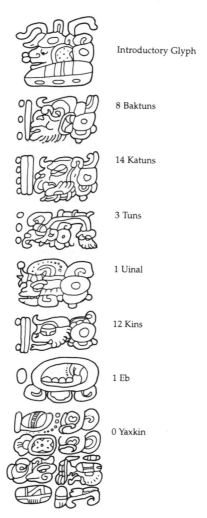

Introductory Glyph

8 Baktuns

14 Katuns

3 Tuns

1 Uinal

12 Kins

1 Eb

0 Yaxkin

Figure 10   Sample Mayan date from the Leyden Plate

destroying some of the greatest scientific creations that the human mind has ever achieved, and the records of hundreds of years of astronomical research.

In his researches carried out quietly in the corner of a German library far away from the jungle of Central America, Förstemann had undoubtedly found the most important key to the Mayan dating system—but even he hadn't quite broken the code. Though he was able to read Long Count dates in their own context of the *Dresden*, he was unable to link them to known dates in our own Gregorian Calendar. To do this more data was needed, and in particular more accurate renderings of date inscriptions as they are found on Mayan monuments. This final achievement, which would enable all Maya Long Counts to be translated into recognizable Gregorian dates, was to fall to other minds. Sporadic attempts were made at photographing inscribed Mayan monuments during the late 19th century, but this was not easy because they were scattered, often in inaccessible places, all over the jungle of Central America. It was not until Alfred Maudsley came along and carried out his detailed survey that a compendium of complete and accurate inscriptions was finally made available to other researchers. The publication between 1889 and 1902 of his *Archaeology* as an appendix to the five-volume *Biologia Centrali-Americana* proved to be another milestone in Mayan research. Now at last it was possible to compare a wide range of inscriptions with Landa's text and the data contained in the Codices.

Perhaps not surprisingly, but again to the dismay of modern Mayanists, the next great leap forward in our understanding of the Mayan calendar was brought about by the work of another eccentric outsider, Joseph T Goodman. He was an entrepreneur in the true American tradition who had become a professional journalist at an early age. By the time he was 23 he edited his own newspaper, the Virginia City *Territorial Enterprise*. Virginia City, near Reno in the state of Nevada, was a boom town. Gold had been found there in 1859, and the easy wealth that this produced meant that it quickly developed into an archetypal Wild West town. Goodman rode the wave, not only running the local newspaper (which incidentally gave Mark Twain his first writing job as a reporter) but dabbling in gold stocks. He was soon a wealthy man and was able to move from the frenetic get-rich-quick atmosphere if Virginia City to the relative calm of California. Here he started another newspaper, the *San Franciscan*, bought a raisin orchard in Fresno, and settled down to a new hobby: Maya studies.

By 1897 he was ready to publish the first results of his efforts, which went into an appendix to Maudsley's archaeological appendix in the monumental *Biologia Centrali-Americana*. Ignoring the prior claims of Förstemann, whose early work he must have been aware of, he claimed to have discovered the Long Count and the 4 Ahau 8 Cumhu starting-date for the calendar. Modern-day Mayanists such as Eric Thompson are convinced he did not have enough genuine material available to him to have worked this out on his own, and that he must have stolen the idea from Förstemann.

Be that as it may, he did make some other startling and very original contributions to Mayanology. The first of these was the discovery that the Maya used special 'head-code' glyphs as an alternative way of representing numbers to the bar and dot system. Just as we have alternative ways of writing numbers—as Arabic glyphs, Roman numerals or even tally marks—so also the Maya made use of more than one system in their Long Count dates. Of much greater significance, though, was an article he published in 1905 in a journal called *American Anthropologist*. Here, under the simple title 'Maya Dates', he presented ground-breaking work that at last made it possible to correlate Maya Long Count dates with dates in our own calendar.

Up until this time all Long Count dates, such as the hundreds written on temples, pyramids and other monuments, were 'free-floating'. That is to say, no one had been able to make the necessary link between Maya dates and our own calendar which would enable all the inscriptions to be dated according to the Gregorian system. From a close study of Landa's *Rélacion*, the Codices and various colonial records, Goodman made the connection that was eventually to allow other scholars to put together a full chronology for the Mayan civilization. Goodman's work on the Long Count was ignored for many years but in the end he was vindicated, and with a slight refinement of three days, his chronology was adopted by one of the most influential of all Mayanists, Eric Thompson.[7] He finally established, once and for all, that the end of the last Great Cycle and the start of the present corresponded to the Gregorian date of 13 August 3114 BC. As a Great Cycle was reckoned to last for 13 baktuns—ie 1,872,000 days—the end of the present age will come on AD 22 December 2012. There is not long to go, for we are living in the closing years of the present cycle.

Mayan Astronomy

The Maya, however, did not keep time only in a theoretical way, counting the days as they passed: they were also expert astronomers. As more and more of their cities have been rescued from the jungle and studied by archaeologists, it has been established that the orientation of temples and other buildings was of paramount importance. The Maya, as well as the other peoples of Central America, were very aware of the heavens around them and the movements of the planets. Often doorways or roof-combs,[8] which are a particular feature of classic Maya temples, were placed in such a way that they could mark the rising, culmination or setting of particular stars. They were especially interested in the movements of the Pleiades star-cluster as well as those of the wandering planets Mercury, Venus, Mars and Jupiter. Needless to say they made close observations of the sun and moon, and this enabled them to predict eclipses accurately.

Förstemann was the first to recognize that the *Dresden Codex* contained tables for the prediction of eclipses. Today we would use algebra but, as far as we know, the Maya did not do things in this way. They used a combination of observational astronomy and reference tables to make predictions for the future.[9] The tables in the *Dresden* not only had to provide the priests with information concerning expected eclipses but to harmonize with the all-important 260-day *tzolkin* cycle. Without going into too much detail, they did this by making their table have a length of 11,958 days, which corresponds closely to 46 *tzolkins* (11,960 days), before going back to the start. This exactly equals 405 lunar months, which is also 11,960 days. In fact so accurate was this table that it has been calculated that it gives an accuracy for the duration of a lunar month which is only seven minutes too short! It has also been worked out that another set of figures provide corrections to the first table, which would enable it to stay accurate to one day in 4,500 years. This is an astounding achievement.

Important as the prediction of eclipses no doubt was, however, of equal if not greater interest to the Maya was the behaviour of the planet Venus. Förstemann realized that five pages of the *Dresden* were given over to computations concerning Venus. It seems that the Maya were not so much concerned with the day-to-day movements of the planet but with its average cycle over long periods of time. Whereas the Venusian year can be as short as 581 or as long as 587 days, the average is 584. It was this number and its multiples that were of particular interest to the priests who devised the table. What has proved to be of even greater interest, though, is their inclusion of two dates which give rise to the so-called 'super-number' of the *Dresden Codex*. This is 1,366,560 days, and relates the start of the *Dresden Codex* back to the beginning of the present age, the Birth of Venus. It is highly significant because it relates, in integral terms, a whole range of important cycles.

In fact 1,366,560 =

$260 \times 5{,}256$　(number of *tzolkins*)
$365 \times 3{,}744$　(number of vague years)
$584 \times 2{,}340$　(number of average Venus cycles)
$780 \times 1{,}752$　(number of average Mars periods)
$18{,}980 \times 72$　(number of Calendar Rounds or Aztec Centuries)

It was this master number from the *Dresden Codex* that first got Maurice Cotterell interested in the Maya when he read about it, for it was very close to another significant number, 1,366,040 days, that he had arrived at from an entirely different route: the study of sunspot cycles. Could the two numbers—which differ only by exactly two 260-day periods—be related? This was to become a matter of major concern for him over the next few years, and his discoveries in this field were to be quite sensational. However, before going into this we need to backtrack, leaving the Maya for the time being, to see how Cotterell arrived at his own 'super-number' of 1,366,040 days.

3

A NEW SOLAR ASTROLOGY

Astrology is a subject that divides the world. The most ancient of all the sciences, it is seen by some as the very epitome of all that is worthy of human interest. Conversely, and perhaps in greater numbers, at least among scientists, there are its opponents who see in this study of supposed astral influences nothing more than blind superstition. Superstition or not, it has not been a purely European or even Eurasian obsession. It seems that all civilized societies have been interested in the movements of the stars, not least the Maya. The surviving Mayan Codices, such as the *Dresden*, are mainly taken up with astrological matters, such as calculations and prognostications for the 584-day cycle of Venus, in addition to tables for working out when to expect eclipses. It is now known that some Mayan buildings, such as the *Caracol* in Chichen Itza, were used as observatories, enabling priests to watch for the exact moment of rising and setting of planets, their interest being primarily astrological.[1] The sheer sophistication of Mayan methods for calculating the cycles of Venus, Mars and other planets is one of the many surprising features of this civilization. But it seems that at the root of their astrological concerns was human fertility.

That astrology itself should attract a degree of scepticism is not surprising given the wild and fanciful claims often made in its name. Are we really to believe that when Jupiter tracks through the sign of our birth it will bring good fortune? Conversely, is a conjunction of Saturn with one of the other planets in a natal horoscope really as challenging for the unfortunate subject as the textbooks claim? In astrology, science and mysticism have been so intertwined, and for so long, that to arrive at a simple conclusion one way or the other is no easy matter. What is clear to anyone who studies people is that it cannot be completely dismissed. There is, as they say, 'something in it'.

This was Maurice Cotterell's conclusion too when as a young communications officer in the Merchant Navy he spent months at a time away at sea. In the close confines of a ship he couldn't help but notice how the behaviour of at least some of his shipmates varied in accordance with astrologically ascribed traits. For example, he noticed that men born under the supposedly more aggressive 'fire' signs were indeed more aggressive. Their aggression additionally seemed to be cyclic, though it was not immediately obvious how this was linked to astrology. Intrigued and having some time on his hands, he decided as a matter of personal interest to make his own investigations into the subject. At home on shore leave, he went into his local library and took out all the books he could find that seemed to have any bearing on the subject. These included not only popular books on astronomy and astrology but others on such seemingly unconnected subjects as bee-keeping— the life cycle and behaviour of bees is after all closely linked to the sun. While searching through all this material he came across the results of a very interesting study carried out at the Institute of Psychiatry by astrologer Jeff Mayo[2] in co-operation with the renowned psychologist Professor Hans Eysenck.[3] On the basis of two scientifically-controlled studies carried out on 1795 and 2324 subjects respectively, they were able to show a correlation between astrological birth sign and extrovert/introvert tendencies (*see* Figure 11).

This could not be explained statistically for the odds against it were 10,000 to 1. As any astrologer might have predicted, there was a definite statistical tendency for people born under the so-called fire and air signs to be more extrovert, whereas those

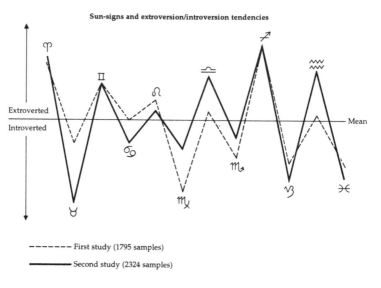

The above is the result of studies done by astrologer Jeff Mayo and the Institute of Psychiatry, under the aegis of Professor H. J. Eysenck. On the basis of two studies of 1795 subjects and 2324 subjects, it can be seen that the positive signs (Aries, Gemini, Leo, Libra, Sagittarius, Aquarius) are predominantly extrovert, and the alternating negative signs are predominantly introvert. The odds against these results happening by chance are 10,000 to 1. The mean is just above 13.50.

Figure 11   Mayo/Eysenck Diagram

born under the water and earth signs were introvert.[4] Because the 12 birth signs alternate in the order fire, earth, air and water, the year therefore divides itself up very neatly into alternating extrovert and introvert months (*see* Figure 12).

Cotterell was aware that because of precession (the slow, backwards shift of the equinoctial points on the sun's path through the sky) the signs of the zodiac no longer correspond in space to the constellations bearing the same names. Precessional changes mean that whereas at the time of ancient Greece the sun would physically have been in the constellation of Aries at the spring equinox, it is now framed by the stars of Pisces at this time. The fact that astrologers still call the first sign in spring Aries[5] and not Pisces is a convention that has not changed and is one of the reasons scientists dismiss astrology as a pseudo-science. Yet the Mayo/Eysenck data indicate that the seemingly misplaced astrological cycle of signs

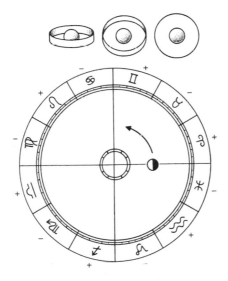

Figure 12   Alternating astrological birth signs

works—people born under the 'sign' of Aries show marked extrovert characteristics even though the sun is not in the actual constellation of Aries itself. There could be only one explanation for this:
what was important in astrology was not the starry background of
the zodiac, which in fact only acts as a clock-face, but some cycle
related to the sun itself. In other words *the root of astrology lay in solar
influence and the variations of the solar year.*

The question that confronted Cotterell now was, what could the
sun be doing that might cause people to be extrovert or introvert
according to the sign of the zodiac they were born under? As a
radio operator he was more aware than most of the way that radio
waves are affected by the state of the Earth's upper atmosphere,
and that this in turn is influenced by the sun. He also knew that at
times when there are many sunspots visible, radio signals are
distorted and much noise is generated, making reception difficult.
It seemed to him now that perhaps astrological effects could also
be somehow connected with these solar variations, but he had no
idea as to how this might come about.

Freckles on the Sun

As the most visible and familiar of all celestial bodies, the sun is something that we all take for granted. Yet how much do we really know about this the parent of our solar system, the body which for so many previous cultures was considered to be the father of the gods? The availability of modern telescopes and computers means that our knowledge concerning at least the outer skin of the sun has increased enormously over the last few years. Yet there is still much that we don't know and perhaps never will. Cotterell, having identified the sun, or rather some solar cycle, as the prime agent in determining astrological types, was now keen to see exactly what was responsible for the recorded effects. He had a hunch that it could be connected with sunspots, but he needed more data before he could be sure that this was so. He also needed to know more about the way they affect the Earth's magnetic field.

Sunspots are areas of relative coolness on the surface of the sun: they only look dark because the rest of the sun's surface is even hotter and brighter than they are. They were first identified in 1610 by Galileo, who used one of the earliest telescopes to observe them. He recognized that they were blemishes on the surface of the sun itself and not merely satellites passing in front of its disc. For unlike the planets Mercury and Venus, which also at times pass across the solar disc, they are not permanent features but are forever changing in both number and position on the sun's surface. Some spots last for only a few hours, others for months, but they all eventually disappear. They also vary in size, some of them being large enough to be seen with the naked eye.[6]

It has long been known that sunspots are not entirely random phenomena. In 1843 R Woolf established that there is a rhythm in the way that sunspots appear and disappear that seems to follow a cycle of roughly 11.1 years. At the beginning of the cycle, spots appear near the sun's poles. As it progresses, so they gradually manifest nearer and nearer the equator. Then, usually before the cycle finally peters out, more begin appearing near the poles. However, the cycle is not perfectly regular, and the maxima or peaks of sunspot activity are not all of equal intensity. There are also extreme minima such as between 1645 and 1715 when there were no spots at all.[7] At those times the dazzling sun presents a clean visage to the wider cosmos that surrounds it.

Causes of sunspots

For a long time astronomers and physicists alike were at a loss to explain sunspots. Whereas on the one hand their transient nature gave the impression of atmospheric phenomena like tornadoes, their periodicity suggested they were being driven by some deeper and unexplained mechanism inside the sun's core. Like the Earth the sun rotates on its own north-south axis. However, there is one crucial difference between the two bodies; whereas the Earth has a hard, rocky crust and therefore turns like a solid ball, the sun is composed of superheated plasma gas and does not rotate uniformly. In fact the sun rotates more slowly at its poles than it does at its equator, giving rise to a solar 'day' of 37 Earth days at the poles compared with only 26 at its equator.[8] Also, like the Earth and most other planets in the Solar System, the sun has a magnetic field. However, this is not a simple field like the Earth's but is more complex. There is still much that is mysterious about the sun's magnetic field but it is currently thought to have two components: a north-south dipole and an equitorial quadripole.

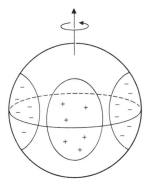

Model of magnetic structure
In these Schematic diagrams, the Sun's magnetic structure at the base of the corona is represented as consisting of two components: a pattern of alternating positive and negative polarities near the equator (left), and tilted dipole field at the poles (right). The two rotate at different rates, and their sum depends on their relative phase.

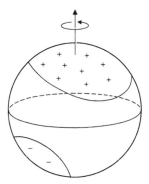

Figure 13   Solar magnetic fields

The north-south dipole field is somewhat similar in orientation to the Earth's magnetic field. The quadripole field looks like four 'bubbles' of magnetism spaced at regular intervals around the solar equator. These bubbles are of alternating polarity: the equivalent of the north and south poles of a magnet—except that there are four 'poles' instead of two (*see* Figure 13). Now because the sun's equator is turning faster than its poles, its magnetic flux lines get wound up into loops, rather like twisting spaghetti on a fork (*see* Figure 14). This has the effect of causing small areas of intense magnetism below the sun's surface. It is thought that the magnetic

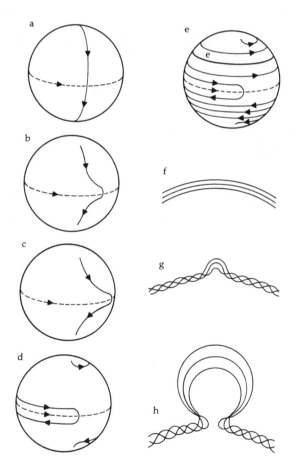

Figure 14   Twisting of solar magnetic flux

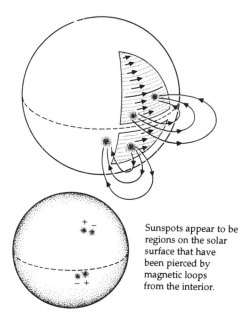

Sunspots appear to be regions on the solar surface that have been pierced by magnetic loops from the interior.

Figure 15   Sunspot loops

loops eventually burst out of the surface and thereby give rise to the familiar sunspots[9] (*see* Figure 15).

Cotterell was now beginning to suspect that these variations in the sun's magnetism were responsible for astrological differences between people, and he therefore made them the focus of his studies. The question was, what could possibly be the mechanism for such effects?

Winds from the Sun

Our knowledge of the Solar System has increased by leaps and bounds since we have been able to send spacecraft out beyond the Earth's atmosphere. Yet it is easy to forget that it is only as recently as the 1960s that it has been possible for us to observe the Solar System from a perspective other than our own planet's surface. It is only now, at the end of the 20th century, that we are able to go beyond our atmosphere and experience space not as some imaginary region but for real. What we have discovered is that far from being the near-perfect vacuum that it was assumed to be even a few years ago, it is filled with radiations, gases and dust particles. True, this matter is widely dispersed, but it is now recognized that there is more of this invisible or 'black' matter in the universe than that contained in all of the visible stars and planets. It now appears that these latter are merely bodies of highly condensed matter floating in a sea of thin, attenuated gas. This is in fact much closer to the ancient belief that space is like a vast ocean through which the Earth swims like a turtle than the isolationist vacuum theories of the last century.

Our family of planets, in a very real sense, lives within the aura

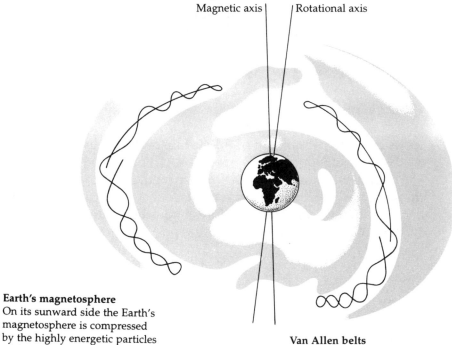

Magnetic axis | Rotational axis

Earth's magnetosphere
On its sunward side the Earth's magnetosphere is compressed by the highly energetic particles of the solar wind, which collide with the earth's magnetic field. On the opposite side, the 'magnetotail' stretches far out into space.

Van Allen belts
The Earth is encircled by zones of radiation known as 'Van Allen belts', in which charged particles spiral to and fro, trapped by the Earth's magnetic field: the belts are therefore inclined at an angle to the Earth's rotational axis.

Figure 16   The magnetosphere and Van Allen belts

of the sun. Our parent star not only gives out visible light but radiates throughout the electromagnetic spectrum. Its emanations include radio, infra-red, visible, ultraviolet and X-rays. In addition to these types of rays, it also projects matter into space as the so-called solar wind. This is a stream of charged particles, ions, that are constantly thrown off its surface into space, particularly from prominences and flares. Though this 'wind' is very thin and attenuated compared with movements of our much denser atmosphere on Earth, it is nonetheless extremely significant. It is the reason, for example, that the tails of comets always point away from the sun, like inflated windsocks. However, it is not only comets that are affected by the solar wind but our planet as well. Stretching around the Earth and containing its atmosphere like an envelope is what is called the magnetosphere. This extends into space and contains two zones within it, called, after their discoverer, the Van Allen Belts[10] (*see* Figure 16). Where the solar wind hits the magnetosphere it distorts it, giving rise to a bow-shockwave.

The type and charge of particles that the sun throws off as the solar wind varies, but in the main they are either electrons, like the cathode rays inside a television set, or they are protons, positively-charged hydrogen nuclei.[11] If we imagine a cross-sectional view of the sun at its equator, we see the four bubbles of its quadripole

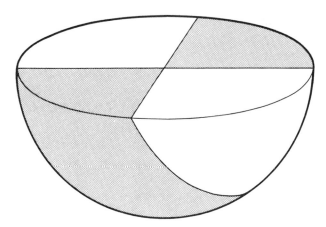

Figure 17   Cross-sectional view of the sun's equatorial magnetic field

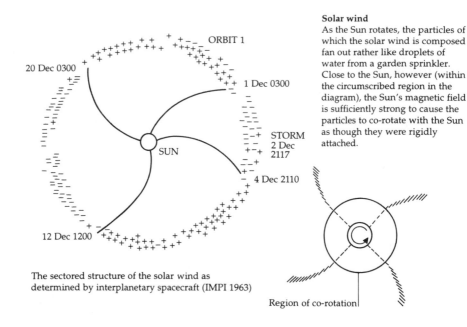

The sectored structure of the solar wind as
determined by interplanetary spacecraft (IMPI 1963)

Solar wind
As the Sun rotates, the particles of which the solar wind is composed fan out rather like droplets of water from a garden sprinkler. Close to the Sun, however (within the circumscribed region in the diagram), the Sun's magnetic field is sufficiently strong to cause the particles to co-rotate with the Sun as though they were rigidly attached.

Region of co-rotation

Figure 18   *The sun throwing off particles like a garden sprinkler*

field (*see* Figure 17). As it spins on its axis, so it throws off charged particles into space, but the nature of these particles and their polarity at any given point in space around the equator of the sun is determined by the magnetic polarity of the bubble in that region. The particles carried on the solar wind from regions of negative polarity are negatively charged (electrons), while those from positively-charged regions are positively charged (mainly protons). The net result is that, rather like a garden sprinkler, the sun throws out particles in all directions, but these are of differing types depending on the source of emission (*see* Figure 18). Data sent back by an interplanetary spacecraft (IMP1 1963) has shown that this is indeed the case.

Besides causing a bow-shockwave when it hits the Earth's magnetosphere, the solar wind is responsible for other, more dramatic phenomena. Many of the charged particles come streaming in through the skin of the Earth's magnetosphere and are trapped in the Van Allen Belts. There they are then accelerated downwards and towards the poles by the Earth's own magnetic field. The result is that they come crashing through the upper atmosphere and, as they do so, produce the bright illuminations known as the Aurora Borealis or Northern Lights (*see* Plate 25).

The solar wind not only gives rise to aurorae but can at times produce much more serious and frightening effects. An example of this happened in 1989. A report from the Geological Survey Group in Edinburgh shows how, in January and February of that year, activity began to increase sporadically over the entire solar disc. On 5 March at 13.54 GMT a massive X-ray flare, lasting for 137 minutes, erupted from the sun's surface. It was believed to be the largest such event this century, and it overloaded the sensors on the equipment being used by the scientists to monitor it. In the region where the flare had occurred a cluster of sunspots could clearly be seen—evidence of a connection between the event and the sun's magnetic behaviour. On 8 March a solar proton event began, and a large quantity of these ions began to flow to the Earth on the solar wind, the activity continuing until 13 March. The arrival of this stream of charged particles, the nuclei of hydrogen atoms, was to have a profound effect on the Earth's own magnetic field. In fact the change in flux was the biggest seen since 1952, and gave rise to a violent magnetic storm. Monitors at the Lerwick laboratory in the Shetland Islands registered a large deviation in terrestrial magnetism of 8 degrees within the space of a few hours. This compares with a normal deviation of only about 0.2 degrees per hour. The intensity of the storm was such that the Aurora Borealis could be seen clearly in southern England. Indeed, reports of similar sightings came pouring in from as far south as Italy and even Jamaica. The rapid changes in the Earth's magnetic field also produced huge surges in power lines, telephone lines and cable networks. In Canada more than a million people were left without electricity as parts of the power grid went down following the overloading of transformers. The Earth's ionosphere, a region itself composed of charged particles and against which radio waves are normally bounced, was totally disrupted making communication by this medium impossible. The background noise also meant that satellite communications were badly affected. So intense was the radiation that astronauts on board the space shuttle *Discovery* were prevented from working outside their capsule. In the end their mission was aborted a day early because of a computer malfunction thought to have been caused by the storm. Even under the blanket of the higher atmosphere there were dangers. A Concorde airliner had to be diverted southwards to avoid subjecting its crew and passengers to the risk of unnecessary radiation. All in all, this one flare—by no means a spectacular event in solar terms—had caused havoc on Earth.

Astrogenetics

Back in 1986 this event was still in the future but Cotterell was already putting together a new theory that linked astrology with solar behaviour. He was convinced that astrological differences between people were caused by variations in the solar wind affecting the Earth's magnetic field, which in turn influenced the future development of a foetus at conception. In other words, a newly fertilized human egg was stamped at conception with the pattern of the prevailing magnetic atmosphere, and this determined its astrological type at birth. This 'conception' theory was radically different from that held by most astrologers who believe that occult planetary and stellar influences at *birth* are what are important. Nevertheless Cotterell was convinced that he was right in this matter and began writing a book on the subject. His findings are summarized in Appendices 1 and 2 but can be read in more detail in his book *Astrogenetics.*

By the middle of the year he had *Astrogenetics* ready in its first draft and sent it out to various leading authorities on astronomy and astrology, hoping either to get some favourable comments or, failing that, at least some positive feedback concerning his theory. Sadly, most of the people he wrote to didn't reply and he could only assume that they either totally disagreed with his findings or were not interested in the thesis. Undeterred, he learned of a forthcoming International Conference on Astrology that was to be hosted by the British Astrological Society at the Royal Free Hospital in London. Informed of his years of research, they agreed that he should come along and tell delegates of his discoveries. True, he would have only ten minutes before lunch to describe two years of work, yet this was better than nothing and it would at last provide an opportunity to give the whole subject a public airing.

As it turned out he was not to be disappointed. Predictably, most of the gathered astrologers were less than pleased with his theory that the time of conception, not birth, was what mattered. To accept such a proposal would mean that the very foundations of their science would have to be changed. Not only that but a significant proportion of their would-be clients have no knowledge of their exact time and place of birth even if they know the date. How many people could be expected to know where or when they were conceived? Even assuming their parents could tell them when the likely act of intercourse that resulted in pregnancy took place, this would still not pinpoint the moment of conception, which could have happened hours or even days later. Given such practical considerations, it was to be expected that his ideas would get only a lukewarm reception at best. However, all was not entirely lost for astrologers were not the only people listening to the lecture. In their midst were members of another profession— journalists. When the event came to be reported the next day in the papers, it was Cotterell's new theory that was given the most attention. In the course of a long article, Diana Hutchinson of the *Daily Mail* called him 'The wizard who gets astrologers seeing stars' and went on to say that he '... seems to prove there is a scientific basis for astrology'.[12] This was followed by radio interviews on BBC World Service, BFPO,[13] and an hour-long phone-in on LBC.[14] At last the subject of sunspots, the solar wind and its effect on human genetics was getting a public airing.

This, however, was to turn out to be only the beginning. Two years later, in 1988, he pulled the whole theory together and published it under the title *Astrogenetics—The New Theory*. Though such magazines as *Nature* refused to review it, the thesis did receive praise from certain more open-minded academics.[15] Meanwhile Cotterell had changed his job and was now working at Cranfield Institute of Technology (now Cranfield University). This was most fortuitous for it offered him a golden opportunity to make use of one of the most powerful computers in the country. On the university's computer, he used a dedicated algorithm to plot the behaviour and interactions of the three magnetic variables involved in the Earth's rotation around the sun. This had never before been successfully accomplished owing to the complexities of the equations involved in synthesizing the three changing variables: the sun's polar field (37 days), its equatorial field (26 days) and the Earth's orbital velocity around the sun (365.25 days). To simplify matters, he used an equation based on snapshots of the sun's and the Earth's combined magnetic field every 87.4545 days. This was done because every 87.4545 days the sun's polar and equatorial fields complete a mutual cycle and, as it were, come back to zero. The computer plugged away at its sums for several hours before eventually spewing forth its vital data in the form of a graph. What came out was sensational. In a long printout of jagged peaks and troughs, looking like some erratic heartbeat, a rhythmic cycle could clearly be seen. This graph of interaction had the fingerprints of whatever it is that drives sunspots—for what could clearly be traced was an 11.49-year cycle marking periods of intense activity. This, however, was not everything. There were clearly other cycles implied by the graphs, spanning much longer periods of time.

Long days of the sun

Cotterell pored over the computer printout for months, unravelling what was to turn out to be his most important discovery to date. The data, in its raw state, represented the relative angles of the sun's and Earth's magnetic fields taken as snapshots at 87.4545-day intervals. However, it was at first far from clear what the graph meant.

The visual record of sunspots as seen by astronomers seems to point to a cycle of 11.1 years. Cotterell was now able to find evidence for this cycle in his computer-generated data. Each 87.4545-day portion of time he now, for simplicity's sake, called a *bit*. A period of 8 of these bits, or 8 × 87.4545 days (ie almost 700 days) seemed to be very significant; this he now called a *microcycle*. Six of these microcycles (ie 48 bits) made a longer cycle of 11.49299 years. This was uncannily similar to the average observed sunspot cycle of 11.1 years. At last he seemed to be finding the correlation for which he had been seeking.

Looking more closely at the data he noticed that there was a cycle of 781 bits of time before the graph repeated itself. This period of 68,302 days (or 187 years) he called the *Sunspot cycle*. This long period was the equivalent of 97 microcycles, but careful analysis of the data showed that whereas 92 of these were indeed of 8 bits in duration, 5 were longer, at 9 bits; they seemed to contain an extra *shift bit*. This suggested that though the true cycle should theoretically be only 776 bits long, in practice the sunspot cycle was pushed forwards by 5 bits. At first this anomalous behaviour was very puzzling. What could be causing it? Going back to his textbooks and studying again the figure of the solar magnetic field, it became obvious that somehow it involved what is known as the sun's *warped neutral sheet*. Just like any other magnet, the sun has an area around its equator where the two polar magnetic fields are exactly balanced so that neither north nor south poles predominate. The result is a thin, neutral sheet, or interface, between the two magnetic zones radiating out into space. However, the textbooks were all agreed that because of the complex nature of the sun's magnetic field, this sheet is not exactly smooth: it is kinked (*see* Figure 19). It seemed that the neutral sheet shifts by one bit every 187 years and that a particular shift bit would therefore shunt along through the whole sequence of 97 microcycles in a period of 97 × 187 or 18,139 years.

This great period of magnetic interaction between the sun and Earth seemed to be the most important of all. It was, however, divided up unequally into three periods of 19 sunspot cycles and two of 20, making 97 in all. It seemed that each time one of these periods came to an end, so the sun's magnetic field reversed. At last Cotterell seemed to have hit on what he was later to see might have been some very ancient knowledge.

Once more Cotterell tried to bring his ideas to the attention of the scientific establishment, but again he was rebuffed. The magazine *Nature* refused to publish an article outlining his new theories on sunspot cycles. When he wrote to the Royal Astronomical Society to see if a paper on the subject could be included in their quarterly journal, again he was refused. They gave as their reason

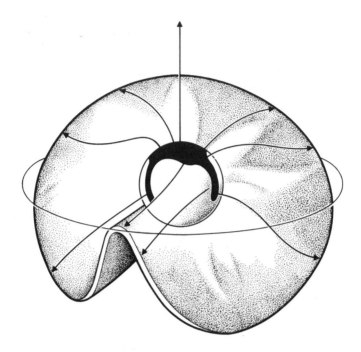

Figure 19 The sun's warped neutral sheet

that not enough was known of the true shape of the sun's magnetic field to construct a working model, and therefore his theories were invalid. However, since the data that Cotterell was working with and which he had used as the basis for his arguments had in fact come from them in the first place, this seemed a lame excuse. Of course the sun's field and the shape of the warped neutral sheet are more complex than the idealized forms given in textbooks, but one has to start somewhere and science is full of assumptions and simplifications without which no progress in knowledge could be made. If these journals were truly the open organs of modern research that they claimed to be, then surely they would want to present these new ideas to a wide audience and encourage the sort of debate that could lead to further elucidation. Reading their curt replies he couldn't help but wonder whether their real reason for rejecting his articles was nothing to do with his science but that he wasn't an acknowledged astronomical academic. Undeterred, he pressed on with his researches, which now took on a new and unexpected direction.

Sunspots and the Maya

Cotterell had come a long way now from his initial studies of astrology and the solar wind. What had begun as a relatively simple theory concerning human behaviour had broadened out into a much larger study of the mechanics behind the sunspot cycle. He had had no idea at the start of all of his researches that this would be the outcome, but he now seemed to have stumbled upon something far more exciting, though perhaps rather worrying. To summarize, the time periods of the sun that seemed to matter were:

a) 87.4545 days (1 bit) = the period of time the sun's two magnetic fields take to come back to their starting positions relative to one another;

b) 8 bits = 699.64 days (1 microcycle);

c) 48 bits = 4197.81 days = 11.49299 years;

d) 781 bits = 68,302 days or 187 years (1 sunspot cycle);

e) 97 × 68,302 days = 18,139 years (1 complete cycle of the warped neutral sheet).

This last period and its subdivisions now interested him more and more. Breaking it down into its constituent parts he could see that there were five time periods included in it which corresponded with changes in polarity of the sun's magnetic field and the shifting of the warped neutral sheet. These were given by:

1) 19 × 187 years = 1,297,738 days
2) 20 × 187 years = 1,366,040 days
3) 19 × 187 years = 1,297,738 days
4) 19 × 187 years = 1,297,738 days
5) 20 × 187 years = 1,366,040 days

It was this last period of 1,366,040 days that was in Cotterell's mind when he first read about the Mayan super-number of 1,366,560 days recorded in the *Dresden Codex*. It seemed too similar to be a coincidence. What is more, his division of the greater period of reversals of the sun's polarity seemed to mirror the Mayan conception of earlier ages. They, like his data, indicated that there had been four earlier ages before our own. It seemed that what they were indeed talking about was the shifting or reversal of the sun's magnetic field. Could this be the mechanism behind the collapse of one age and the start of another?

Reading further in a book called *Early Man and the Cosmos*,[16] he came across a curious reference to another Mayan number, 1,359,540. This 'lucky number', which is rather similar to that contained in the *Dresden*, refers to the inauguration date of the Temple of the Cross at Palenque.[17] Like the *Dresden* 'super-number' it can be divided by no fewer than seven calendrical or planetary cycles, indicating that it had more of a ritual than calendrical significance. Realizing that this could be an important clue to the connection between his own sunspot numbers and the Mayan calendar, he decided that he would go and investigate the matter for himself. Now in no doubt that he was on to something, he made the necessary arrangements and booked a trip to Mexico. It was to be a journey that would change his life.

4

MAURICE COTTERELL IN MEXICO

A Mexican adventure

Mexico City today is a thriving, bustling metropolis with a population that according to some estimates exceeds 25 million. This makes it the largest city in the world, more than double the size of London or New York, yet with a fraction of their infrastructure. It is still a city of contrasts, for though its centre is rapidly being transformed with shiny new skyscrapers, it is ringed round with squatter camps. To cope with the never-ending flood of poverty-stricken immigrants is impossible, even with the best will in the world. No sooner are amenities such as running water and electricity brought to one mushrooming shanty town than another appears on scrubland near by. As a result the city sprawls in all directions, as far as the eye can see. Arriving on a British Airways jet, Cotterell now found himself in the middle of all this hubbub, gasping for breath in the thin fume-laden air.

Anxious to see as much as he could in the short time available, he made his way to the old quarter, which is built on the original island of the Aztecs. Here, surrounding the main square or *zocalo*[1], are many Spanish buildings, including the presidential palace and the cathedral. This last turned out to be a sad sight, for like most of the other old churches in the city it is steadily sinking into the ground.[2] It is only held up from collapsing by an internal network of scaffolding, which destroys any sense of beauty or grace it may once have enjoyed. The presidential palace with its famous murals by Diego Rivera[3] depicting the history of Mexico (*see* Plates 9, 10 and 11) was in a rather better condition. Made from the stones of demolished Aztec pyramids, it is one of the oldest of all the buildings in Mexico City but seemed to have withstood the ravages of time rather better than the ponderously heavy cathedral. Near by were the last remnants of Tenochtitlan, the base of the Templo Mayor, once the largest of the Aztec pyramids. Cotterell learnt that it was only in 1978 that the site was fully excavated, after a power company digging a cable ditch came across a huge altar stone.[4] The archaeologists in charge of the dig had been excited to discover that the Aztecs had reconstructed their temple many times, building each new pyramid on top of the previous. This was done because at the end of a Calendar Round of 52 years everything had to be renewed. Even the pyramids, it seemed, had to have a new skin when the calendar dictated it.

Cotterell next visited the *Museo de Antropologia*, the country's principal museum. This lies south-west of the *zocalo* at the end of the great *Avenida Paseo de la Reforma*, the main artery of the city. It is one of the world's great archaeological museums with a suitably elegant setting in the middle of Chapultepec Park. Opened only in 1964 in a splendid modern building, it houses a vast collection of pre-Columbian artefacts including the Aztec Calendar Stone and the statue of Coatlicue which so impressed Bullock. Different halls, arranged around an open and airy courtyard, are devoted to collections from the various pre-Columbian cultures. As well as sizeable collections of Olmec, Zapotec, Toltec and Mayan artefacts, there is a whole hall given over to the ancient city of Teotihuacan. In this room, along with many statues and pots, there is a full-scale reproduction of part of one of its most famous buildings, the Pyramid of Quetzalcoatl.

The next day he was to visit Teotihuacan itself. This site lies some 25 miles north-east of Mexico City and is a popular tourist destination because of its ready accessibility. First excavated around 1889

by the maverick archaeologist and leading *cientifico* Leopaldo
Batres,[5] the ruins of Teotihuacan are both the largest and in many
ways most enigmatic of all Mexico's archaeological sites. The city
flourished throughout the classic period, at the time when the Maya
built Palenque, and was abandoned, for reasons unknown, in about
AD 750. In his dig, Batres found evidence that the city had been
destroyed by a great fire. At first sight this suggested that it had met
its end at the hands of invaders, for who else would have put it to
the torch? Yet there was another curious anomaly: many of the
buildings also showed evidence that they had been deliberately
filled with rubble and buried so that even their roof timbers were
still intact. It was as though they had been preserved in aspic. This
in itself must have been an enormous task, involving the digging
and transporting of tons of earth and rock with the sole purpose of
burying an abandoned city. Yet there was no clear answer to why
either the Teotihuacanos themselves or their supposed invaders
should have done this. Batres could only suggest that it was done
to protect the sacred sanctuaries from the eyes of the profane.

Teotihuacan today is still impressive to look at, if somewhat
lacking in atmosphere. Arranged at regular intervals along the
42-metre-wide and four-kilometre-long Avenue of the Dead are
23 palaces and temples. But these are dwarfed by the massive
Pyramid of the Moon that stands at the northern end of the
avenue, and the even larger Pyramid of the Sun,[6] which lies just
to its east and nearly halfway down the avenue. At the southern
end of the avenue and on the same side of it as the Pyramid of the
Sun lies a square containing the smaller Quetzalcoatl Pyramid.
This building is remarkable, for like the Templo Mayor of Tenochtitlan it shows evidence of having been rebuilt several times, with
layers like onion skins. This alone suggests that the idea of periodic renewal was not an Aztec invention but goes back to very
much earlier times.

The death of the gods

Unfortunately, unlike the Maya, the Teotihuacanos have left us no
written texts to explain the substance of their beliefs, though we

can glean some idea from the artistic representations of their gods. The Pyramid of Quetzalcoatl is particularly helpful in this respect because it carries a frieze showing alternating rows of sculptures of the feathered serpent god Quetzalcoatl[7] and the rain god Tlaloc. Clearly, then, these two were venerated in the Valley of Mexico long before the time of the Toltecs.

The true significance of the Pyramids of the Sun and Moon is also unknown. We only know them by these names because that is what the Aztecs called them. It was also they who gave the city its present name, Teotihuacan, meaning 'Place where the gods are born', for they had their own mythology associated with the site. The Aztecs believed that at the end of the previous age the gods gathered in darkness at Teotihuacan to decide which of them should become the new sun to light the world. According to one of their myths a rather arrogant god named Tecuciztecatl volunteered for the privilege, but the rest of the gods elected the more humble and elderly Nanahuatzin as a second contender. A great funeral pyre was built and Tecuciztecatl was invited to jump into it. When he couldn't pluck up the courage to sacrifice himself in this way, they then asked Nanahuatzin. He immediately ran and jumped into the flames. Seeing this, Tecuciztecatl found his nerve and he too threw himself upon the pyre, ashamed that he had been outdone by his humble rival. This was not the end, however, for phoenix-like they were both reborn: Nanahuatzin became the new sun god, Tonatiuh, and Tecuciztecatl became the moon.[8] Unfortunately, the sun would not move in the sky but hung motionless on the eastern horizon. Tonatiuh demanded the fealty and blood of the other gods before he would get to work travelling along the ecliptic. After some deliberation the other gods agreed and, one by one, gave themselves up to have their hearts removed by Quetzalcoatl. Fortified by this blood offering Tonatiuh became Nahui Ollin, the Sun of Motion.

The Aztecs used this story of the self-sacrificing gods, which they almost certainly inherited from the earlier Toltecs, to justify their own bloody religion. They reasoned that if the gods themselves had had to die to keep the sun moving in the sky, then humans had a duty to follow their example and make sure the sun god was kept properly fed.[9] The connection between this Aztec myth and the site of Teotihuacan has never been explained, but it is possible that something did happen there that involved a great, fiery ritual. The evidence that the city was abandoned after being burnt is striking, and certainly for the Aztecs it became a sacred burial ground.

Mountain of the Bat god

Moving on from the Mexico City area, Cotterell flew to Oaxaca.[10] The Oaxaca Valley has a long history of settlement but was seized by the Aztecs only 40 years before the coming of Cortes. The Spanish colonial city that was built on the earlier Aztec ruins is in many ways the most attractive in the whole of Mexico. At an altitude of 1600 metres it has an agreeable climate, and when Cortes arrived he fell in love with the place and intended to retire there.[11] But what makes Oaxaca particularly interesting is not so much its old world charm as the nearby ruins of Monte Alban, the most breathtaking site in all of Mexico. Here, perched on a mountain top overlooking the Oaxaca Valley, was a ceremonial centre fit for the gods themselves.

Founded by Olmec immigrants perhaps around 800 BC, Monte Alban is a remarkable feat of engineering. First the mountaintop was artificially flattened—itself an enormous task—and then a huge area was laid out with ball-court,[12] tombs and other buildings. Then around 300 BC another people, the Zapotecs, entered the Oaxaca Valley. They took over Monte Alban, building pyramids, temples and tombs of their own. Like the Maya, the Zapotecs had a written language, though all that remains of this is a few inscriptions that will probably never be deciphered. Just as at Teotihuacan, the site was carefully abandoned by the Zapotecs, who buried their temples and pyramids. However, the site was later used by their rivals in the valley, the more militaristic Mixtecs. They emptied the Zapotec tombs and re-used them for their own dead. By the time the Aztecs arrived, Monte Alban was just a hilltop, its secrets preserved until Batres brought in the spades.

Years of work on the site have brought dividends. An intact

Mixtec burial tomb yielded a vast quantity of gold jewellery as well as many carved bones. In the Mexico Museum of Anthropology, Cotterell had seen one of the most important finds from Monte Alban, a curious mask of a bat god. He was now to see many ceramic representations of this same deity, who seemed to be the messenger of death.

Something else that caught Cotterell's attention was a famous group of sculptures known as The Dancers. These are a set of reliefs which depict figures in various postures and which, when they were first discovered, were thought to represent people dancing (*see* Plates 31 and 32). Today it is believed that they have a medical significance. The building in which they were found is one of the oldest at Monte Alban and is thought to have functioned as a hospital. Some of the sculptures would appear to represent patients with obvious abnormalities; others seem to be connected with aspects of fertility.

Moving on from Monte Alban, Cotterell next visited the Zapotec site of Mitla, some 40 kilometres down the road. This was entirely different, being built on relatively low-lying ground. Here the Zapotecs constructed a ritual centre that again served as a cemetery. This time, however, the buildings were decorated in a most extraordinary manner. Whereas the temples at Monte Alban were all of hewn stone, arranged in step-pyramid fashion with sloping sides, those at Mitla were rectangular boxes decorated with large panels of mosaic. These were of most intricate design, made out of small pieces of rock, all carefully ground into squares and diamonds, and fitted together without cement. There were around 15 different designs altogether, apparently signifying such things as the elements and the seasons. Once more it seemed that the rain god was important, for the favourite designs were a group of three that mostly occurred together and which are interpreted as symbolizing clouds, rain and lightning.

Leaving the Valley of Oaxaca behind, Cotterell now pressed on with his tour, flying eastwards to Villahermosa. From here it was only a bus ride to his most important destination: Pacal's jungle city of Palenque.

The Lost City

In many respects Palenque has changed considerably since its discovery by Father Ordoñez in 1773 and the publication of the classic *Incidents of Travel in Central America, Chiapas and Yucatan* by Stephens and Catherwood in 1843. Two things that have not, however, are the tropical heat and the mosquitoes. At the edge of the steaming jungle, the oppressive atmosphere still challenges all but the most intrepid of travellers. Perhaps this is one of the reasons why the site was abandoned by its builders, for in many other ways it is the most impressive pre-Hispanic city in the whole of the Americas. But the area in which it stands was not always jungle. Between AD 600 and 800, during what is now termed the Late Classic, it was densely populated. It was in fact one of a number of competing cities in the central region of Mayaland, its origins like its abandonment still something of a mystery. Although not very large—indeed it is considerably smaller than the famous Yucatan city of Chichen Itza that rose to prominence later on in the 10th century—it commands respect for the quality of its buildings. Most archaeologists and visitors alike agree that it is the most beautiful of all Mayan cities, combining aesthetic proportion with elaborate decoration. What we see today, though, is only a pale shadow of how it must once have looked, for when it was built the majority of the buildings were covered with brightly-coloured stucco friezes.[13] Only small portions of these have survived to the present day, so we have to rely on the etchings made by the early explorers, particularly Catherwood, to understand how they must formerly have looked.

Only a small part of Palenque has been fully excavated and many buildings away from the centre are still either wrapped in jungle creepers or buried under earth mounds. The large number of official, as opposed to domestic, buildings that have been found testify to its having been an important ceremonial centre. We can only guess at the sort of colourful rituals that were performed but, judging by the majesty of the buildings, they must have been elaborate. The man who seems to have been most responsible for building this magnificent city was of course Pacal,[14] who ascended to the throne at the age of 12 and was 80[15] when he died in AD 683.

Archaeologists are generally agreed that he had his burial crypt built for him beneath the Temple of Inscriptions, though the building was finished off by his son Chan Bahlum. If so, then Pacal was also responsible for the inscriptions that give the pyramid its present name. That the pyramid was designed from the outset to be a mortuary temple is clear from the fact that both the sarcophagus and lid are too large to be moved from their crypt. They must have been placed there before the pyramid, with its inscriptions, was built around them. This makes sense of course, for even assuming it would fit through the door of the crypt, who would want to go to all the trouble of having to carry a heavy sarcophagus up the outside of a pyramid only then to have to take it back down a narrow internal staircase? A small practical consideration, perhaps, but certainly one worth heeding.

Lord Pacal was clearly highly intelligent, and he must have been

Figure 20   Pacal grasping a serpent

initiated into whatever secret wisdom the Maya possessed. All the evidence gathered, both from his tomb and from other inscriptions at Palenque, suggests that during his lifetime he was regarded as little less than a god. After he died his pyramid was, at least for a time, a place of pilgrimage and the centre of some sort of ancestor cult. It was this pyramid even more than the Temple of the Cross that Cotterell now wanted to see.

After a long bus ride from Villahermosa he arrived in Palenque, and the next day he wasted no time in setting off for the archaeological site. Before him stood the magnificent Pyramid-Temple of Inscriptions. Pausing only to catch his breath, he scaled this edifice which till then he had been able only to imagine. Following in the footsteps of Alberto Ruz over 30 years earlier, he thereupon made his way down the internal staircase of the pyramid. It was a long way and unbearably humid, the limestone walls saturated with the perspiration of the thousands of visitors who had made the same journey before him. Halfway down, the staircase turned sharply to the right and led on to an antechamber where the skeletons of six sacrificial victims had been buried so that they could protect and accompany their master on his journey to the next world. Excited, Cotterell scrambled down the last few steps to where the triangular slab gave access to Pacal's tomb. Standing in the gloomy half-light he felt a shiver run down his spine as he peered into the crypt. There, still covering the now raided tomb of Pacal, was the great Lid of Palenque.

He had already seen many other pre-Columbian artefacts both at Monte Alban and in the National Museum of Anthropology at Mexico City, but nothing had prepared him for the eerie timelessness of this tomb. The great Lid, with its complex interlocking design, seemed to belong to another world—a place where logic and reason are turned upside down. A work of art, yes, but something more than this: a riddle. Now he understood why von Däniken and others had been so obsessed with this one antiquity, for like Pacal's jade mask, with its half-open lips and quizzical expression, it challenged the onlooker to probe into its mysteries while denying a straightforward answer. Seeing it now for the first time, something of its magic seemed to pass into him. Cotterell could no longer ignore it nor pretend it was just an inscribed stone tablet: it was alive, and now he had to probe its secrets, almost as if it was a matter of destiny. Blinking as he returned into the light, he made his way carefully back down the outside of the pyramid. Around him were scattered the remains of other once noble buildings, while the sun above still blazed down, almost melting the very fibres of his sweat-sodden shirt. None of this seemed to matter any more; he could no longer worry about such things. In his core he had changed: a door had opened, one that beckoned him onwards to find out more concerning Pacal and his mysterious land of calendars.

Away from the monuments, in the village of Palenque, were the usual tourist stalls selling everything from leather goods to exact scaled-down replicas of the Lid. He bought one of these and then, hungrily searching for anything that might give him more information, he purchased every book that they had on the subject of the Maya. Laden down with all these trophies he made his way back to England via the post-Classic Mayan cities of Uxmal and Chichen Itza in the northern Yucatan. He was not to know it then but he was about to make an extraordinary discovery: Lord Pacal and his people were in possession of knowledge which we are only now just beginning to rediscover.

The Breaking of the Code

Back in England, Cotterell got down to the business of unravelling the mystery of the Maya. Closeting himself away, he immersed himself in the books he had brought back from Mexico, all the time looking for clues to the central enigmas of the Lid and the Mayan sacred number 1,366,560. Before he could go any further with this research, he had to get to grips with the Mayan calendar—or rather calendars, for they had more than one. As we have seen, the simplest of these was also used by the Aztecs, Zapotecs, Toltecs and others. It was based on the interaction of two cycles: a 'vague year' of 365 days and a 'sacred year' of 260 days. The use of the 260-day *tzolkin* is of very great antiquity. It seems to go back to at least the time of the Olmecs and is still used for magical purposes by some of the more remote Maya tribes right up to the present day. Although its origins are obscure, it was clear to Cotterell that it was highly significant over and above any magical connotations that individual day names might carry, for the number 260 divided exactly into both his own number of 1,366,040 and the Mayan super-number of 1,366,560 days, the first 5254 times and the second 5256. This seemed significant. More importantly, while working at Cranfield Cotterell had made a vital discovery. In analysing the way that the sun's polar and equatorial magnetic fields interacted, he discovered that they came close together every 260 days. This seemed to bear out his suspicion that the Mayan numbering system was connected with solar magnetic cycles.

Cotterell was especially intrigued to learn how the Maya and others wove together their two cycles to the extent that each day was given two names, one based on its position in the *tzolkin* and the other stemming from the 365-day vague year, the combination relating to the Aztec Century: a period of either 52 vague years or 73 260-day counts, as appropriate.

For Cotterell this figure of 260 was later to become the vital key in breaking the code of the Mayan numbering system. Whereas other scholars had made the breakthrough that enabled the dates in Mayan inscriptions to be translated into dates in our own calendar, he felt there was still no satisfactory explanation *why* the Maya used cycles of 144,000, 7,200, 360 and 20 days duration. Furthermore, he reasoned, why would the Maya omit the important time period of 260 days from their inscriptions? And why did they, as he had discovered, attach such importance to the number 9? Cotterell now decided to insert the 'missing' 260-day figure into the cycle sequence. He then multiplied each cycle by 9, added the totals together, and arrived at a remarkable result—the Mayan magic number, which was virtually identical to his own sunspot figure of 1,366,040.

$$\begin{array}{ccccc}
144,000 & 7,200 & 360 & 260 & 20 \\
\underline{9} & \underline{9} & \underline{9} & \underline{9} & \underline{9} \\
1,296,000 + & 64,800 + & 3,240 + & 2,340 + & 180 = 1,366,560
\end{array}$$

Cotterell felt that he had hit the jackpot, for it now seemed to him that the cycles of the Mayan numbering system were used to draw attention to the importance of the 1,366,560-day cycle. More-over, he believed that his theories about the sun's magnetic behaviour provided him with a unique understanding of the astronomical importance of the 260-day cycle, without which the Mayan numerical code could not have been broken.

Having mastered the intricacies of the basic calendar, he now turned his attention to the famous Aztec Calendar Stone, which he had also seen in Mexico City. Reading a pamphlet he had picked up in the Mexican Museum of Anthropology he learned that this stone celebrated the Aztec belief in former ages. At the centre of the wheel was the image of Tonatiuh, the sun god. He had his tongue poking out to symbolize the fact that he gives breath or life. To the Aztecs, Toltecs and others, however, the sun was not something that could be taken for granted, nor was it wholly benevolent. They believed that it needed constant human sacrifice to keep it moving, to make sure that it did not set permanently and bring to an end the fifth and last age.

Arranged around the face of the sun god were symbols repre-senting the four previous ages. Each age had been under the rulership of a different god, and each had apparently ended in some sort of cataclysm. Wanting to know more about this, Cotterell turned to the late accounts given to Spanish friars by descendants of the survivors of Cortes' invasion. It was clear from these that much knowledge had been lost concerning the details of pre-Columbian beliefs on these matters, but enough had been recorded to give some indication of what this knowledge was all about. Turning first to the story as relayed in an anonymous manuscript from 1558 entitled *Leyenda de los soles*, seemingly de-rived from one or other of two earlier documents, the *Chimalpopoca Codex* and the *Cuauhtitlan Annals*, he was able to find evidence for a belief in time-cycles based on periods of 52 years—Aztec Cen-turies. This account gave precise details of time periods that were clearly of symbolic importance:

First Sun	*Nahui Ocelotl*	Duration, 676 years (52 × 13)
Second Sun	*Nahui Ehecatl*	Duration, 364 years (52 × 7)
Third Sun	*Nahui Quihahuitl*	Duration, 312 years (52 × 6)
Fourth Sun	*Nahui Atl*	Duration, 676 years (52 × 13)

According to this account, the second and third ages—or 'suns'—were of much shorter duration than the first and last. When they are added together, however, they give a period of 676 years, the same as the other two. What this implied was that these four suns were only three-quarters of a full cycle, and that a fifth age of 676 years would be needed to complete a full round of 52×52 years. Though interesting from a numerological point of view, this account did not seem to be based on real time periods or to have much to do with the Mayan magic number of 1,366,560 days. It rather seemed to emphasize the limitations of the Aztec calendar which could not go beyond the 52-year basic time division.

Turning to the *Vatico-Latin Codex*, Cotterell found a much fuller and at first more mysterious Aztec account of bygone ages:

- **First Sun**
  Matlactili. Duration 4008 years. Those who lived then ate maize and were giants. The sun was destroyed by water. It was called Apachiohualiztli (Flood—deluge), permanent rain. Men were turned into fish. Some say that only one couple, Nene and Tata, escaped, protected by an old tree living near the water. Others say that there were seven couples who hid in a cave until the waters went down. They repopulated the Earth and were gods in their own nations. The goddess who presided over this era was Chalchiuhtlicue ('The one with the Jade skirt'), wife of Tlaloc.

- **Second Sun**
  Ehecatl. Duration 4010 years. Those who lived then ate a wild fruit known as the Acotzintli. The sun was destroyed by Ehecatl (god of wind) and man was turned into a monkey in order to cling to trees to survive. This happened in the year One Dog (Ce Itzcuintli). One man and one woman standing on a rock were saved from this destruction. This time was called the Golden Age and was presided over by the god of wind.

- **Third Sun**
  Tleyquiyahuillo. Duration 4081 years. Men, the descendants of the couple who were saved from the second sun, ate a fruit

called Tzincoacoc. The world was destroyed by fire on the day
Chicunahui Ollin. This age was given the name of
Tzonchichiltic ('Red Head') and was presided over by the god
of fire.

- **Fourth Sun**
  Tzontlilac. It began 5026 years ago. This age, in which Tula was
  founded, was called Tzontlilac ('Black Hair'). Men died of
  starvation after a rain of blood and fire.

This account put the ages in a different order, indicating that
there was some uncertainty among the later Aztecs about what it
really should be. Because this did seem to be a more reliable
account, however, Cotterell decided to use it for his further researches. Thinking about this account, and particularly the role of
the goddess Chalchiuhtlicue (('The one with) the jade skirt'), he
suddenly recalled the Lid of Palenque. Might not the goddess
Chalchiuhtlicue, or her Mayan equivalent,[16] be the figure represented at the centre of the Lid? No one had ever looked at this
figure as representing a female before, but it seemed to fit. In
descriptions of this goddess it was said that besides wearing a jade
skirt she had a jade necklace from which hung a gold medallion.
She was also said to hold a round lily leaf in her left hand and to
have water flowing out of her feet. On the Lid all these details were
present (*see* Figure 21). Here was a very female-looking figure with
legs apart as though giving birth. She held what seemed to be a
leaf, and flowing from her was what could be interpreted as
streams of water. Round her neck were beads and again what
seemed to be some sort of medallion. There was no doubt in
Cotterell's mind: this was the image neither of a spaceman nor of
a man falling backwards into an afterlife world—it was the
goddess Chalchiuhtlicue!

Having made this discovery, he now began a systematic search
of the Lid for evidence of other gods in the design. The first and
most obvious was Ehecatl—god of wind and first-born of the
gods. An aspect of Quetzalcoatl ('feathered serpent')—known to
the Maya as Kukulcan—Ehecatl was usually depicted as a bird
with a long tail. Looking at the Lid it was clear that the figure at
the top was meant to be just such a bird, a quetzal, whose green

Figure 21 Chalchiuhtlicue, goddess of water

feathers were highly prized by both the Maya and the Aztecs (*see* Figure 22).

The other two gods of the ages were at first harder to find and required some lateral thinking. Then at last it came to him: look at the Lid from the other way round! Turning it upside down he could immediately identify them. First there was Chaac, the rain god, the Mayan equivalent of the Aztec Tlaloc. He could be seen at the bottom of the Lid with six long tusk-like teeth (*see* Figure 23).

Below or above him (depending on how you looked at the Lid)

Figure 22 Ehecatl, god of wind

Figure 23   Tlaloc, god of celestial fire and rain

was the god Tonatiuh, shown as on the Aztec Calendar Stone with his tongue poking out, symbolizing that he gave life. One important difference was that unlike the Aztec Tonatiuh, who was shown with a full set of teeth in his open mouth, this god had most of his teeth missing. He seemed to have worn them away, implying the end of his age (*see* Figure 24).

Between the figures representing Chalchiuhtlicue and Ehecatl there was a shape on the Lid which at one level seemed to represent the Tree of Life or suckling tree. At the centre of it was a cross, however, and Cotterell was in no doubt that it signified the sun—as it does in many cultures throughout the world (*see* Figure 25).

By discerning meaning in the images of the gods inscribed on the Lid he had broken the first code. The Lid of Palenque, though

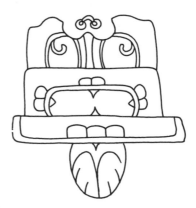

Figure 24   Tonatiuh, sun god

Figure 25 The sun-cross between Ehecatl and Chalchiuhtlicue

personal in that it acted as the cover for Pacal's tomb, was univer-sal in its imagery. *It was a book of symbols that was intended to be, and indeed perhaps was, read.* Not only that, it was a cultural icon that recorded the passing of the ages, and was therefore similar in significance to the Maya as the Calendar Stone had been to the Aztecs. It recorded major events in world history that related to the mythology of the Maya and in a sense illustrated their holy book of Creation, the *Popol Vuh*. Cotterell had long known of the existence of this sacred book of the Quiché Maya, which as we have seen was first published in French by Brasseur de Bourbourg in 1861. Getting out his much-thumbed English translation, Cotterell read its first sentence:

> The *Popol Vuh*, as it is called, cannot be seen any more ... The original book, written long ago, once existed but is now hidden from the searcher and from the thinker ...

Pondering on these words it occurred to him that the author might have been talking quite literally. Perhaps there was a hid-den version of the book, put where no one could find it, still less interpret what they had found. The name *Popol Vuh* means 'coun-cil book',[17] and among its fairytale-like stories of the birth of humanity, and the doings of heroes such as the twins Xbalanque and Hunahpu, there is a serious intent. Undoubtedly what we read about this book today, particularly in translation, is only a superficial interpretation of what is in reality a highly esoteric work of art. Hidden beneath the poetry is a deeper meaning, a subtext of catastrophism cloaked in mythology. Cotterell began to wonder if the Lid of Palenque was not itself the original *Popol Vuh*: the one that had vanished and was 'now hidden from the searcher and from the thinker'. He was convinced that there were deeper levels of code relating to the Lid which could, if one but had the key, be deciphered. To break this code was now his greatest desire.

The Overlays of Lord Pacal

It was the numbers of the sunspot cycle, particularly 1,366,040 days, that had brought Cotterell to Palenque, but his visit to that ancient site had now turned his attention in another direction entirely. It was not the hieroglyphs for the Birth of Venus, 1,366,560, which filled his dreams on returning to England but Pacal's eerie tomb at the bottom of its staircase. His mind kept coming back to the Lid with its strange decorations. He felt sure there was some deeper meaning to all of this—a message, if you like—sealed up for future generations. He had, of course, already associated the principal figures on the Lid with the passage of solar ages, and that this interpretation was correct he was in no doubt. Still he had this nagging feeling that he was only at the beginning of the mystery, that there was a deeper, more esoteric explanation to the Lid. Almost in desperation he now turned his attention away from the central motifs to the surrounding border area, which also seemed to contain some sort of code.

Around the edges of the Lid is a curious border containing images, some of which are now recognized as representing the sun, moon, planets and constellations. Among these images are human faces, placed deliberately, it would appear, like characters in some well-known story. Cotterell was convinced that just as the main body of the Lid was carved with representations of the gods ruling over the ages, so the border had its own message. Looking at it, one thing immediately stood out: two of the corners were missing (*see* Figure 26). Now there was no record of the Lid's having been damaged since its first discovery by Alberto Ruz in 1952, and certainly not of the corners having been chipped. It seemed, therefore, that they had either been broken off at the time the Lid was being put into the chamber or that it had been designed in this way in the first place. In any event this seemed very strange, for everything else about the Lid seemed absolutely perfect. Would the Maya have covered the sarcophagus of their most important king with a lid that had been accidentally damaged? More to the point, is it likely that exactly the same accident could have happened to two corners? It seemed more likely to him that the breaking off of the corners was deliberate, and indeed part of the intended design. The question was, why?

Cotterell was already beginning to see that whoever it was who designed the Lid (probably Pacal himself) liked riddles and enjoyed playing with design elements in such a way that they

Figure 26   Borders of the Lid

interacted with one another. Could he have done the same with the border? Was the chipping of the corners done intentionally to draw attention to something? In short, was there a message to be read in this?

He reasoned that the Maya believed each part of the microcosm to be only one part of the macrocosmic universe, and each individual to be likewise a similar piece of Creation. This idea extended to the self, so that each individual could be apprehended as a tiny piece of oneness, which in turn led to the dualist perception of 'I am you' and 'You are me'. He could see that this was epitomized in their pantheon of gods representing the opposing forces of nature. Both the nature of the physical earth and of humanity were split into dualities that were really complementary, such as day and night, birth and death. Yet these apparently dual natures had a habit of changing into their opposites, so that night would inexorably become day and day would become night. Similarly birth would lead to death and death to birth. Good would in time become bad (through excess) as surely as bad would become good (following aversion to pain and suffering).

This new insight he had into the psyche of the Maya provided the next key to the decoding process. For if I am you and you are me, if night becomes day and day becomes night, then perhaps the missing corners are not really missing at all. Maybe they are just not visible unless you look for them in the right way, to see how 'missing' can turn into 'found'. Looking at the problem in this way gave Cotterell a new perspective and led him into a different line of reasoning. Perhaps, put simply, there was indeed a message: 'Complete the corners and you will find something else.'

Looking at the right-hand border, the broken code at the top should have consisted of five large dots linked together in an X-shaped cross by smaller dots (*see* Figure 27). That this was so was indicated by the appearance of this same symbol halfway down the border. Very well then; the message seemed to be that this symbol needed to be completed—but this still left the question of how? Looking at a graphic representation of the Lid complete with its border, Cotterell surmised that if a copy of it were laid on top of it, with the borders overlapping, then the corner could, as it were, be made complete. The copy would, in effect, supply the

Figure 27   The broken corners can be overlapped

missing part of the puzzle. Accordingly, he made two acetate copies of the Lid and placed them one on top of the other. Sliding them around, he was able to make the corners match in such a way that the broken symbol resembled the one halfway down the right-hand side. He then examined the rest of the border and was amazed to see that it too now made sense. What had been seemingly chaotic images were now married up with their second halves and it was possible to see what they also were meant to represent.

Turning to the opposite border, he tried the same process of overlaying and again was surprised by what he found. What had been seemingly meaningless glyphs suddenly burst into life. Instead of half-figures, difficult to see and appreciate, he was now confronted with clearly symbolic designs that made sense in terms of Mayan religious mythology. The most obvious of these was a dragon figure, symbolic of fertility, that he could now clearly see in the left-hand border (*see* Figure 28). More subtly, the dragon also contained the face of a jaguar, the two seemingly fused together. Lower down the border was what looked like a monkey, its arms outstretched above its head as though hanging from a tree. Below the monkey there was a stylized snake's head—perhaps signifying the feathered serpent god Quetzalcoatl. In all, the whole pattern was curiously reminiscent of the story of Creation contained in the Mayan epic, the *Popul Vuh*.

Like the Aztecs, the Maya believed that there had been four other creations before our own. During these the gods fashioned different races of people first out of clay and then out of wood. These early races were incapable of fulfilling what was to be the prime purpose of humanity, to cultivate the earth and supply the gods with prayers and sacrifices. They were therefore destroyed, only a few individuals remaining. In the course of the last destruction the survivors were turned into monkeys, who by hanging on to branches were able to escape total annihilation. Thus the Maya, like modern Darwinists, believed that the monkey race preceded the creation of modern humanity. Could the border code of a hanging monkey somehow refer to this episode of the *Popul Vuh*? Cotterell was inclined to think so.

Turning his attention to the lower border of the Lid and carrying

Figure 28   Revealing the secret glyphs in the border

out the same technique of building an image by overlapping, he found something else. In the middle of this border is a human face with a curious 'banana' on its nose. To remove the banana it was necessary to push the two noses together (*see* Figures 29 and 30).

Now, looking at the larger image of the Lid, it was clear that there is a similar banana on the nose of its central image (*see* Figure 31). What would happen if he pushed two of these images together in such a way that the bananas disappeared on these images too? Carefully juggling the images and twisting them round so that the two faced each other, he slid them together to remove the banana.

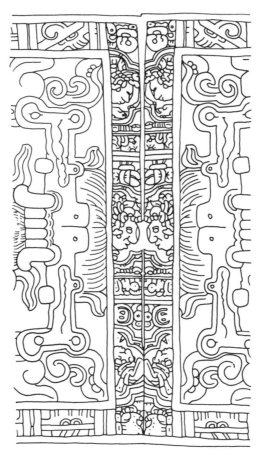

Figure 29   'Banana' nose border

Figure 30 'Banana' noses together

Incredible as it seems, this too produced a meaningful image. Suddenly he was able to see the looming image of a bat hovering where the two faces met (*see* Plate 23). In fact there were two bat images: one flying face-on towards the onlooker, and the other seen from the rear and flying away.

Figure 31 Figure from centre of Lid with 'banana' on nose

Cotterell knew that the bat god had figured prominently in the mythology of many different cultures of Mexico, including that at Monte Alban. When he had visited the Museum of Anthropology in Mexico City, he had been particularly struck by an image of this deity made out of 25 pieces of jade. It seemed that the bat, because of its association with the night and its silent flight, represented death. In the *Popul Vuh* two of the most important characters are a pair of hero twins called Hunahpu and Xbalanque, whose task it is to overthrow the evil lords of the underworld. In the course of the story a killer bat, Camazotz, snatches off the head of Hunahpu, which then has to be replaced with a gourd.[17] Later, through various trickery on the part of the brothers, the head is retrieved and magically fixed back on his body. It therefore seemed no accident to Cotterell that the image of a bat should appear, hidden as it were, on the Lid. It occupied an important place in the mythology of the Maya.

Another composite picture to come out of the Lid was that of a jaguar. This, it was said by the Maya, represented the fifth age of the creation. Cotterell found this by placing the five-dot central border code of one acetate over that of another. The jaguar features prominently in Mayan as well as Olmec art, and it was amazing to see this emblem of the fifth age brought out in this way through the five-dot patterns (*see* Plate 24). It had been puzzling him for some time why the Lid showed only four gods of previous ages whereas the Aztec Calendar Stone showed five. Now he knew why: the crafty Maya had hidden it from the prying eyes of the casual onlooker.

He now took a fresh look at the Lid itself, without the use of overlays. It was clear to him that the motif of a cross standing over the reclined figure somehow represented the sun. The use of a cross to symbolize the sun is almost universal across the world, pointing to the very great antiquity of this sign. However, this symbol also had a second meaning, that of the Ceiba Tree. The Mayan version of the universal Tree of Life had 400,000 nipples instead of fruits. It stands, in other words, as the tree of Creation from which all life draws its nourishment. Some of these nipples seemed to be represented on the cross-branch of the Lid tree as pegs. What was even more interesting, though, was that the sun-cross had loops depicted on it. Could these be symbolic of the magnetic loops on the sun that give rise to sunspots? If so, then how could the Maya have possibly known about such phenomena? These were questions for which there were no answers.

Carrying on with his overlay technique, Cotterell was able to find over one hundred images and even stories on the lid that he could relate to Mayan mythology. Was this pure invention on his part or were they really there? He himself was in no doubt of their reality but he now wanted to consult with experts to see what they had to say.

An academic roasting

The Museum of Mankind is a building which few people—even Londoners—know exists. Tucked away in a back street behind Piccadilly, it looks more like an oldfashioned polytechnic or college hall than a department of the British Museum. Inside it is quite spacious, but what strikes the visitor most is its rather grand hall, as though the building were really designed to be a gentlemen's club or the London residence of some country grandee. Opposite the main entrance is a large staircase flanked by two massive plaster casts of Mayan sculptures.[18] It beckons the visitor upwards to where the main collections are housed. These include a wide range of ethnographic artefacts, from an Easter Island *Maui* with its pursed lips and sightless eyes, to African masks and Polynesian spears. Though the Museum's concern for multicultural values is all too clear, it is difficult to say just why some artefacts are deemed to belong in this building and not in its much more illustrious sister, the British Museum. Until recently, October 1994 to be precise, there was almost nothing from the Americas, bar an enormous totem pole, to be found in the British Museum itself. This deficiency has now been rectified with the opening of a new Mexican Gallery, but it used to be the case that American antiquities were absent from the British Museum and had to be sought in the much more politically correct Museum of Mankind. This had one advantage in that there are not the same number of tourists thronging its rooms and galleries, but conversely there is the sense that one is intruding into a private world, like walking into a great house only nominally open to the public.

Each of the great museums in London has a twin function, to be both an institution with a duty to provide an opportunity for the public to view its collection and an academic body with responsibilities to care for the collection in its keeping and to carry out research. In addition to an army of yawning guards, standing or sitting in every room to which the public has access, the museums employ a large number of scholars. In the British Museum itself there are whole departments tucked away behind mahogany doors and occupying large segments of the building. The staff who man these departments have at their disposal libraries and research facilities that are not open to the general public, but they are required, under the terms of the Museum's charter, to offer assistance and advice when asked. Just as anyone is free to apply for a pass to the famous British Museum Reading Room, which is also closed to the public, so they can contact members of staff either by letter, phone or in person and ask for information. This is a very important right, for at the end of the day it is the taxpaying public who fund these institutions and support their work.

While writing *The Orion Mystery* I had quite a few dealings with the Egyptologists of the British Museum and found them always to be courteous and helpful. That is not to say that they agreed with everything we had to say, but they were at least willing to talk to us. I was therefore very surprised to hear how Maurice Cotterell had had enormous difficulties not just in having his ideas accepted but in even getting an appointment at The Museum of Mankind. In October 1992 he telephoned to arrange an appointment to discuss his work with an assistant keeper at the Museum. He had already tried by letter but not having received a reply he decided that the phone was the only way to get heard. When he eventually got through, he was refused point blank. Undeterred, he contacted the Mexican Embassy in London and got talking to their cultural attaché, Mr Ortez. He was very interested in the work and could see the value in it, but even he could not arrange an interview with the Museum because the staff were too busy.

Two months later Cotterell went to see Mr Ortez in person, and this time they had more luck with the Museum: an assistant reluctantly agreed to give him ten minutes of her time. He raced across London accordingly, feeling as if he had been granted an audience with the queen. As it turned out he was wasting his time, for she barely listened to what he had to say before turning on him and telling him in a scolding tone to get out and read some books by proper authorities on the matter.

As far as he could tell, her central criticism of his theories was that the Maya had no acetates at their disposal, so whatever he might have discovered using this method must therefore be invalid. On the face of it this was a valid point. Of course the Maya didn't have acetate copies of the Lid to play around with as he had, but did they really need them? There could be another explanation. If he had been given the time Cotterell could have pointed to the *Popol Vuh*, which said:

> ... and the Kings knew if there would be a war, and everything was clear before their eyes; they saw if there would be death, and hunger, and if there would be strife ...

For Cotterell, the *Popol Vuh* was the book of the past, the present, and the future. It also contained a revealing reference to the superior intelligence with which the founding fathers were endowed:

> ... They saw, and could see instantly far, they succeeded in knowing all that there is in the World. When they looked, instantly they saw all around them and they contemplated in turn the arch of the heaven and the round face of the Earth. The things hidden (in the distance) they saw all, without first having to move; at once they saw the World ... great was their wisdom.

As far as Cotterell was concerned, the Maya had no need of acetates. Their writings and their superior knowledge of astronomy, architecture and science were proof enough of this. Although he did not know precisely how they had acquired their highly developed spatial abilities, he felt he had the evidence for it in front of him in the images he had decoded from the Lid. The Maya were certainly far more advanced than their neighbours, being almost alone amongst the Indian tribes of North America in having a written language. Uniquely they made use of the Long Count calendar, which in its complexity far surpassed that of the Aztecs, Toltecs, or any other pre-Columbian civilization. They built their cities and temples with the sort of artistic flair one associates with a high culture, and they—or at least their ancestors—are widely credited with the first cultivation of maize as a staple crop. All these notable achievements point to exceptional intelligence, at least among their rulers.

Reasoning in this way, Cotterell could see how they could have produced the complex design on the Lid without recourse to the modern invention of acetates. Western education has many strengths but also notable weaknesses. This is most apparent in the use we make of our minds. Whereas in the past people thought nothing of learning long epic poems and reciting them, today the average person is hard pressed to remember a few lines of Shakespeare. But although learning by rote has gone out of fashion in the West, it is still the way that knowledge is passed on in many developing countries. For example, in Islamic countries it is still considered normal for children to learn the entire Koran by heart. The ancient Romans took the development of memory a stage further by combining it with visualization. When an orator had a complex speech to give, he would not rely on mere inspiration to provide him with the words he needed in the right order. Instead he would organize his thoughts by visualizing a familiar place, perhaps a theatre, in his mind's eye. Then he would deliberately place thought symbols representative of the subjects he needed to discuss in various locations around the theatre. When he came to give the speech he would recall the image of the theatre and, as he mentally moved around it, he would recall the thought symbols and lecture on the points represented by each of them.

This method of thought training was very popular at the time of the Renaissance too, and is still used as a method of developing mindpower by professional magicians (among others). In order for it to work, it is necessary to develop the imagination—that is to say, to be able to think clearly in visual images. This is not as difficult as one might suppose, for it is a natural faculty of human beings. It does, however, require a certain amount of mental strength to hold an image clearly. It is therefore not inconceivable that instead of having to rely on physical acetate overlays to see the complex designs hidden in the pattern embossed on the Lid, whoever constructed it was able to do this in his or her mind's eye.

Cotterell had no time to explain any of this at the Museum before he was unceremoniously shown the door. He was left absolutely dumbfounded by her attitude towards him, all the more so because she categorically refused to give him any letters of introduction to Mexican archaeologists when he told her he was planning to go back to Mexico. Far from being encouraged in his work, he felt like he was being obstructed. But why? What was it about this subject that had produced such a violent outburst? Were they always so rude to strangers, or was it just that he was an outsider proposing something new? Whatever the reason he was soon to find out that she was not alone in her attitude. Other archaeologists would turn out to be even more hostile. As it was now becoming clear that he was not going to get any help from this quarter, he decided he had better make his own arrangements and try to get some appointments once he was out there. The last time he had visited Mexico it was purely a learning trip, to find out more about the Maya and in particular about the pyramid tomb at Palenque. This time he would return with something of his own to show. Come what may, he intended to make known his discoveries concerning the Lid of Palenque in the country of its origin. It would prove to be a fascinating experience.

A Mexican Breakfast

It had begun as an ordinary February day in Mexico City. The traffic roared through the busy boulevards, the usual crowds of vendors, beggars and commuters began pouring out onto the streets. The thin air was heavy with pollution, making it difficult to breathe. In short, everything was normal in this the largest metropolis on Earth, the city which stands on the ruins of the Aztec capital, Tenochtitlan. In one of the wealthier suburbs of this great city, a close friend of the president's wife drew back the curtains and turned on her television set. In a studio on the other side of town, two presenters fidgeted, waiting to go on air as soon as the

commercial break ended. Both of them were women in their mid-
to late twenties, as smartly dressed and made up as any European
or American TV hostess. Yet written in their faces and behind the
mask of modernity was the tortured history of their country. The
one girl, the more senior, was clearly of Spanish stock. To her right
and acting as interpreter was her assistant, equally pretty but with
the unmistakable features of a Mayan Indian. Their guest that day,
the focus of their attention, was Maurice Cotterell, and he was
about to reveal his discoveries for their benefit.

Maurice had brought with him a large folder of notes and A4
acetate copies of the slab. Under the watchful eye of the camera
and to the excitement of the two girls, he began to explain how it
contained in condensed form an encyclopaedia of ancient Mayan
knowledge. Laying the acetates side by side, he showed them how
the borders of the slab contained hidden images, such as a tiger,
the Mayan version of the Great Bear constellation and a stylized
dog, the planet Venus as the evening star. Now putting the acetates one on top of the other, he revealed further images such as
the bat god of death and Quetzalcoatl, the feathered serpent. He
concluded his magic show by asserting that the Maya were a
highly intelligent people and that they had evidently carved the
slab in order to preserve their knowledge for posterity. He hoped
that Mexican archaeologists would take this work further, for he
believed that he had at last found the key to the mystery of the
Maya and why they had disappeared.

Within minutes of the program going out on air, the switch-
board at the television station was jammed. It seemed that half of
Mexico City had been glued to their screens, learning for the first
time about a theory British archaeologists had done their best to
suppress. Among the callers was the First Lady's friend, herself
the wife of a cabinet minister. Both she and the president's wife
were members of the prestigious Voluntary Cultural Society of
Mexico City, and it just so happened that they were about to hold
one of their biannual meetings. Exhilarated, she asked if Maurice
would be willing to come along and talk to the society about his
discoveries. Thus it was that two days later he found himself in an
official government building standing before an audience of about
forty ladies, including the wives of other government ministers.

As they had no overhead projector, he had to hold up the acetates against a white background while he explained his theories. Although the room was crowded and it was impossible to see what was going on from the back, this didn't seem to matter for many of the ladies had already seen the TV interview. They were ecstatic over the very idea of such a discovery concerning one of their nation's most treasured relics from the past, and were quite uninhibited about saying so. Some of the ladies were in tears; others kissed him proclaiming him the reincarnation of Pacal. All wanted to shake his hand and were keen to offer whatever help they could to further his work. The First Lady, in a gesture that brought applause all round, awarded him a medal with a yellow ribbon— the highest honour bestowed by the society. She also promised to arrange meetings for him with some top Mexican archaeologists. Since this had been one of the chief reasons for his coming to Mexico in the first place, he was extremely grateful to her—but at the same time he was apprehensive after his bad experience at The Museum of Mankind. Would things be any different now? He hoped so, but casting his mind back to what had happened before he had to admit the omens were not good.

Meetings with the Inquisition

Following his disastrous appointment at The Museum of Mankind, Cotterell knew that in promoting his theories he could expect little or no help from professional archaeologists. Nevertheless it was important that he should discuss his findings with them, if only as a matter of courtesy. Not only that but he needed intelligent feedback on how his ideas fitted with the accepted consensus concerning the Maya. He was therefore keen to meet with the Mexican academics. When he had arrived in Mexico City he had attempted, without success, to see the Director of the Templo Mayor Museum, who was apparently out of the country. Following the TV program, however, and the publication of articles concerning Cotterell's work in the papers, he suddenly returned and an appointment was duly arranged.

If the meeting in The Museum of Mankind had been frosty, this one was full of fire. The director turned out to be a man in his fifties, stocky, his Spanish appearance giving him the look of a conquistador. His English was not very good but it seemed that he didn't need to be told: he had already made up his mind that Cotterell's theories on the Lid of Palenque were heretical. Red in the face and foaming at the mouth, he took hold of one of the acetate overlays and began tearing at it, trying to pull it apart. When it wouldn't give way he became all the more angry and virtually tossed Cotterell out onto the street outside the Museum. It was a bravura performance intended to show the contempt felt by the establishment for an outsider who had dared to cross the Atlantic and challenge the home team on their own ground. Once more Cotterell had the feeling that he had unwittingly trodden on forbidden territory, and he now knew what the ancient Maya must have felt like when Bishop Landa took their holy books and turned them into a bonfire. It seemed that some things in Mexico just don't change.

On arriving in Mexico City, Cotterell had taken the precaution of hiring a guide to show him round the city and arrange for introductions. She was now able to secure him an appointment with two of the staff at the Anthropological Museum—the equivalent of London's Museum of Mankind. Here he met with two younger archaeologists in their thirties, one a man and the other a woman. They were very friendly, invited him to sit down, and listened attentively for about three hours as, stage by stage, he went through his unlocking of the Lid of Palenque and how it tied in with sunspot cycles. He couldn't help but wonder, however, if their more positive reaction might perhaps stem from a direct instruction to be nice, possibly by the First Lady herself.

That night he returned to his hotel room and was preparing to go to bed when something appeared under the door. It turned out to be a business card from a man with the forename Miguel who was the Director of a Mayan Agricultural College. There was something odd about the card and Cotterell suspected he was an impostor. For one thing, the telephone numbers on the card were crossed out and a fresh number written on the back. For another, why should such a card be delivered by hand in this curious manner? It would have been just as easy to have telephoned. The scrawled message said that he, Miguel, had seen the program on television and was anxious to meet Maurice personally to discuss some of his ideas. They arranged a meeting for the following morning, which was a Saturday, but unfortunately it was necessary to make it brief because another interview had already been arranged through the local newspaper, *Nova Dadis*, with an archaeologist at the independent Museum del Carmen.

Miguel turned out to be a man in his sixties, dapper, and with penetrating eyes. He was accompanied by a young man in his twenties who he said was his son, though it seemed more likely that he was a grandson. Again Cotterell had the uneasy feeling that all was not as it seemed—that the man was an impostor or even a spy. It was hard to say why he had such a strange reaction, perhaps something to do with the strange manner in which he had made his acquaintance. Miguel seemed more like Carlos Castaneda's Don Juan than the director of an institute. Well, perhaps he was. At any event the meeting went along very amicably. Once more Cotterell explained his theories, but this time his listener was much more attentive to the details of what he was saying. At last he seemed to be speaking to someone who knew and understood what he was talking about when he mentioned time-cycles, and who was keen to find out more concerning the role of sunspots. He asked intelligent questions, not doubting the validity of the overlays but wanting to know whether Cotterell thought the cycles of the sun could have been linked to Mayan ideas on crop rotation.[19] Why did they use cycles of 144,000, 7,200 and 360 days for their crops? At that time Cotterell was unable to give him a positive answer on these points but promised he would look into the matter and contact him again in due course. The next day he phoned the numbers given on the card—but no one had heard of his visitor from the Mayan Agricultural College. Later he was to write to him care of the address he had been given, but again to no avail. It seemed that Miguel had vanished as mysteriously as he had first appeared.

Later that day he went to the Museum del Carmen and met up with Dr Yolotos Gonzales who, like the lady he had met in England, was of retirement age. Unlike the hostile gentleman at the Templo Mayor Museum she was interested in the material and agreed that Maurice had definitely hit on something important with his decoding of the Lid. She was convinced that the work was worthy of further investigation but warned him that there would be obstacles. Not everyone would be in favour of what he was saying, if only because it was novel. He should expect opposition from the archaeological establishment, a body which from the time of the dictator Porfirio Diaz has had enormous influence on Mexican affairs. Not yet clear just what this warning meant, Cotterell carried on with his tour and went to visit two leading Mexican banks as well as several publishers who had expressed interest in his work as outlined in the press. Both groups were extremely supportive and assured him that publication of the work, whether for private distribution to esteemed clients of the bank or as a commercial proposition to the general public, was guaranteed. It would be a formality to put together a concrete proposal, and then it would be a matter of drawing up contracts.

Before returning to England Cotterell made another journey to the pyramids of Palenque. This time he noticed something else, something quite disturbing. On the occasion of his first visit he had been so overwhelmed by the general impressions of Mexico and the sheer mysteriousness of the site that he had not really paid much attention to the state of the monuments themselves. Now, walking around the site in a more objective and detached frame of mind, he could see how they were suffering from the effects not only of mass tourism but more damagingly from the Mexican oil boom. The once pristine, white limestone of the pyramids and palaces were now stained black by the oily soot produced by the refineries only a few miles to the north in the swampy margins of the Gulf of Mexico.

The oil boom of the 1970s following the OPEC embargo has had a devastating effect not only on the nature of the region of Tabasco but also on its archaeological heritage. Many Olmec remains such as basalt heads, sculptures and indeed a whole mosaic have been moved from their original site on the island of La Venta to a park of the same name in the provincial capital of Villahermosa. Here they are arranged in a sort of outdoor archaeological museum where visitors can walk around and look at the sculptures in a semi-jungle setting. Meanwhile the sites from which these precious artefacts have been taken are exploited for their oil, all other archaeological traces being erased in the process.

The impact of the oil industry, probably the most powerful in the world and certainly of crucial importance to the Mexican economy, can scarcely be overestimated. While it has undeniably brought wealth to what were once malarial swamps, its side-effects have been quite catastrophic. The acid rain produced by Villahermosa and other cities is eating steadily into the limestone of Palenque, and already many inscriptions are becoming hard to read. It is, however, set to grow further—once oil has been found, history shows that nothing will be allowed to stand in the way of its extraction. Drilling has recently taken place at Palenque, within a hundred yards of the Pyramid of Inscriptions itself. Cotterell could only sigh and pray that things would go no further. Yet with so many hungry mouths to feed, it is not surprising that the Mexican government gives the oil industry a high priority. Revenues from tourism, though important for the economy, are tiny compared with that generated from black gold. As long as this continues, antiquities will remain under threat. With the collapse of the Mexican peso and the risk of political meltdown owing to high-level corruption, the threat to archaeological monuments can only become greater.

With fresh resolve to draw the attention of the world to the plight of Mayan monuments, Cotterell packed his bags and set off back to England. He condensed his ideas concerning the overlays and the Lid of Palenque into a two-volume work entitled *The Amazing Lid of Palenque*, which he published at his own expense, lodging a copy as required with the British Library. Now even if the academics didn't like his theories they would at least be available to future researchers. He also went over the heads of the establishment, directly contacting the *Daily Mail*. Like the staff on the Mexican breakfast program, they were enthusiastic about his ideas and printed a long piece with the heading THE MAN WHO BROKE THE CODE OF MAYA CARVING. It was this piece that brought him to my attention and which indirectly led to our collaboration on the present book. However, it was not the Lid of Palenque or Cotterell's discoveries using acetate overlays that really attracted me: it was his remarkable work relating sunspot cycles to the Mayan calendar and human biology. He had by now taken this far beyond its early stages recorded in *Astrogenetics*, and it was this more than anything, I felt, that needed to be brought to public attention. With his solar-genetic theory he seemed to have rediscovered something which, if true, is of vital importance to everyone on planet Earth.

5

LAND OF THE RATTLESNAKE

In search of the Maya

Cotterell's theories concerning sun cycles and the Maya amazed me both in their simplicity and universality. Could it really be that the Maya, living under conditions that we would today equate with the Stone Age, had such precise knowledge concerning sunspots? Did they indeed remember and record in their myths some devastating tragedy that had all but wiped out humanity? Were they really able—through astrology, numerology, dreams or whatever—to make prognostications about the future? All these were questions that now occupied me and I realized that I would only find the answers if I went to Mexico myself. What I would be looking for was not just the more obvious and tangible remains of this vanished civilization but their cultural atmosphere and, if possible, some pointers towards the esoteric side of their religion. This, I was now beginning to understand, was closely linked to the teachings of the great god-human or avatar that the Aztecs called Quetzalcoatl and the Maya Kukulcan. Perhaps it was from him that they learnt about sunspot cycles or at least obtained their astronomical knowledge. I felt sure that underneath the myths and superstitions there was a real human being, a wise teacher, who had once instigated a religion based upon self-transformation. I wanted now to know what this religion had been about, and if possible to identify this teacher and when he had lived.

In December 1994 I had the opportunity at last of following in Maurice's footsteps. By now I had read a great deal about the Maya, Aztecs, Toltecs and so forth, and looked forward to seeing the ruins of this amazing civilization for myself. My wife Dee, who is the photographer of the family, arranged to take time off work and come along as well. She had accompanied Robert Bauval and me on my first trip to see the pyramids of Egypt, and was keen to see how the Mexican ones would compare. Arriving in Mexico City, we were agreeably surprised by how attractive the centre still is and at how many old colonial buildings have survived the ravages of time. Though earthquakes[1] are an ever-present reality in this part of the world, the greater threat to buildings appears to be subsidence. I was amazed to see that many of the old churches have sunk by up to nine feet in the soft soil beneath them, and can now be reached only by bridges and stairs. Other buildings, such as colonial mansions, show great cracks in the walls as they too sink into the bed of Lake Texcoco. With the help of UNESCO, money is being poured in to save the architectural treasure that is old Mexico City, but it still seems to be too little too late. Perhaps no amount of money is sufficient to hold back the forces of nature forever.

At the *zocalo* there was a demonstration by Maya Indians angry about the appointment of a new governor for Chiapas region. Huddled in small groups under makeshift tents of coloured plastic, they looked tired and dejected. It seemed that the Zapotista rebellion of the previous spring was still rumbling on with little satisfaction for the Maya.[2] In front of the square was the great cathedral, which had apparently taken nearly 500 years to build and was now falling down. Incongruously for a Christian monument, it had a large plaque on its front emblazoned with the old Aztec symbol of Tenochtitlan: an eagle standing on a cactus and clutching a serpent in its beak. I was soon to discover that this symbol is now the coat-of-arms for the whole Mexican nation, and is to be found everywhere from public buildings and T-shirts to the coinage (*see* Figure 32). With mixed emotions, for the Catholic Church still commands enormous respect at all levels of society, the Mexicans are reclaiming their past, and this Aztec emblem seems to represent for them all that was great about their country before the arrival of Cortes.

Behind the tumbling cathedral I came across the ruins of the Templo Mayor with its succession of building plans like tree-rings. I shuddered to think of the 20,000 souls who had had their hearts torn out in the dedication ceremonies for just one of these buildings, but then the Aztecs—like other Indians—believed in reincarnation and that the souls of those so sacrificed would go straight to heaven. It took an effort of imagination to see the blackened volcanic stones before me as the base of the glittering, brightly-painted, twin-towered pyramid illustrated in my guide-book. They looked more like the foundations of some bleak Lancashire cotton-mill. Then I called to mind the writings of Fray Bernardino Sahagun, the first missionary to befriend the Indians and to make a serious record of their traditions before they all

Figure 32 Eagle clutching a serpent from the outside of the Mexican Museum of Anthropology

disappeared. He wrote that at the end of each 52-year period the Indians were mortally afraid. On the last night of the old cycle, terrified that the world was about to end and the sun not rise again, they took to the hills. There they studied the sky, waiting for the Pleiades star-cluster to reach the southern meridian.[3] When it carried on moving (as of course it always did), there was great rejoicing, for then they knew the world wasn't going to end after all. A new fire was lit, like an Olympic torch, and brands sent all over the kingdom in celebration of the new cycle that had been granted by the sun god Tonatiuh. Meanwhile old crockery was smashed and the Templo Mayor was refurbished with a new skin. It seems that the Aztecs were keen on making fresh starts, even though it must have cost them much in terms of time and material possessions.

Looking at the ruins of the Templo Mayor I couldn't help but notice the many serpents' heads protruding from the base like so many gargoyles. I hadn't expected this, thinking that Mexican pyramids, though stepped, were smooth-sided. In fact, as I was to discover the next day, there was a precedent for this at the early site of Teotihuacan. In the Mexican Museum of Anthropology there was a large number of Aztec sculptures many of which depicted serpents. Some of these were so lifelike in their execution that it seemed they might almost slither away. The connection between the Aztecs and Teotihuacan became apparent when I went into the room where a few years before Maurice had examined the replica of the Quetzalcoatl Pyramid. Hanging on a wall was a representation of the sun god as executed by the Teotihuacanos. Like the later representation of Tonatiuh on the Aztec Calendar stone it had its tongue poking out. But this god did not have the round, fleshy face of Tonatiuh: it was shown as a skull. Clearly the Teotihuacanos were also concerned about the connection between the sun and death.

The next day we visited Teotihuacan itself and climbed to the top of the Sun Pyramid. It offered a marvellous panorama over the surrounding area and I could well understand the awe with which the Aztecs regarded this ancient site. I could also imagine what it must have been like when Cortes rallied his men there against the forces under the command of Snake Woman. At that time the pyramids and temples were covered over with turf and brush, but even so—or perhaps more so—they would have provided cover and an elevated position for the beleaguered Spaniards to occupy. The death of Snake Woman and the flight of the remaining Aztecs was the day on which the Americas were lost as far as the Indians were concerned.[4] After that it was only a matter of time before other Europeans arrived to complete the job begun by Cortes. Standing on the Pyramid of the Sun and surveying the Avenue of the Dead before me, I wondered how much he knew about the myth of Quetzalcoatl. Did he know that the Aztecs believed that this god-man would not only avenge himself on those who had driven him from his kingdom but would one day return to Teotihuacan? Did Cortes lead his men there because he knew of this prophecy and the psychological advantage it gave him? Whatever the case, Cortes survived the battle to fight another day. A year later he fulfilled the prophecy almost to the letter by overthrowing the Aztecs and establishing Spanish rule.

Coming down from the Pyramid and braving the onslaughts not of wild Aztecs but of souvenir hawkers, I made my way to the Citadel and the Quetzalcoatl Pyramid. Unlike the replica frieze that I had already seen in the Museum of Anthropology, this has lost all of its colour. Even so, it was staggering to look at. Underneath a later rather plain-looking pyramid, archaeologists had found the remains of an earlier construction. This was altogether more lively, with alternating heads of what are believed to have been the two chief gods of the Teotihuacan pantheon, Quetzalcoatl and Tlaloc (see Plate 16). The sculptures of Quetzalcoatl, which are arranged one above the other in steps, seemed to amalgamate serpentine characteristics with those of a large-toothed predator, perhaps a jaguar, each head having a frilly ruff round its neck like the rays of the sun. What was also interesting about these heads was that they were remarkably similar to those I had seen the previous day on the sides of the Templo Mayor. Clearly, though buried under the later pyramid they were not forgotten by the Aztecs. I was not entirely convinced, however, that these heads did in fact represent Quetzalcoatl as the guide books suggested: they seemed rather too demonic and elemental to be symbolic of the wise teacher for whom I was searching.

The Tlaloc faces were altogether more abstract with round goggle-eyes and a snaky skin. If the 'Quetzalcoatls' were representations of a sky god associated with the sun, then Tlaloc was definitely earth-bound. It seemed to me that the pair formed a duality, like the Chinese *yang*-tiger and *yin*-dragon. Could it be that there was an oriental link here? In that Quetzalcoatl was supposed amongst other things to be a god associated with wind and Tlaloc was the god of rain, there seemed to be a curious parallelism.[5] Unable to pursue the matter further for the time being, I left it there.

Leaving the Mexico City area we passed on through Oaxaca and Monte Alban, before eventually arriving in Palenque itself. Here everything was pretty much as I had expected, having closely examined many pictures of the site. Seeing it all first-hand, however, was quite an experience. The overwhelming feeling was one of surprise at how such a place could have been built at all, given the intense heat and humidity; to work under those conditions must have been absolutely exhausting. I was also surprised by the scale of the site, only a part of which has been excavated. It stretches way into the surrounding jungle, which looms large and vibrant all around. Going into this was like entering the lungs of some primaeval beast, its hot, sauna-like breath all-pervasive. Here there were trees a hundred feet high that are recognizable to us in England as house-plants. Great roots stretched out like tentacles and a burbling brook rushed off down the hill, in part to fill an ancient Mayan watercourse, itself probably built during the reign of Pacal or his son Chan Bahlum.

As we walked through the ruins there was much evidence of the interest the Maya took in the sun and stars. Standing in front of Chan Bahlum's Temple of the Cross it was possible to see how it was aligned with his father's Temple of Inscriptions. This line, if continued, points towards the midsummer sunset. The implication was clear: the dead Pacal was like the setting sun, who in some way passed on responsibility and power to his son Chan Bahlum, the new ruler.[6] The sense of dynastic continuity was emphasized in the series of bas-reliefs, now sadly faded, that decorate the inner sanctuaries of the temples belonging to the Cross Group. Clearly the Pacal dynasty enjoyed a sort of Divine

Right of Kings, which as we have seen was linked to Mayan sacred numerology.[7]

Inside the largest building on the site, the so-called Palace, I was interested to see that one room is now thought to have been some sort of observatory because it has a frieze near the ceiling displaying representations of certain planets and stars. On one of the outer walls of this same building there are still to be seen the remains of some of the stucco reliefs drawn by Count Waldeck.[8] One of these shows a young king seated on a double-headed jaguar throne and receiving a crown from an attendant figure (*see* Figure 33). This brought to mind the very similar throne of Tutankhamen I had

Figure 33 Plaque showing the jaguar throne, 'Palace' of Palenque

seen in Egypt only a couple of years before. What was it about
these spotted cats, I wondered, that so attracted kings that they
wanted to make their thrones in imitation of them? How was it
that such a similar design to the throne of Tutankhamen could
have sprung up thousands of miles and centuries later on the other
side of the Atlantic? It was a mystery.

Walking down from the Palace I came to a building known as
the Count's House apparently because Waldeck had once used it
as his living quarters. Here, protected by a thatched roof from the
harsh glare of the sun, was an unusual stucco face (*see* Figure 34).
It was executed in quite a different style from other stucco work
present on the site and, perhaps because he looks as though he is
wearing glasses, has been identified as the Mexican rain god,
Tlaloc. This has been puzzling archaeologists greatly in recent
years because it is considered to be in the Teotihuacan style.
Evidence of pottery fragments and obsidian implements proves
that the Teotihuacanos traded with the Maya, but this mask

Figure 34   Teotihuacan-style Tlaloc in Palenque

appears to indicate close cultural and religious links in addition between these very different Amerindian races.

Leaving Palenque we went north to see something of the Yucatan Peninsula, where the Maya survived the great catastrophe that seems to have engulfed so much of Central America in around the 8th century. It was here that in many ways Mayan art reached its pinnacle. Following Maurice's itinerary we proceeded first to Uxmal (pronounced *Oosh-mal*), artistically the finest of the Yucatan cities. The most eye-catching feature of the site was the Pyramid of the Sorcerer (*see* Plate 17), a tall building with rounded corners and very narrow steps. Climbing up this structure, and even more, going back down it, was something of an ordeal and not to be recommended to anyone who suffers from vertigo. Next to it was a small courtyard, and standing here looking back up the pyramid there was an extraordinary sight. What had seemed while we were up there to be a normal chamber, one that might be expected in a pyramid temple, had from ground level something of a surreal appearance. The entire chamber and its surrounding stonework made up one enormous face—that of the rain god Chaac (*see* Plate 18). One can only imagine what rituals were performed in this chamber but clearly they must have been concerned with rain. It was obvious from the huge number of sculpted masks of the rain god that were to be seen elsewhere throughout the ruins of Uxmal that Chaac was a very important god. The masks, mostly placed one above another on the corners of important buildings, reminded us of the Tlaloc faces on the Quetzalcoatl Pyramid at Teotihuacan, except that these ones seemed to have curious elephants' trunks (*see* Plate 19). The purpose of these has been a mystery for over 150 years: John Stephens in his 1843 travelogue remarks:

> ... The reader must suppose this stone projecting in order clearly to understand the character of the ornament last presented. It measures one foot seven inches in length from the stem by which it is fixed in the wall to the end of the curve, and resembles somewhat an elephant's trunk, which name has, perhaps not inaptly, been given to it by Waldeck, though it is not probable that as such the sculptor intended it, for the elephant was unknown on the continent of America.[9]

Below he includes a diagram of the object in question, a curious hook shape with 10 little roundels sculpted on it (*see* Figure 35). Looking at this I was immediately reminded not of an elephant's trunk (a fatuous suggestion but typical of Waldeck's romanticism) but rather of a constellation of stars—perhaps Ursa Major or Ursa Minor. Later I was to have further thoughts on this and see how this might not be so far from the truth.

Rain was of extreme concern to the inhabitants of Uxmal for there are no rivers in the area nor even *cenotes*, the natural wells that are a feature of the Yucatan. They were entirely dependent on artificial cisterns to get them through the dry months of the year and needed to store as much as possible of whatever rain fell. For this reason the floors of the temple courts were built with a slight gradient so that they would steer rainwater into the waiting cisterns. We had seen something like this before in Monte Alban where, because the temples were built on a hilltop, there was a similar water shortage. Here in Uxmal, however, the scale of the enterprise was staggering and was clearly meant to deal with monsoon conditions.

Another favourite symbol at Uxmal was the feathered serpent god Quetzalcoatl in all his various forms. There were serpents

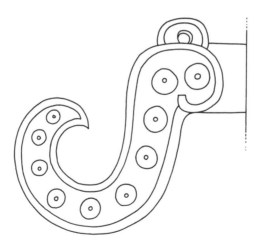

Figure 35   Waldeck's 'elephant's trunk'

Figures 36 & 37   Serpent friezes at Uxmal

everywhere on the temples, sometimes double-headed, at others single (see Figures 36 and 37). Feathered serpents formed what had been the balustrade of the ball-court, and sported along the fronts of friezes in a collection of buildings now known, rather imaginatively, as the Nunnery. It was clear from all of this that the twin cults of Quetzalcoatl-Kukulcan and Tlaloc-Chaac were as dominant here as they had been in Teotihuacan. I wondered whether there could have been some sort of connection between the two sites, and if so what relationship they might have had to one another. Textbook archaeology seemed to be rather light on this subject, referring only to vague trade links between Teotihuacan and the Maya, but I suspected there was something deeper here. Comparing the art at Uxmal with that of Teotihuacan, Tenochtitlan and Monte Alban it was clear that it was here, in the Yucatan, that what for want of a better term we might call the Quetzalcoatl school had its highest expression. The detail in the reliefs on the walls and the complexity of the symbolism involved spoke not of post-Classic decadence but of Renaissance. We seemed to be looking at the handiwork of a people who, far from retreating into oblivion, were filled with creative energy, vitality and strong beliefs. It seemed that we were getting closer to the origins of this strange religion.

The following day we went to Chichen Itza, the most famous of all the ancient sites in Yucatan. In the older part of the city, as at Uxmal, we saw the same images of serpents and rain gods repeated over and over again, the style of the buildings being very similar to those at Uxmal. However, the main areas of the city showed a markedly different, military flavour owing to its unusual history. For unlike Uxmal, which remained more or less purely Mayan right up until its abandonment, Chichen Itza was colonized by invaders from the west: the Toltecs. They brought with them military discipline but also an Aztec-sized appetite for human sacrifice. That this was so was attested by the many reliefs of jaguars and eagles feasting on the hearts of sacrificial victims, as well as whole walls covered with carved human skulls. When looking at these it was hard to feel any love or sympathy for the conquerors, still less to believe that their leader was a good and honourable man. Yet the traditions state that he too was a Quetzalcoatl. I needed now to investigate this connection further.

Chichen Itza and the legend of Quetzalcoatl

The Mayan city of Chichen Itza seems originally to have been built at roughly the same time as Uxmal, in the Terminal Classic period.[10] At some time in the 10th century, however, the Yucatan was invaded from the sea by Toltec warriors. According to legends told to the Spanish in the 16th century, they were led by a god-king called Topilzin-Ce-Acatl, who took the title Quetzalcoatl or Kukulcan. It seems that this was the same king mentioned in the legends of the Aztecs, who had once ruled over the Toltecs of Tula before being driven out by his rival Tezcatlipoca or 'Smoking Mirror'. The legends speak of him as a peaceable leader who, having left his home, arrived in the Yucatan and established a new capital at Chichen Itza. Friar Diego de Landa has this to say:

> The opinion of the Indians is that with the Itzas who settled Chichen Itza there ruled a great lord named Cuculcan [sic], as an evidence of which the principal building is called Cuculcan.
>
> They say that he came from the west, but are not agreed as to whether he came before or after the Itzas[11] or with them. They say that he was well disposed, that he had no wife or children, and that after his return he was regarded in Mexico as one of their gods, and called Cezalcohuati [Quetzalcoatl]. In Yucatan he was also reverenced as a god because of his great services to the state, as appeared in the order which he established in Yucatan after the death of the chiefs, to settle the discord caused in the land by their deaths.[12]

After telling us how Kukulcan went on to found another city called Mayapan, meaning 'standard of the Mayas', Landa goes on to say: 'Cuculcan lived for some years in this city [Mayapan] with the chiefs, and then leaving them in full peace and amity returned by the same road to Mexico.'[13]

Modern Mayanists point out that there is considerable ambiguity and confusion in Landa's account owing to the fact that there was clearly more than one migration into the Yucatan. The Quetzalcoatl or Kukulcan that is described must have been a Toltec leader. The Itzas, however, were a later much-despised people, who came to Chichen Itza sometime in the 13th century and gave their name to the formerly Toltec city of Chichen. In any case the coming of the first Quetzalcoatl cannot have been the peaceful event that his later historians describe. The evidence from inscriptions at Chichen itself is of a violent invasion and the overthrowing of the local Maya dynasty. The murals in the Temple of the Warriors show in graphic detail how the Toltecs took control of the country, first winning a naval engagement against local Maya who came out on rafts to try to drive them away and then fighting another great battle in a city, which may have been Chichen itself. Having won the field of battle, they made slaves of their enemies, sacrificing the leaders to the sun god.

Looking at these scenes of warfare, it was difficult for me to square them with the image of the supposedly peaceable Quetzalcoatl as depicted by Landa. Nor, it seemed, was this just some aberration brought on by the necessities of war. It was clear from other buildings, such as the Temple of the Jaguars, that human sacrifice was as much part and parcel of Toltec culture as it was with the later Aztecs. Elsewhere, in the ball-court, it was clear that the game was played to the death, the winning (or perhaps losing) team's leader being beheaded so that his spurting blood could give sustenance to the sun. Heart-sacrifices were also a regular feature of their religion. At the Temple of the Warriors there was abundant evidence of this, with depictions of jaguars and eagles eating human hearts (*see* Figure 38). I felt disgusted by these images and could only feel sympathy for the Mayan slaves who must have supplied the raw material for this grisly sacrament. If this Quetzalcoatl really was the god-king whose return was prophesied to the Aztecs, then perhaps Cortes was indeed his reincarnation. For it seems that he showed as much ruthless disregard for life as Cortes in his desire to take dominion over a foreign people. I couldn't help but feel, however, that this was not the whole story. There seemed to be something missing—something that was only hinted at by Landa when he said that there was disagreement about whether Cuculcan came before, with, or after the Itzas.

It was clear to me by now, if it hadn't been before, that the cult of Quetzalcoatl–Kukulcan was something far bigger than this 'king' and very probably much older. As at Uxmal, the cult, in the form of the feathered serpent, was strongly in evidence in the way many of the buildings were ornamented. This form of decoration

Figure 38   Eagle eating human heart, from the Temple of the Warriors, Chichen Itza

reached its climax with the extraordinary Pyramid of Kukulcan, the one referred to by Landa as the city's 'principal building'. He visited it himself and made the following observations:

> This structure has four stairways looking to the four directions of the world; they are 33 feet wide, with 91 steps to each that are killing to climb. The steps have the same rise and width as we give to ours ...
> ... When I saw it there was at the foot of each side of the stairways the fierce mouth of a serpent, curiously worked from a single stone.[14]

These magnificent heads are still to be seen and I was able to take a good look at them. They are far from unique, however, and are to be found at the foot of virtually every stairway of every building of any significance in Chichen Itza. Most often the serpents were paired and had rather short bodies serving as the entrance pillars to a temple. These were always topped off with an L-shaped tail that included a stylized rattle. Elsewhere on the walls of temples there were feathered serpent's head masks from which human heads popped out (*see* Figure 39). I wondered if this implied the snakes were giving birth to these people, who were perhaps initiated priests. I had seen similar masks at Uxmal and somehow they seemed highly significant. Clearly there was something in this and it had to have a connection with the Quetzalcoatl religion, but as yet I didn't understand it.

Returning to the Pyramid of Kukulcan, it is now well established that it has, as Landa suggests, a cosmological significance. The choice of 91 steps to each side, with one extra at the top to reach the temple, is no accident: they clearly represent the 365 days of the year. Furthermore, the orienting of the Pyramid to the four cardinal directions was also for definite reasons. Landa tells us in his book that the Maya of the Yucatan used to carry out special New Year festivals that varied year by year. The 20 names for the days of their months were grouped into four sets of five. The initial one of each group was used to determine what he calls the

Figure 39 Feathered serpent with human head coming from its mouth

'Dominical letter' of the year and the directional god with which it was associated. He writes:

> Among the multitude of gods worshipped by these people were four whom they called by the name Bacab. These were, they say, four brothers placed by God when he created the world at its four corners to sustain the heavens lest they fall. They also say that these Bacabs escaped when the world was destroyed by the Deluge. To each of these they give other names, and they mark the four points of the world where God placed them holding up the sky, and also assign one of the four Dominical letters to each, and to the place he occupies; also they signalize the misfortunes or blessings that are to happen in the year belonging to each of these, and the accompanying letters.[15]

Later he tells us how it was the custom in each Yucatan town to have two heaps of stones at each of its four gates facing the cardinal directions. It was at these that ceremonies were carried out to drive away demons prior to ushering in the New Year. Given the calendrical significance of the steps on the Quetzalcoatl Pyramid and the orientation to the cardinal directions, it seems obvious that this building was meant to symbolize the central pivot or shaft of the world around which the universe turns. Yet it has another amazing feature that was never witnessed by Landa because it was discovered only after the building had been restored during the 20th century. Twice a year, at the equinoxes, the sun plays an amazing trick, which must have seemed like a miracle to anyone not initiated into its secrets. During the afternoon on these two days, shadows are cast on the balustrades which take the form of moving serpents gliding down the side of the pyramid. We can only speculate on what this symbolized, but perhaps it seemed to the onlooker as though some magical, ghostly Quetzalcoatl were in a sense coming back to life.

The serpent does not have the building entirely to himself, however. Just as in Teotihuacan the Pyramid of Quetzalcoatl was found to contain an inner structure complete with alternating heads of their two chief gods, so this pyramid also shows evidence of having been rebuilt on more than one occasion. Archaeological investigation has revealed a hidden staircase underneath the present outer skin that leads upwards to an internal chamber. Contained in this is a remarkable throne in the form of a red-painted jaguar with spots made of green jade. Seeing him staring out through white, shell eyes there, I was reminded again of the plaque I had seen at Palenque depicting their king, Pacal, seated on his own jaguar throne. It seems that the Toltecs, who built the later pyramid, had borrowed this symbol of power from the Maya—but where had the Maya got it from?

Also at Chichen Itza is another interesting building which I visited: it is called the Caracol, a Spanish name meaning 'snail' (*see* Plate 26). This curious structure is circular in cross-section and has an inner spiral staircase leading to an upper chamber—hence its name. Here small windows point in various directions and it is now believed that these were used for observations of the planets, particularly Venus. Clearly the priests of Chichen Itza were interested not only in the sun and its equinoxes but in observing other stellar bodies as well.

Leaving the ruins and their stifling afternoon heat behind us, we proceeded to Merida, the provincial capital of Yucatan. It was here that Don Francisco de Montejo, formerly one of Cortes' officers, established a base in 1542. From humble beginnings Merida was to become a thriving Spanish town, with pleasant squares and colonial-style houses. The source of its wealth was an unpromising looking cactus called the *henequin*, which grows in abundance under the hot tropical sunshine. When the leaves of this plant are shredded, they produce the extremely tough fibrous material called sisal which is used in the making of string. Today the boom in sisal is over: it has been replaced for the most part by cheaper, stronger, synthetic materials. However, it is still used for making twine, baskets, shoes, hammocks and the Panama hats that are sold by street-traders on every Merida street-corner.

Walking around Merida it is still possible to feel something of the old colonial charm, but it is not easy. Over the last 20 years or so Montejo's city has been swollen by immigration to over a million inhabitants—all of whom seem to be constantly on the move. The narrow streets are packed with pedestrians and every imaginable kind of motorized vehicle, all competing for precious space. Although the city is laid out according to a grid system and the streets are all numbered—a boon to the traveller who doesn't know his way round—the incessant noise, pollution, and sheer pressure of people makes shopping an occupation that is both stressful and dangerous.

We were staying in the aptly named Hotel Casa del Bahlam, which translates as 'House of the Jaguar', and wanting to obtain more information about the sites we had seen decided to look for a bookshop. We did not have to look very far, for there was one between the hotel and an Opera House, which, incongruously, was putting on a production of *The Nutcracker Suite*. Inside the shop, like everywhere else, there was a fine patina of black dust, largely deriving from leaded petrol. Fortunately, most of the books on sale were protected by plastic bags, though this gave them a rather second-hand feel. Finding a shelf of English-language books, and looking eagerly for anything that might help explain more about the Mayan sites and Quetzalcoatl, I came across a series of very curious booklets. These, it seemed, were all written by the same author, one José Diaz Bolio, and had titles such as *Why the Rattlesnake in Mayan Civilization*, *The Geometry of the Maya and their Rattlesnake Art*, and *The Rattlesnake School*. Suspecting that I might have unwittingly stumbled across something quite important, I bought several of the booklets and took them back to our room to read. I was to discover that they were not just curiosities but the key I had been looking for to explain why all the pre-Columbian civilizations, and not just the Maya, were seemingly so obsessed with serpents. Staying up half the night I read them all, and having discovered that Diaz Bolio lived in Merida, decided I would have to seek him out the next day.

Meetings with a Remarkable Man

Taking a taxi to the suburbs, I arrived just after sunset. I was greeted affably at the door by José Diaz Bolio himself, who turned out to be a man in his eighties (*see* Figure 40). No longer sprightly, he was nonetheless still sharp of mind and only too willing to talk to me about his theories concerning the origins of Mayan culture. It seemed that for some 50 years he had been studying Mayan art and architecture, but in an unorthodox fashion. He had in the course of his long life been a soldier, a poet and a musician, as well

Figure 40　José Diaz Bolio

as an archaeologist. I could see all of these careers written into his craggy visage, and could imagine him as a young man fighting in the revolutions that convulsed Mexico for so many years. The steely determination that must have served him well through many painful years was still present, and I was aware that I was not talking to any ordinary old man. Like Carlos Castaneda's Don Juan he had a special presence. He was a man of knowledge, of wisdom, who had seen the world and who was not afraid now to face eternity.

Spread before us on the table were over 20 books and booklets, all written and published by him without any help from outside sources. Against all the odds he had forced his ideas onto the world, in spite of the opposition of not only the establishment—which believed him to be somehow dishonouring Mexico by telling the truth about Mayan civilization—but even of his friends. Now, sitting peaceably in his little cottage, he concentrated as he attempted to pass on to me something of the spirit of his ideas. The key concepts were very simple to grasp but their ramifications were vast. For according to Diaz Bolio the Maya, and indeed all the other cultures of Central America worthy of the name civilization, were deeply involved in a rattlesnake cult. This, he assured me, was not a hypothesis but a fact, which he had proved over and over again in his work during the past 50 years. It was shocking to the authorities not because they hadn't realized how central the serpent is in Mayan art but because, as he saw it, the Maya quite literally derived their knowledge of the world 'from the mouth of a rattlesnake'.

By now spellbound I sat bolt upright in my chair as he told me about his thesis which, to give it a name, he calls the cultural ramifications of the rattlesnake. He explained how in the early years of his researches he used to keep rattlesnakes in the house and study their behaviour first-hand. It was not enough for him to read about them in encyclopaedias or to consult expert opinion, he wanted to see and feel them for himself. Next to us were two rattlesnake skins in a plastic bag and I began to feel uncomfortable, wondering whether there might be a live rattler hiding under the sofa or in some other inaccessible place. He assured me that these days he didn't keep live snakes, but there had been times in the past when pets of his had escaped, causing untold commotion with the neighbours. These days, however, things were calm, and he concentrated on writing, publishing, and giving a few private lectures to interested students. By now we had struck up a good rapport and information began to pour out of him, though not in a very ordered fashion. I tried my best to keep up with what he was saying, using a tape-recorder to make sure I did not miss anything important. My main task was to see to it that the conversation covered the ground I wanted, for I was convinced that his rattlesnake concept was the missing link in our understanding of Mayan chronology.

We carried on in this fashion for several hours, by which time he was becoming tired and I was feeling heavy with new information. I had a plane to catch the following afternoon but I promised to come and see him again in the morning to finalize certain arrangements concerning the distribution of his books in England. With that I returned to the Hotel Casa del Bahlam to set about putting these new ideas in some sort of order, and to ponder their relevance to Maurice's work on sunspot cycles.

The Teachings of Don José

At the start of our conversation, Don José, as I shall now call him, explained that at the root of the ancient Mayan religion lay the veneration of the rattlesnake. That this was at least in part true was evident from the many sculptures of serpents with rattlesnake tails seen in front of their temples and pyramids. However, it went very much deeper than this—and it was not just any old rattlesnake. It seems that the particular one that was important to them was *Crotalus durissus durissus* and its subspecies, which they called the *Ahau Can*—'Great, lordly serpent' (*see* Figure 41). This species of snake is only found in the Yucatan Peninsula and neighbouring

Figure 41   The Ahau Can, Crotalus durissus durissus

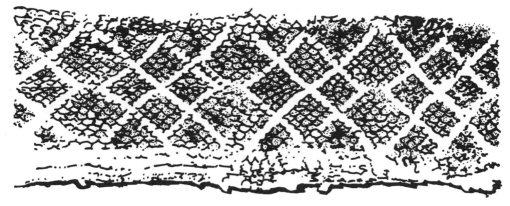

Figure 42   The back of a Crotalus *rattlesnake*

areas, yet its cultural significance seems to have stretched far and wide from the United States to Argentina in South America. He believed that the reason *Crotalus* was so important to the Maya was manifold but most significantly it had to do with the pattern on its back.

Many snakes have patterned skins. *Crotalus durissus durissus*, however, has a particular design along its back of interlocking squares and crosses (*see* Figure 42). According to Don José this pattern is reflected in a very large proportion of the art and architecture of Central and South America—so much so that one could call it the central inspiration of all Amerindian art. He showed me a picture from a temple at El Tajín, Veracruz, that exactly matched the pattern of *Crotalus* and it was quite clear that this was no accident (*see* Figure 43). I also remembered the mosaic-friezes from Mitla and how they were composed of zigzag lines made out of little stones. These too, I now realized, were based on the same snakeskin patterning. The tiny carved stones that made up the mosaics were just like the scales of a snake and matched the way in which its pattern was made out of regular diamonds of colour. The principle difference between the designs of the Zapotecs and the one I was now looking at from El Tajín was that whereas the latter was a like-for-like representation of a serpent's skin, the Mitla mosaics were more expressionistic. The Zapotecs had taken the basic design and produced variations on the theme

Figure 43   Architectural design based on Crotalus *at El Tajin*

in the way that a composer might write a symphony based on a simple melody (*see* Figure 44). Don José assured me that this was so, and that not only was this the case in architecture but in all the other arts too, including even the simple embroidery on the costumes of peasants. This explanation made sense to me, for the preponderance of zigzags in Indian design had to owe its origin to something important, and the inspiration for it had to be something in the environment: why not the skin of a rattlesnake?

This, however, was just the beginning. Don José proceeded to show me how the *Crotalus* pattern is in fact made up of interlocking individual squares, and that each of these contains a cross-shape. It was this simple design of the cross within the square—which he has named the *canamayte* pattern (*see* Figure 43)—that made this rattlesnake so sacred to the Maya. It was also the basis of their science, for it taught them geometry.

Studying the *canamayte* pattern, I could see how this might certainly have been an important inspiration behind the development of not just Mayan but all American Indian architecture. Laid flat, the most natural thing would be to orientate the square in such a way that its sides pointed towards the four cardinal points. This would mean that the cross would also be directed in this way. The natural way of expressing this in three dimensions would be as a pyramid, oriented to the points of the compass and with a staircase running down the centre of each of its three sides. This is exactly

Figure 44   Zapotec mosaic from Mitla: clouds, rain and lightning

how many of the pyramids of the Maya and others were in fact built, the most obvious example being the Chichen Itza Temple of Quetzalcoatl itself, which I had visited only the previous day. More complicated sites, such as the hilltop of Monte Alban, were designed on *canamayte* principles, again involving orientation to the cardinal points but this time using multiple squares. In his books, and particularly in one called *The Geometry of the Maya and their Rattlesnake Art*, Don José supplies a series of diagrams showing how the *canamayte* was probably used to define not just the floor-plan of buildings but their elevations too. Turned on its side and on one corner, the profile of the *canamayte*, made out of the scales of a snake, closely resembles the steps of a pyramid in profile. Other architectural features, such as the cross-sections of doorways and the placing of temple roofs, could also have been derived from the simple *canamayte*.

But according to Don José it was not only the laws of space that the Maya learnt from the *Ahau Can*, their lordly serpent: it taught them about time as well. One of the curious things about snakes is that they slough off their skins. For *Crotalus durissus durissus* this happens once a year, in mid-July, around the time in Yucatan when the sun reaches the highest point in the sky for the second time in the year.[16] There is therefore a natural correspondence between sun and serpent, that annually renew themselves together. This link between sun and serpent was further heightened for the Maya by the way the *Ahau Can* was believed to grow an extra rattle each time it moulted. According to local folklore, it is possible to tell the age of a snake by counting the number of rattles it carries on its tail. Because of this the heart-shaped rattles symbolize the year, and are still kept by the Maya for good luck.

Don José was to come up with even more startling information linking the rattlesnake cult with the Mayan calendar itself. According to him the *C. durissus* loses and replaces its fangs every 20 days. This period of time is, of course, the Mayan *uinal*. He pointed out that the standard glyph for this looks like the open jaws of a snake with two very obvious and prominent fangs. Could it be, he said, that the Maya counted their days in twenties because they recognized this as the basic cycle of renewal for their favourite serpent? Even if this were not the case, I had to agree that it was at the very least a remarkable coincidence that their calendar dovetails so neatly into the perceived cycle of the *Ahau Can*.

According to Don José the ancient Maya called themselves *chanes*—that is to say, serpents. They were extremely devout and had to perform certain initiation practices in the name of their religion. Just as a male Jew or Muslim child has to be circumcised, or a Christian baptised to be accepted as one of God's chosen, so Mayan babies—or at least those of the nobility—had to have their heads flattened. Because this was a very painful process that sometimes resulted in the baby's death, it cannot (as anthropologists are wont to suggest) have been done simply for reasons of fashion; no parent would subject a child to such pain unnecessarily. The only convincing reason for doing it was that it served a religious purpose. Don José asserted that head-flattening was performed to give the child what he called a *polcan*, or serpent-head (*see* Plate 28). In this way the child was initiated into the family of *chanes*, the ones who were the people of the serpent: its children. For these people the *Ahau Can* and everything to do with it was as much of a religious and cultural emblem as the Cross is to a Christian. It filled their lives and they proclaimed their adherence to its values at every opportunity, whether it was the building of a temple or the embroidering of a smock. According to Don José there was another initiation that is still practised in some parts of the Yucatan involving a live rattlesnake. In this the right hand is passed over the snake nine times to the left and then the left nine times to the right. This is done to confer artistic talent, particularly in embroidery.

What then was this cult whose totem was the *Ahau Can*, and to whom does it owe its origins? Don José had two explanations, which perhaps are really one and the same. The first was that at some period in remote antiquity some native, more intelligent than the rest, noticed the pattern on the back of *Crotalus* and began imitating it in his art. From such simple beginnings perhaps a school, using the geometry of the *canamayte* pattern as its inspiration, developed practical techniques of architecture and pleasing patterns for their clothing. The snake would also, on account of its ability to shed its skin and emerge fresh each year, have symbolized resurrection and therefore immortality. As a solar animal whose life was closely geared to the annual cycle of the sun, it would have been a simple process of transference to believe that *Crotalus* was somehow endowed with solar intelligence. In this way, as in the Biblical story of Adam and Eve prior to the Fall, it was the snake itself who was the teacher of mankind. As the wisest of the animals it taught the Maya calendrics, mathematics and the basic patterns of their art. By virtue of its skin patterning and lifestyle it unwittingly put in place the basic elements of civilization. This, if you like, is the rationalist explanation, the one that could perhaps find some support amongst anthropologists. But there is another one.

It is a curious irony that the best analogy to the second explanation is the story of St Patrick, who, according to the legends, banished all snakes from Ireland shortly after bringing the Christian Gospel to its shores. It is said that Patrick, wishing to explain the doctrine of the Holy Trinity to the Irish, bent down and picked a three-leafed shamrock, its three-in-one design a suitable symbol for what he wished to convey. Thereafter the humble shamrock was revered as somehow holy and Irish, so that today it has come to symbolize not just the Trinity but Ireland herself. However, it was not really the shamrock which taught the Irish about Christianity but St Patrick who made use of it as a symbol. Looking at the snakeskin patterns I wondered, could not something similar have happened in the Yucatan long, long ago? Could there have been a 'St Patrick' washed up on the shores of Yucatan, who seeking to make himself understood, made use of a local snake to teach the people he met the elements of an advanced religion? Could the *canamayte* pattern, like the shamrock, have become a cultural icon on account of its association with such a wise man? This, I felt, was a more likely explanation than the simple one of cultural evolution. I was also beginning to suspect that this 'St Patrick' might be the real Quetzalcoatl, and I was now to find out his name: Zamna.

In his book *The Rattlesnake School*, Don José gives the name Zamnaism to the ancient religion of the Maya. Zamna (or Itzamna) was the head of the Mayan pantheon of gods and was, according to Don José, the prototype of the later Quetzalcoatl. He writes:

> Zamna, the main Mayan god-hero, appears to be the original pattern or model for the Quetzalcoatl Toltec deity. Being earlier than the Toltec invasion of Yucatan, he has the same attributes as the latter. Zamnaism was a non-bloody and non-violent religion. Human sacrifices were introduced into Yucatan by Tula's Quetzalcoatl-Topilzin-Ce-Acatl, who left here, as also among the Maya-Quiché of Guatemala the flourishing practice of beholding the tribes sacrificed in his presence. In his boyhood the author [Don José] saw at Izamal, Yucatan, a great stucco head of Zamna, destroyed later by disrespectful hands.[17]

Fortunately an etching of this great head of Zamna was made by Frederick Catherwood in 1844, so we are able to see what it looked like (*see* Figure 45). It is nothing like the later representations of Itzamna that one sees in the Mayan Codices, which portray him as an aged god. This sculpture—monolithic in

IZAMAL
Gyantic Hea

Figure 45   Catherwood's print of the giant head of Zamna at Izamal

scale—has its mouth open, implying that he is giving voice to some important teaching. Although, as Don José says, the head of Zamna at Izamal has long since fallen prey to vandals, I did see something similar to it among the ruins of Palenque. There at the foot of the Palace was another great stucco head. It wears a plumed headdress and stares out meditatively (*see* Figure 46). That a head of Zamna should be there is certainly no coincidence, for the religion practised at Palenque was certainly in some way related to the Quetzalcoatl–Kukulcan cult. The name Palenque is

Figure 46   Giant head, probably of Zamna, at Palenque

derived from Spanish and means 'place that is fenced off'—in other words a pallisade, which presumably the Spanish village was at one time. Nachan is possibly its original name: this is what it was called by its first Spanish visitor, Friar Ramon Aguilar, when he was taken there by his parishioners in 1773. In the book *A History of the Creation of Heaven and Earth* that he wrote afterwards, based he says on documents destroyed by Bishop Nuñez de la Vega of Chiapas, he refers to Palenque as the 'Great City of Serpents'.

Ordoñez's book concerns a legendary leader, Votan, who brought his people to Palenque and whose symbol was a serpent. Could this Votan, who is said to have come from the Atlantic, have been a prophet of Zamna, a Mayan equivalent of St Patrick? This, I was beginning to see, might be the real story behind the Maya serpent cult, so I now began to turn my mind to these possibilities.

Before leaving Merida and returning to England, I went round to see Don José again, this time taking my wife Dee with me. We found him sitting on his bed in his pyjamas because he had been ill during the night. He seemed somehow older and frailer than the previous day, a stark reminder that at 88 years of age his body could no longer keep up with his mind. We discussed his major works, *La Serpiente Emplumada* and *Mi Descubrimiento del Culto Crotalico*, and the possibility of my getting them published in English. I promised I would do my best, for his sake hoping in my heart that this could be done quickly. Then to our great surprise, he suddenly burst into song. A strong, tenor voice filled the air as he sang extracts of Italian opera. Though perhaps straining a little on some of the high notes, his voice was still true and able to hold a tune without going flat—something that I, at half his age, would find impossible. 'It is a very strange thing,' he said, 'although my body is old and I am unable now to do much of what I would like, I still have my voice. It is because I trained as an opera singer!'

Dee and I felt overjoyed at the sheer exuberance of this human spirit that refused to give in to old age. Before we left he signed copies of his books for me and we promised to keep in touch. Then, in a gesture both meaningful and apt, he gave me two rattlesnake skins to take to England as souvenirs of our visit. When I got back I passed my hands over them nine times, in each direction. Perhaps now I would, at least in part, be initiated into the cult of *Crotalus durissus durissus* and with its help find out more about the esoteric side of Zamnaism.

6

THE NEW FIRE, THE CHACMOOLS, AND THE SKULL OF DOOM

The shaking of the rattle

Our trip to Mexico had been much more fruitful than I had expected. I now felt sure that I was on the track of a possible route of transmission for the extraordinary knowledge of the Maya. It was clear from what Don José had told me that the rattlesnake cult was an extremely important element in their belief. But I felt this was only part of the story. It seemed to me that he was looking at the subject from a rather earth-bound perspective; there was a more cosmic element to all of this than the reptilian *Crotalus*. Everything about the Maya pointed to their having been extremely good astronomers as well as numerologists, and their interest in the sky seemed to be at the root of whatever it was they wished to express by the term Quetzalcoatl or 'feathered serpent'. I was rather surprised when at Palenque our guide had pointed out that the Maya followed the movements of the constellation of Orion which, he said, was nearly always visible at night at that latitude.[1] The interest in Orion, though, seemed to be of secondary importance compared with their fascination with the Pleiades star-cluster[2] (*see* Plate 37). This small cluster of stars is part of the constellation of Taurus and may be described as a miniature version of Ursa Major. It occurred to me that it might well have been what Catherwood's 'elephant's trunk'—as repeated over and over again on the temples of Yucatan—really represents. Without knowing in advance where it might lead, I decided to look into this matter further.

Back at home, in front of my computer, I began by investigating the mysterious events surrounding the Pleiades star-group and the Aztec New Year festival. The Maya called the Pleiades the *tzab*, meaning 'rattle'. It seems that they regarded them as having much the same function as a snake's rattle, which is shaken as a warning before it strikes. If Friar Bernardino Sahagun's report is to be believed, the Aztecs must have had a rather similar conception. In his books he prints a picture showing how the Aztecs depicted the Pleiades as nine stars contained in a sort of daisy chain of seventeen other stars (*see* Figure 47). English translations of his works are very hard to come by but fortunately Don José quotes the relevant passage in one of his booklets, *Why the Rattlesnake in Mayan Civilization*. Because it is important I will quote the passage in full.

> The measurement of all times that these Indians [the Mexicans] carried out was as follows: the largest measurement of time was of 104 years, and they called it a century; half of this period, which is 52 years, they called a sheaf of years. This number of years they have counted since ancient times; it is not known when it began, but they quite faithfully believed that the world would come to an end at the termination of one of these sheaves, and they had prophecies and oracles that

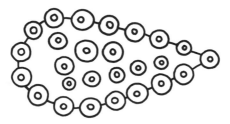

Figure 47   An Aztec illustration of the Pleiades; from Sahagun

the movements of heaven would cease then, and they took for a signal the movement of the *Cabrillas* (Pleiades) in relation to the night of this feast, which they called *Toxiuh molpilli*; for on that night the Cabrillas were in the middle of the sky at midnight, corresponding to this Mexican latitude.

On this night they lit the new fire, and before they lit it they put out the fires of all the provinces, towns and houses of all this New Spain, and all the satraps and ministers of the temples went in great procession and solemnity. They went from here, from the Temple of Mexico [Templo Mayor] early at night; they went to the summit of that hill near Ixtapalapa and which they call Uixachtecatl; and they climbed to the top at nearly midnight, to where there was a solemn *cu* [Mayan name meaning 'god and temple', a term that the conquistadores learnt when they landed in Yucatan] made for that ceremony; and if they were too early, they waited until they arrived; and when they saw that they [the Cabrillas or Pleiades] passed the zenith, they understood that the movement of the heavens was not to cease, and that it was not the end of the world, but that it would last another 52 years, and that the world surely would not come to an end. At this hour great multitudes were in the hills surrounding this province of Texcoco, Xochimilco and Quahtitlan, waiting to see the new fire, that was the signal that the world would continue on; and as the satraps brought out the fire with great ceremony in that hill's *cu* it then appeared all around the hills, and when those who were there saw it, they were so happy that they yelled and their yells reached up to heaven, for the world was not coming to an end and they undoubtedly had 52 more years.

The last new fire ceremony they held was in the year 1507; they held it with all solemnity because the Spanish had not yet arrived. In 1559 the next *gavilla* (sheaf) that they called *toxiuh molpilla* ended. On this occasion they did not hold a public celebration because the Spanish and their priests were in the land; by now in 1576 [the year in which Sahagun is writing], therefore, 17 years of the present *gavilla* have passed.

When they brought out the new fire and held the ceremony, they renewed the pact they had with the idol, that of serving him, and they renewed all the statues of him which they had in their homes and rejoiced, knowing that the world was safe. It is clear that this method of measurement was the Devil's invention, in order to renew the covenant they had with him every 52 years, frightening them with the approach of the end of the world, and making them believe that he extended time and granted it to them as his gift, moving the world forward.[3]

Clearly Bernardino Sahagun, good Franciscan that he was, was in no doubt that the festival of the New Fire, like almost everything else in the Indians' religion, was connected with idolatry and devil worship. This is hardly surprising, given the prevalence of so many strange-looking sculptures of Tlaloc, Coatlicue, and so on, not to mention serpent motifs—in Spanish eyes emblems of the Devil himself. Even so, he must have been impressed by something the Indians told him or he would not have taken the trouble to record the ceremony in such detail. It looks very much as though his strong protestations concerning the Devil were put in more for reasons of political expediency than anything else. He himself was obviously fascinated by the astronomical significance of the *Toxiuh molpilli* ceremony.

Looking at his account more closely, it is apparent that the Indians must have had some sophisticated, probably astronomical, system for telling the time. They clearly regarded as crucial the moment when the Pleiades cross the southern meridian at midnight. However, they would not have been able to detect that moment simply by observing these stars. The Pleiades rise and cross the meridian every day and, except when they are invisible in daylight, may be observed to do so. However, there is only one day in the year when they do so precisely at midnight, and the Mexicans must have had other means for calculating which day this was. I was now curious myself to find out what day it was, so taking Sahagun's date of 1507 for the last such ceremony, I tried working it out using the SKYGLOBE computer program. The results that I came up with were fascinating—but before going into this there are some other matters that need first to be covered.

In the *Rélacion*, Diego de Landa records that a similar fire ceremony was carried out by the Maya in the city of Mani. It seems that at one time this fire festival had been widely celebrated by all the Maya of Yucatan, but after the destruction of Mayapan[4] (around 1450 according to Landa) it was confined to Mani alone. He relates:

> In the twelfth chapter was related the departure of Kukulcan from Yucatan, after which some of the Indians said he had departed to heaven with the gods, wherefore they regarded him as a god and

appointed a time when they should celebrate a festival for him as such; this the whole country did until the destruction of Mayapan. After that destruction only the province of Mani kept this up, while the other provinces in recognition of what they owed to Kukulcan made presents, one each year, turn and turn about, of four or sometimes five magnificent banners of feathers, sent to Mani; with which they kept this festival in that manner, and not in the former ways.

On the 16th of Xul all the chiefs and priests assembled at Mani, and with them a great multitude from the towns, all of them after preparing themselves by fasts and abstinences. On the evening of that day they set out in a great procession, with many comedians [professional rejoicers], from the house of the chief where they had gathered, and marched slowly to the temple of Kukulcan, all duly decorated. On arriving, and offering their prayers, they set the banners on the top of the temple, and below in the court set each of them his idols on leaves of trees brought for this purpose; *then making the new fire* they began to burn their incense at many points, and to make offerings of viands cooked without salt or pepper, and drinks made from their beans and calabash seeds. There the chiefs and those who had fasted stayed for five days and nights, always burning copal and making their offerings, without returning to their homes, but continuing in prayers and certain sacred dances. Until the first day of Yaxkin the comedians frequented the principal houses, performing their turns and receiving presents bestowed on them and then taking all to the temple. Finally, when the five days were passed, they divided the gifts among the chiefs, priests and dancers, collected the banners and idols, returning them to the house of the chief, and thence each one to his home. They said and believed that Kukulcan descended on the last of those days from heaven and received their sacrifices, penances and offerings. This festival they called Chicc-kaban.[5]

There is a note from the translator of Landa's work, William Gates, that tells us more about this festival at Mani:

We probably have here a survival from an earlier adjustment of the calendar, as shown both by the month names and the ceremonies. *Xul* means 'end', 'termination', and on the 16th they created new fire, and continued offerings and other ceremonies for the last five days of the month, paralleling those later carried on before the New Year beginning the 1st of Pop. *Kin* means 'sun', 'day', 'time', so that *Yaxkin* means 'new time'. And so even in the later changed arrangement they kept the month Yaxkin for the renewal of all utensils with preparation for the very sacred ceremonial carving of the new images in the following month Mol, and carried through into Ch'en.

In Landa's time the 16th of Xul fell on Nov. 8th, Yaxkin beginning Nov. 13th, and Mol ending just at the winter solstice, Dec. 22nd.[6]

We know from earlier on in Landa's *Rélacion* that the Maya used the stars and planets to tell the time. He writes:

> To know the hour of the night the natives governed themselves by the planet Venus, the Pleiades and the Twins [Gemini]. During the day they had terms for 'midday', and for various sections from sunrise to sunset, according to which they recognized and regulated their hours for work.[7]

Now when, using the computer, I checked on what day in 1507 the Pleiades crossed the meridian at midnight, I was very

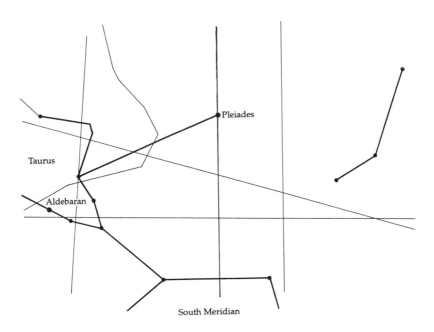

Figure 48 The Pleiades crossing the meridian at midnight on 11 November 1507

surprised to find that it was 11 November (*see* Figures 48 and 49). This lies right in between 16 Xul (8 November) and the start of Yaxkin (13 November). We know that the festival, with its fast, lasted for five days, so this must have been during the period when the Pleiades were crossing the meridian at midnight each day, the central day of this period having the closest timing. So it seems that for the Maya the New Fire ceremony was an annual event, though for the Aztecs it was only celebrated once every 52 years. It is probable that at the time it was widely celebrated outside of Mani it would also have been held at Chichen Itza. If this is so, the most likely place they would have performed the New Fire ritual would have been in the temple on the summit of the Kukulcan Pyramid—the place most sacred to that god. It is noteworthy that the sides of this pyramid resemble the scales of a rattlesnake and

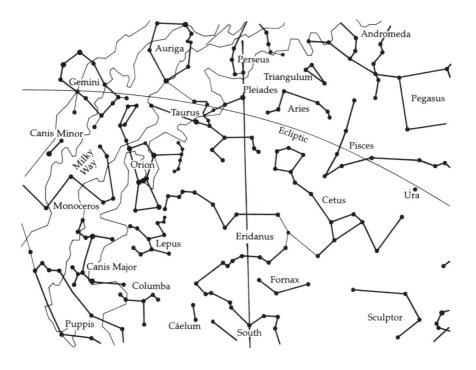

Figure 49   Southern and eastern sky at midnight on 11 November 1507

that its *ad quadratum* architecture is, as we have seen, probably based on the *canamayte* pattern. Once more, it appears, there is a link between the Mayan rattlesnake cult and later Mexican religions associated with Quetzalcoatl–Kukulcan. However, there is clearly an association older than all of this. The most important of the Mayan gods was Zamna, the father figure and teacher of all wisdom. He, it seems, was the prototype of the later Quetzalcoatl–Kukulcan and must originally have been invoked in the New Fire ceremony. Landa refers to Zamna as having been the Mayan equivalent to the Egyptian god Osiris.[8] It seems that just as Osiris was associated with the constellation of Orion,[9] so Zamna and his later incarnation (Quetzalcoatl–Kukulcan) was somehow linked with the Pleiades.

In his book *Aztec and Maya Myths*, Professor Karl Taube of the University of California writes that the New Fire festivals were closely connected with the idea of world renewal after the Flood. In effect they were annual celebrations of an event believed to have taken place when the world was recreated by the gods at the beginning of our own age. Rather as the Mass renews the contract Catholics feel they have with God on account of the events surrounding the death and resurrection of Christ, so the New Fire festival renewed the contract between the Maya and their gods, particularly Zamna. As we have seen, the Aztecs celebrated it at the start of each 'sheaf' of 52 years, but Karl Taube suggests that similar festivals were held by the Maya at the start of other important Long Count periods, such as the beginning of a new katun:

> The new year celebrations were annual re-enactments of the destruction and re-creation of the world. The graphic accounts of the Flood and the erection of world trees in the three books of Chilam Balam reveal that the ritual installation of the Katun and other Long Count periods were thought of in very similar terms.[10]

By now I was beginning to understand that the Pleiades star-group performed something of a similar function for the Indians of Central America as Orion and Sirius did for the ancient Egyptians. For the latter the dawn rising of Sirius heralded the flooding of the Nile and the beginning of their new year. It was on this event more than any other that they organized their calendar, and the day itself was attended by great festivities. Similarly the Maya and others seemed to be watching for the culmination of the Pleiades at midnight before lighting the new fire and starting a new cycle, whether it was a year, Calendar Round or katun. The Aztecs watched for the culmination of the Pleiades at midnight, which would have happened around 11 November, but I wondered if this star-group might have been followed at other times of year as well. One other date crying out for investigation was 12 August, for it was on this day in 3114 BC that our present cycle was said to have started. This, after all, ought to be the date of the original Fire, when the gods gave birth to the sun and moon on funeral pyres at Teotihuacan. Accordingly I once more set up SKYGLOBE to run on the computer, entered in the appropriate data, and adjusted the time factor to when the Pleiades were on the meridian. Once more I was in for a surprise, for it turned out that on that day (and always around that time of year) they hit the meridian just before dawn. Not only that but the sun was preceded by Venus as the morning star (*see* Figure 50). In other words, on this day the Pleiades were performing the same function as Sirius had for the Egyptians in announcing the dawn, the 'Birth of Venus' and the start of a new time-cycle. What was even more telling, though, was that plastered across the southeastern sky were the familiar constellations of Taurus, Orion and Canis Major which played such a big role in the lives of the Egyptians. Could there be a connection, I wondered? Why had the Maya chosen to start their calendar at a time when these particular stars were so prominent? At this point I had no definite answers to these questions, so I turned my attention to other matters.

The Chac-Mools and the fire ceremony

In 1873 Augustus le Plongeon, the son of a French Naval commodore, came to Merida with his young English wife. From there, having learned to speak the local Mayan dialect, he set off for Chichen Itza. At that time the northern Yucatan around Merida was given over to large sisal plantations and the local people were

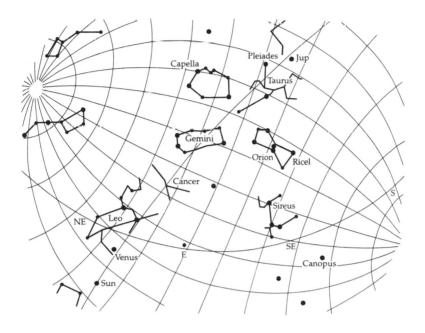

Figure 50   The Birth of Venus before dawn on 12 August 3114 BC

treated by the big landowners as little more than slaves in their own country. Because of his kind nature and the fact that he spoke to them in their own tongue, the local Mayans were prepared to take le Plongeon at least partly into their confidence concerning their traditions. Like Brasseur de Bourbourg before him, he was convinced that the Maya retained lost knowledge of a high order. This, he was given to understand, involved magic and divination. Searching around amongst the ruins of Chichen Itza, he found a glyph on the wall of what he called the Gymnasium, which apparently said 'Chac-Mool' and pinpointed the spot where he should dig to find an effigy of this being. Digging a hole which eventually went down 24 feet, he came across a curious statue of a reclining man looking to one side and holding a plate on his stomach. This, he decided, must be the Chac-Mool he was looking for (*see* Plate 36).

The statue found by le Plongeon and now residing in the Mexico City Museum of Anthropology has turned out to be one of several similar sculptures. All are modelled in the same uncomfortable-looking posture, straining up on their elbows from a reclining position and peering over their right shoulder as though looking at something in the distance. At Chichen Itza there is a reproduction of a Chacmool to be seen on top of the Temple of the Warriors, standing between two rattlesnake columns, and a smaller one by the red-jaguar throne inside the Kukulcan Pyramid. There are one or two more dotted around Chichen and yet another in the Merida Museum. But even though the Chacmools are some of the most readily recognizable statues in the whole of Mexico, and have become cultural icons for the whole Yucatan region, their true function remains a total mystery. Most guidebooks contain the same orthodox opinion that they were somehow connected with the Toltec practice of human sacrifice, perhaps as tables on which to throw the still-beating hearts of victims. However, there is no evidence for this and if they did have this purpose, why does the figure look away over his shoulder rather than towards the offering? Other ideas that they acted as chairs or loungers are equally unconvincing; they are uncomfortable to look at, let alone sit on. So what were they, then?

Don José has his own ideas about the Chacmools and is outraged by the accepted orthodoxy that they were simply used as receptacles for the hearts of victims. In his small guidebook to the ruins of Chichen Itza he writes concerning the one inside the Kukulcan Pyramid:

> So-called Chacmool. This name is scandalously false. The real one will perhaps never be known. The statue represents a priest or deity lying down on its back with bent knees. It holds a four-rattle-square with a solar disc in the centre. It expresses the idea of heaven with one rattlesnake in each corner.[11]

Further on in the same little book he describes the 'Tomb of the Chac-Mool', also known as the Platform of Venus.

> Here we have two wrong names for an unknown object. In it was discovered [by le Plongeon] the famous so-called Chac-Mool. The platform has beautiful rattlesnake symbols and, as a characteristic, the

Pop sign that belongs to the first month of the Mayan calendar. The use of this platform is unknown, as is that of other temples.[12]

Elsewhere Don José says that the Aztec New Fire was brought out of a sacred wooden object placed on the chest of a sacrificial victim.[13] Reading this got me thinking: could the so-called Chacmools of Chichen Itza be substitutes for such a victim? If so, what was their purpose? My first guess was that they were gods of the New Fire, and that at the appropriate time a fire was lit on the small platform each of them holds on his stomach. In Friar Bernardino Sahagun's account, reproduced above, it was said that the Aztecs also brought with them for the New Fire ceremony something called a *cu*, which was both a god and a temple. Could it be that this was their equivalent of a Chacmool, a statue of a fire-god which also acted as an altar?

Another question that posed itself was, how was this fire lit? Sahagun's account tells us that the Aztecs lit their New Fire soon after midnight, when the Pleiades had crossed the meridian. He does not tell us how they did this but we can presume it was done either by striking flints or rubbing together wooden sticks. However, this need not have been so in the case of the Mayan festival for the new year; this continued over five days and there is no suggestion that the fires were lit at midnight. Landa tells us that the idols brought along on these occasions were laid on a bed of leaves. Why, I asked myself, did they do that? Because he then tells us that once the New Fire was lit, incense was kept burning throughout the rest of the five-day ceremony, I began to suspect that this was connected with the 'idols' and their leaves. It seemed likely that the incense-burners were placed near the idols and replenished as needed from piles of fragrant leaves. However, looking at the symbolism of the ritual it seems to me likely that the Maya obtained their New Fire not from flints or sticks but directly from the sun itself. They could easily have done this using some sort of burning-glass to refract the dawn rays of the sun so as to set fire to a bonfire placed near the Chacmool 'idol' or *cu*.

The Skull of Doom

An at first sight unrelated yet most extraordinary discovery was made in 1927 in what was then called British Honduras and is now Belize. A few years earlier an eminent archaeologist, Dr Thomas Gann—Reader on Central American Archaeology at Liverpool University—had announced the discovery of an ancient city on the Rio Grande river not far from the Guatemala border. This is a most curious site for it seems to predate the Maya and who its builders were is not known. In an article contained in *The Illustrated London News* and dated 26 July 1924 he writes:

> The buildings consist of great stone-faced, terraced pyramids, approached on one side by broad stone stairways. The first structure cleared of bush and humus was a truncated pyramid 90 feet in length by 75 feet in breadth at the base, and 30 feet high. . . . The whole pyramid was completely faced with nicely cut blocks of sandstone and limestone, to the lower surfaces of many of the latter of which a layer of chert ¾ inch in thickness adhered. No mortar of any similar material was used in binding these stones together. . . .
>
> Before leaving, we christened the city Lubaantun—literally 'the place of fallen stones' in the Maya language. This city differs from all other known Maya cities in that there are no stone palaces and temples standing upon the great pyramidal substructures, and in the entire absence of stone sculptures and of the great monoliths upon which were inscribed the dates of their erection, put up at 20-year intervals, and later at five-year intervals by the Maya throughout Central America and Yucatan.

Gann finishes his article:

> In the Rio Grande (Lubaantun) ruins we have one of the earliest Maya sites, going back to a period prior to any of the ruined cities at present known in Central America.

It was in this place, hardly accessible even today, that in 1927 a rather sinister artefact was discovered by the 17-year-old daughter of a colourful figure named F A Mitchell-Hedges: a perfectly-made crystal skull. Now we know that the Indians of Central America were extremely skilled in working obsidian or volcanic glass; numerous obsidian tools, weapons and ritual instruments have been found throughout Mexico and into the Maya regions. This skull is different, however, in that it is made of rock crystal and is so perfectly crafted that even the jaw moves. Yet no one, to my knowledge, has been able to put forward a plausible explanation as to how the skull was made in the days before iron tools. It is reckoned that it would have taken 150 years of solid work to smooth down the almost diamond-hard crystal using sand abrasives. The fact remains, though, that the skull exists and was evidently made during or before the time of the lost city of Lubaantun, which is said to predate all other Maya ruins. I concluded, therefore, that if the ancestors of the Maya had the technology to smooth crystal into rounded shapes, then it is likely their descendants did too. It is therefore not inconceivable that the Maya were able to make convex lenses that were at least sufficiently well made to act as burning-glasses. Reading further what Mitchell-Hedges himself had to say, I began to wonder whether the skull was in fact itself intended to be such a burning-glass.

> The Skull of Doom is made of pure rock crystal, and according to scientists it must have taken over 150 years, generation after generation working all the days of their lives, patiently rubbing down with sand an immense block of rock crystal until finally the perfect skull emerged.
>
> It is at least 3,600 years old and according to legend was used by the High Priest of the Maya when performing esoteric rites. It is said that when he willed death with the help of the skull, death invariably followed. It has been described as the embodiment of all evil. I do not wish to try and explain this phenomenon.[14]

Without dwelling on the supposed macabre possibilities of such a crystal skull, I was interested to note that he says there was a legend associating them with Mayan high priests and their esoteric rituals. Could one of these rituals, I thought, have been the bringing of the New Fire? Without testing it out for its efficacy in this respect it is difficult to say with any certainty that it could have performed this function, but the rounded cranium would surely have had lens-like properties. If so, I believe it could have been used to focus the rays of the sun to start a fire.

While in the Mexico City Museum of Anthropology I had seen, in the Teotihuacan Gallery, a representation of the sun as a skull inside a disc of rays. This skull pokes out its tongue in a gesture that is said to be giving life, a curiously contradictory symbol. Meditating on this I realized that the way the sun actually gives life to the world is through its radiations. Moderate amounts of radiation bring about plant growth, but too much and it kills the very vegetation that once fed upon it. It therefore seemed to me that the Teotihuacan skull symbolized these dual attributes of the sun itself as bringer of both life and death; the 'tongue' being rays of sunlight (perhaps also the solar wind) directed towards the Earth. I now wanted to see what further connection this might have with the concept of solar ages, so I began looking deeper into Aztec mythology.

As it turned out, I did not have to look very far, for in the Aztec myth associated with Teotihuacan there is an old diseased god, Nanahuatzin, who has to die on the funeral pyre so that he can be reborn as Tonatiuh, the sun god of the present age. In another myth, this same Nanahuatzin is responsible for splitting open rocks and bringing maize to the surface of the Earth so that it can provide sustenance for humanity.[15] Taking these two myths together, I could see that Nanahuatzin must on the one hand represent the power of vegetation to bring forth sustenance, and on the other the dead, woody material left over at the end of the harvest. By burning this material (especially old corn plants) energy is freed, which the Aztecs believed would then be recycled as sunlight. Viewed in this way, their bonfires assumed a ceremonial importance, for they were the means of returning life to the sun and thereby ensuring future crops. This was as true for the Maya as it was for the Aztecs, for they too associated fertility with fire. They operated a slash-and-burn system of farming, knowing that freshly cleared land was the most fertile for crops.

Returning to the crystal skull it seemed to me that we were dealing with much the same symbolism of death and life. Unlike the skull from Teotihuacan it has no tongue but it is transparent to light. Indeed, it is this quality that must have motivated its makers to carve it out of crystal. I reasoned that the crystal skull did not need to have a tongue because it was the means of focusing the power itself—the light of the sun. Mitchell-Hedges, who seemed to know more about the subject than he was prepared to admit,[16] asserted that the skull was used for esoteric rituals. Whatever these rituals may have been, it seems fair to suggest, given what we know of Maya–Aztec symbolism, that these involved the sun. The most obvious way of making use of the properties of a rounded crystal is the refraction of light, which suggests that the high priest would have held the skull in such a way that it refracted a 'tongue' of sunlight through the open mouth. In short, the 'skull of doom' was no such thing but an elaborate burning-glass used in the ceremony of the New Fire.

A further article by Dr Thomas Gann in *The Illustrated London News* on 1 November 1924, just a few months after his announcement concerning Lubaantun, was to lead me to further insights concerning this ceremony. In this second piece he describes his investigations around the Mayan city of Tulum, and then his finding of a new site, which he names 'Chacmool':

> The ruined city of Chacmool is situated on a peninsula dividing the San Espiritu from Ascension Bay. It had never before been visited by Europeans, and the Indian who guided us to it had come across it accidentally when in pursuit of a wounded deer. The architecture is similar to the other east coast sites—stucco-covered stone buildings standing upon stone-faced pyramids. Here, within a small insignificant temple, we discovered an image of the Chacmool, a gigantic human figure 8 feet high, made of extremely hard cement, reclining upon its back and elbows, the heels drawn up to the buttocks, the forearms and hands extended along the side of the thighs, and the head raised and turned to the right.
>
> It was by the merest accident that we discovered this statue, for it was completely buried in the accumulated dirt and rubbish of centuries, through which the tops of the knees projected for a few inches. On removing the debris from round about it, we came upon a shell gorget, two greenstone beads, an earplug, fragments of the bones of a tapir, and a small pottery incense-burner. This was an extremely important discovery, because these Chacmool figures are purely of Toltec origin, and are found at only one other Maya site—namely Chichen Itza, where, after its conquest by the Toltecs, their religious and artistic influences were strongly developed. We named the city Chacmool after its tutelary deity.

The pictures accompanying the article show a typical Chacmool figure, just like the ones to be found at Chichen Itza, as well as the incense-burner shaped like a man with his tongue poking out. The assumption implicit in Gann's article is that this newly discovered Chacmool must have been a copy of those at Chichen Itza. If, as he says, it is 8 feet high, however, then it is certainly the largest yet discovered. Why, I asked myself, should the Toltecs (or whoever) have chosen to cast a huge Chacmool statue at a remote site on the coast when they were satisfied with near-human-sized ones at home in Chichen Itza? This just didn't make sense. It seemed to me much more likely that this was the original Chacmool, and that le Plongeon's at Chichen Itza was the copy. Unfortunately Dr Gann does not tell us whether the Chacmool faced the sea, but in any case the fact that it was a coastal town seemed important and started me thinking again about Maya origins. Don José had been insistent that the rattlesnake cult had its origins in the Yucatan; the crystal skull (which I was now convinced was intended to be used as a burning-glass) had been found in the Yucatan; the Chacmool figures all belonged in the Yucatan. Could it be that all of these things had a common origin; that, as le Plongeon, Brasseur de Bourbourg and others had asserted, the Mayan civilization was brought from elsewhere by ship to the Yucatan? The importance of these coastal sites seemed to point in that direction, and I was now keen to investigate further the theory that the Maya of Yucatan, and indeed Palenque, might have been influenced in their cultural development by contacts with overseas traders.

7

TRANSATLANTIC TRADITIONS

Ancient Mariners and the Origins of the Maya

Ever since the ruins of Palenque were first discovered by Bishop
Nuñes de la Vega in 1691, there has been speculation about who
the builders of the city might have been. Today archaeologists
have no doubt that Palenque was the work of local Maya Indians
living in the Classic era between the 7th and 9th centuries AD. Yet
there have always been others who have thought that pyramid-
building was something that was brought to the Americas from
outside, that even if the actual pyramids and temples of such
Mayan cities as Palenque were built by locals, the inspiration, and
probably the technology, came from outside. According to Father
Ordoñez, the first to write about Palenque, it was founded in
remote antiquity by a people from across the Atlantic led by a man
called Votan, whose symbol was a serpent. He claimed to have
read in an old Quiché Mayan book, subsequently destroyed by
Bishop de la Vega, that Votan and his people came by sea from a
land called Chivim. They stopped off on the way at the 'Dwelling
of the thirteen' (perhaps the Canaries) and another greater island,
presumably either Cuba or Hispaniola. Arriving on the east coast

of Mexico, they sailed up the Usumacinta River and made their way to Palenque. Votan and his followers are said to have worn long robes and to have exchanged ideas with the natives, who, it seems, were quite friendly towards them and gave their daughters in marriage. Thus it was that Palenque was founded. Votan himself was said to have been the author of the original book found by the bishop, and he evidently made four subsequent voyages back home to Valum Chivim, which Ordoñez identified as the Lebanese city of Tripoli. During one of these journeys Votan is said to have visited another great city in which a temple was under construction that was intended to reach to heaven. Bishop Nuñes, in a publication of his own entitled *Constituciones Diocesianos de Chiapas*, suggests this city must have been Babylon.

Needless to say, academic archaeologists are less than impressed with the story of Votan, which is regarded as purely fictional. However, his association with jade caused a bit of a stir when the tomb of Pacal was opened and the face was found to be covered by a jade mask. Looking at the stucco reliefs of Pacal and his son Chan Bahlum, which depict them as having Middle Eastern noses and generous lips, it is not hard to see why Ordoñez believed the dynasty was of African descent. Not only that but it seems that Pacal was exceptionally tall compared with the average Mayan, as was the man whose skeleton is contained in another recently opened tomb.[1] Given this evidence, one has to ask could there be some substance after all to the story of Votan? Indeed, could Pacal himself have been descended from Votan? It is a curious fact that whereas academic opinion among archaeologists is today rock-solid behind the 'no interference' hypothesis for Indian civilization—ie that the civilizations of the Americas prior to Columbus was entirely self-sufficient—this theory is currently under attack from specialists in other disciplines.

The idea that the inspiration and motivation behind the building of New World pyramids comes from outside the Americas was also the conclusion of such early chroniclers and explorers as Carlos de Sigüenza and his friend the Italian traveller and writer Giovanni Careri. Though Sigüenza accepted that the majority of Indians were descended from tribes who came from the northwest and probably from Asia before that, he was convinced that at least some immigrants had come by boat from across the Atlantic. These people, he believed, had brought with them the custom of building pyramids as well as many other cultural ideas. Careri, in his book *Giro del Mondo*, echoed these sentiments, pointing out that even Aristotle knew that the Carthaginians made voyages beyond the Pillars of Hercules (the Gibraltar Straits).

The Carthaginian connection was to be a recurrent theme in many of the books that followed, and it was not a random choice. The Mediterranean city of Carthage was extremely well located on the North African coast, near present-day Tunis. It was well-protected, had sheltered harbours and, because it was surrounded by good agricultural land, was also self-supporting. However, rather like mediaeval Venice, its prosperity depended upon overseas trade. The Carthaginians were descended from Phoenician emigrants and, like the rest of their race, were great sea-farers. It is recorded by Herodotus, for instance, that the Carthaginians circumnavigated Africa some 2000 years before Vasco da Gama. They also had trading stations in many lands and cities including Memphis (the ancient Egyptian capital), Jerusalem and Babylon. As merchants they had a monopoly of supply on many raw materials, including tin, and to maintain this, kept their trade routes beyond the Pillars of Hercules a closely guarded secret. In fact they controlled all trade in the western Mediterranean: foreign vessels were forbidden to go west of the island of Sardinia. To enforce this exclusion zone required a powerful navy—and this they certainly had. Unfortunately their anti-free-trade stance was eventually to lead them into conflict with their most powerful neighbour, Rome.

The Carthaginian empire was no small-fry and at its height included parts of Spain, much of northwest Africa and the Balearic Islands. Beyond the Pillars of Hercules they had a colony on the island of Madeira and others way off the African coast on the Canary Islands. They also sailed to Britain on a regular basis, for in ancient times this was the most important source of tin. This metal, which has given its name to the plated metal canisters in which baked beans are stored, had a very different purpose then: it was needed for making bronze. Because bronze was used for making weapons and armour, it was probably this trade more than any other that brought Carthage into conflict with Rome.

Though today the Carthaginians and their former capital city are almost entirely forgotten, with a huge population of around one million people it was, in the 3rd century BC, Rome's most powerful rival. One exploit that is remembered took place during the inevitable Romano–Punic wars, for Hannibal, who led his army, including elephants, over the Alps and into Italy, was a Carthaginian general. His eventual defeat by Scipio in 202 BC was the death knell for the Carthaginian Empire, and the beginning of Roman hegemony in the western Mediterranean.

The Carthaginians were not the first to go beyond the Pillars of Hercules in search of tin and other precious metals. Long before their rise, international trade between the Mediterranean and beyond was dominated by their ancestors, the Phoenicians. Their chief ports were in Canaan on the coast of what is now Lebanon and Israel. A Semitic people, like the Israelites who were their neighbours, they evidently supplied much of the material needed to build Solomon's famous temple at Jerusalem. According to the Bible they also provided him with the craftsmen, particularly carpenters, needed to build the wooden inner sanctuary of his magnificent temple at Jerusalem. Given their expertise in building wooden ships, this was a task for which they were obviously eminently suited. As their original homeland came under increasing pressure from the empires of the east—first Assyria, then Babylon, Persia, and finally Greece—so the centre of gravity of their world shifted westwards to Carthage, which rose to be the greatest of all the Phoenician cities.

Even before the rise of Carthage, however, there were colonies of Phoenicians beyond the Pillars of Hercules. The most important of these was in southwest Spain, in the region of the modern port of Cadiz, and went by the name of Tartessus. The city of Tarshish, as it is referred to in the Bible, was the home port for a fleet of oceangoing vessels that were much larger than the small coastal craft that generally hugged the coast of the Mediterranean Sea. The ships of Tarshish, with their highly skilled crews, were well known in the ancient world as they supplied many luxury goods. In particular, they brought back silver from mines in northwest

Spain as well as ivory and slaves from the West African coast. Where these things came from was a mystery to their customers in the eastern Mediterranean, for they kept this information secret.

That the ships of Tarshish, the great merchantmen of the Bronze Age, came from Spain is not really surprising, given that their main function was to sail the rough seas of the Atlantic and not the Mediterranean. Cadiz or Tarshish is an ideal port for exploring the world beyond the confines of southern Europe. For just as ancient Troy stood at the gateway between Europe and Asia, so Tarshish gave access to the wider world of the Atlantic. It was this that brought both wealth and reputation to a place which otherwise stood on the fringes of the known world.

In view of the nature of merchant-sailors and their desire to explore the seas and seek out fresh supplies and markets, it would be surprising if the ships' captains of Tarshish never thought to cross the Atlantic. This, in fact, would have been no more difficult for them than it was for Columbus, for like him they were able to make use of prevailing winds and tides. Considering that people today almost routinely cross the Atlantic in small craft—everything from rowing boats to pedalos—it is ludicrous to suggest that ancient mariners were incapable of such a feat. They had oceangoing craft at their disposal and it is certainly possible that at least some of the silver of the Ancient World came from Mexico.

In the peace treaty that followed the defeat of Hannibal in 202 BC, Carthage lost her fleet and all her possessions outside of Africa. For a trading nation this was an absolute disaster, and it is therefore not at all inconceivable that some at least of her captains and admirals, on hearing what had happened, decided to go west to form a new colony away from the emergent power of Rome. As we shall see later, startling evidence has recently come to light indicating that this may indeed have been so. In essence the story of Votan may not be a myth after all—he could have been a Carthaginian émigré.

This, however, could not be the end of the story in relation to the Maya. Even if Votan, the supposed founder of Palenque, were a Carthaginian, Libyan, Celt or possibly Roman, it would not explain the extraordinary nature of the Mayan calendar, nor its start date of 3114 BC. All of these Old World empires are much too recent, going back only to around the first millennium BC. There was, however, one other trading power that made its presence felt throughout the Mediterranean and beyond, at a time long before the rise of Phoenicia: Egypt. Texts and murals inscribed on the walls of the mausoleum of Queen Hatshepsut (XVIIIth Dynasty, *c*. 1400 BC) depict a trading voyage with a distant land. It is generally assumed that this was Somalia in the horn of Africa, but it may have been southern Arabia or even India. Nobody would suggest that this mysterious land may have been America but these murals do at least indicate that the Egyptians were not so inward-looking as many people think. Going back many generations before Hatshepsut, to the pyramid age (*c*. 2700–2200 BC), we now know that the Egyptians were even then capable of building boats to the highest standards. Not only do we see these illustrated on the walls of many of their tombs but archaeologists have actually found full-sized boats buried in pits next to the Great Pyramid of Giza. One of these, in a remarkable state of preservation, has been reassembled and is now kept in a special museum on the south side of the pyramid. Though the boats found near the pyramids appear to have been for river use and would not have been suitable for sailing out on the open sea, they are further proof, if proof were needed, that there were craftsmen living at the time the pyramids were built who were capable of building large ships out of wood.

During the pyramid age the Egyptians had other craft besides wooden ships. Inscribed on the walls of tombs going back to at least the middle of the third millennium BC are pictures of boats made from bundles of papyrus stalks. Now whereas Egypt was, and is, short of wood, it had papyrus growing in abundance. Mostly this was used for making scrolls, or papyri, from which is derived our modern word *paper*, but this versatile plant had other uses. The property that most interested the boatbuilder was the fact that papyrus stems float on water. By tying bundles of papyri together it was therefore possible to make rafts that were capable of carrying cargoes up and down the Nile. By the time the pyramids were built, the design of papyrus boats had been developed and refined to the point at which they were capable of sailing out on the open sea. The pictures we see carved on tomb walls near the pyramids show these sailing ships equipped with masts, rigging, rudders and cabins. They also have rising prows and sterns, indicating that they were not just river craft but were intended to cope with waves.

The theory that it may have been possible for the ancient Egyptians to sail across the Atlantic to America on papyrus ships was put to the test in 1970. With seven friends, the Norwegian writer and explorer Thor Heyerdahl set sail from West Africa on just such a boat—the design of their craft being based, as near as possible, on Egyptian tomb paintings. In an earlier trip, which he recorded in his famous book *The Kontiki Expedition*, Heyerdahl had proved that it would have been possible for people to have sailed from South America to Easter Island[2] on rafts made of balsa wood. It was during this earlier project that he discovered that the Peruvian Indians of Lake Titicaca made use of papyrus boats. Seeing these he realized that they were remarkably similar in design to others he had seen used by tribesmen on Lake Tana at the source of the Blue Nile. Suspecting that this was a case of technology transfer, Heyerdahl now wanted to prove that it was possible for people to have crossed the Atlantic in the remote and distant past. It was his belief that the ancient Egyptians had come to Lake Titicaca, bringing with them not only the technology of building reed boats but also the idea of pyramid-building.

At only their second attempt, Heyerdahl and his crew succeeded in crossing unaided from Africa to the island of Barbados in the West Indies in just 57 days (a distance of more than 6000 kilometres). Not only that but their boat *Ra II* was virtually undamaged by the voyage. They had proved that, using only the materials and technology of the time, it was technically possible for pyramid-age Egyptian mariners to have made such an Atlantic crossing.

The evidence from North America

It was one thing for Heyerdahl to prove that people could have navigated the Atlantic in ancient times, but the question still remained: did they? In his fascinating book *America B.C.*, first published in 1976 and revised in 1989, Harvard Professor Barry Fell presented startling evidence that America has indeed been repeatedly visited and settled by peoples from Continental Europe and Africa from as far back as 5000 BC until relatively recent times (some 1000 years before Columbus). Unfortunately, many archaeologists and historians, for reasons more to do with national pride than with science, refuse to acknowledge the mounting evidence that this is indeed the case. For example, although Roman amphorae have been discovered at Guanabara Bay, on the sea-bed off the coast of Brazil, the authorities have refused to allow a full investigation to take place.[3] Similarly, Roman coins dated to around AD 375 have been found on a beach at Beverly, Massachusetts[4] but archaeologists continue to insist these must have belonged to an unknown, modern collector who, if they are to be believed, must have been exceptionally careless. In 1972 further Punic (that is, Carthaginian) amphorae were found off the coast of Honduras in Central America.[5] Permission to investigate the wreck from which they came was again refused, this time because it was felt that to acknowledge such a thing would be an affront to the memory and reputation of Christopher Columbus. Given this kind of attitude in academic circles, it is little wonder that our knowledge of ancient contacts between the Old and New Worlds is so scant.

Equally contentious are finds of Carthaginian and Celtic in-scriptions in America. According to Professor Fell (who is an acknowledged expert on epigraphy, the study of inscriptions) there are writings in Punic to be found at quite a number of sites in the United States. He and his friends of the Epigraphic Society have identified numerous tombstones, cairns and stone-built 'root cellars' as dating from the Bronze Age and as having been con-structed by European seafarers. As well as Punic inscriptions there are also short texts in Ogham, the written language of the Celts. In pre-Roman times these people inhabited France and Spain. It is Fell's contention that, as Julius Caesar himself reports in his writ-ings, the Atlantic Celts were first-class mariners, with vessels capable of withstanding the pounding of Atlantic rollers. Fell has found American inscriptions that seem to confirm this, including records concerning ships from Tarshish. In *America B.C.*, Fell translates one of these, from the Tartessian Punic in which the original was written. Under the outline carving of a ship's hull the text says: 'Voyagers from Tarshish this stone proclaims'.[6] The stone in question apparently marked the spot where ships from Tarshish would regularly dock to exchange cargoes with settlers who either worked silver mines further inland or trapped animals for their pelts.

What was of greater interest to me was that in 1976 another important find was made, this time in Mexico itself. While excavating the ruins of the Mayan city of Comalco on the Caribbean coast, archaeologists discovered that many of the bricks used to build the city carried inscriptions. Though most of the inscriptions found on these bricks were (as one might have expected) Mayan, two were found to be written in a neo-Punic script in ancient Libyan. One of the bricks shows a rough calendar, with the months marked by their initial letters. The other shows a figure with the inscription 'Yaswa Hamin', meaning 'Jesus protect'. They could therefore be dated as coming from some period between the time of Christ and the 3rd century AD, and added some support to the Votan legend.[7]

Early Egyptian artefacts and inscriptions are harder to come by, possibly because being older they have worn away or maybe because nobody has yet recognized them for what they are. However, texts which are recognizably written in the later and less formal hieratic style have been found on Long Island and on a stele from Davenport, Iowa.[8] What does seem very 'Egyptian' though, is the concept of building step-pyramids to function as tombs. Could the concept of pyramid-building have been brought to Central America by Egyptian, Carthaginian or other seafarers? Though it is all too easy to scoff at such a proposition on the grounds that the pyramids we know of in the New World are all much younger than their equivalents in Africa, this idea—as we have seen—has not been without its supporters. However, the most obvious place to start looking for evidence of such a connection turns out not to be within the Maya lands themselves but further west, at the greatest of all pre Columbian cities: Teotihuacan.

Teotihuacan and the Egyptian connection

The great Pyramids of the Sun and Moon at Teotihuacan north of Mexico City have, rightly, been compared with the pyramids of Giza. Colossal in size, it is almost beyond belief that their builders were able to erect such huge monuments with the primitive tools then available. Yet the site at Teotihuacan contains much more than just these two structures, impressive as they are. The vast area that the city covers means that it must, in its day, have been the largest metropolis in all the Americas. Indeed, even in the Old World there would have been few cities to match it.

Teotihuacan, like Mexico City today, was built on a grid system of streets. Its most imposing feature, however, besides the great pyramids, is a grand avenue that runs for some ten kilometres before culminating in a plaza in front of the Pyramid of the Moon. At either side of this avenue are small temples and stepped platforms, many of which served as tombs for the nobility. Though little is known about the origins or spiritual practices of the builders of Teotihuacan, it seems that to the Aztecs, perhaps indeed in recognition of the original function of this part of the city as a necropolis, this avenue was known as the Way of the Dead.

The whole idea of a necropolis, or city of the dead, is very Egyptian. We now know that the Egyptian Great Pyramids of the IVth Dynasty were not built piecemeal merely to satisfy the whims of despotic pharaohs but were also raised according to a definite plan. Like Teotihuacan, Giza was built to represent something very definite. The towering pyramids of Giza are not only the most massive edifices on Earth, they are also symbolic of an amazing stellar religion. As Robert Bauval discovered and he and I documented in our book *The Orion Mystery*, they were laid out to represent the Belt of Orion, the most recognizable constellation in the sky. The Egyptians conceived of the Milky Way as a celestial counterpart of their own river, the Nile. Every year they waited in anticipation for the Nile flood that was both a blessing and matter of concern. They needed the fertile mud that the river brought down from the highlands of Ethiopia, and they needed the fields to be irrigated, but at the same time they feared that the river might rise too much and flood their homes. They believed that the annual flood was controlled by the gods, and in particular by Egypt's patrons, Osiris and Isis. It seemed to them that the trigger for the flood, which occurred in midsummer, was the first appearance of the Isis star, Sirius, after its annual period of invisibility. This was heralded by the earlier rising of Orion, and they therefore watched the stars of this constellation, which borders on the Milky Way, with keen anticipation.

There was, however, another aspect to all of this. The Egyptians believed in a heavenly afterworld to which they hoped their souls would go after death. The Pyramid Texts, which are carved into the walls of certain of the later pyramids, provide abundant evidence that they conceived of this as being in the constellation of Orion. All burials took place on the west bank of the Nile which, with its pyramid fields, symbolized the region of Orion on the banks of the Milky Way. In the language of ritual, the bringing of a dead body across the Nile for burial was seen as somehow connected with the soul's crossing of the celestial Nile, the Milky Way, to reach the heavenly paradise of Orion where Osiris reigned. The Milky Way, then, was a river of the dead—the original Styx over which the dead must cross if they are to reach the afterworld. The function of the Egyptian pyramids, in as far as we understand them, was to assist the pharaoh in this journey by making use of the science of correspondences: as above, so below. By crossing the Nile, undergoing certain rituals, and being buried in a pyramid, the pharaoh's soul was believed not only to go to the stars of Orion but indeed to become a star itself. This, in outline, was the theory of transformation that underlay the Egyptian religion and continued to be its inner mystery long after the pyramids themselves were abandoned.

The connection between the Egyptian pyramids and the Milky Way is very clear for anyone who wishes to study the matter.[9] What is also of significance, however, is that there is a similar connection with at least some of the Mexican pyramids. Among many of the tribes of North America there is a belief that the Milky Way is a path through the sky along which the dead have to travel on their way to the higher heavens. Often it is conceived of as having a gate at both ends, where it crosses the ecliptic. One of these intersection points or 'gates' lies between the constellations of Gemini and Taurus—next to Orion (*see* Figure 51)—and the other is on the opposite side of the ecliptic between the constellations of Scorpio and Sagittarius (*see* Figure 52). The Earth has a slight wobble as it spins which causes the way we see the heavens to change cyclically over a period of roughly 26,000 years. This wobble is known as precession, and one of its most noticeable effects is to change the sign of the zodiac that rises at the spring equinox every 2160 years. We are currently at the end of one sign, Pisces, and about to enter the next, Aquarius. However, the ecliptic or sun's path through the heavens always intersects the Milky Way at the same points regardless of precessional changes.

The idea that the Milky Way has two gates is not confined to the Americas but was also part of the Pythagorean and Orphic

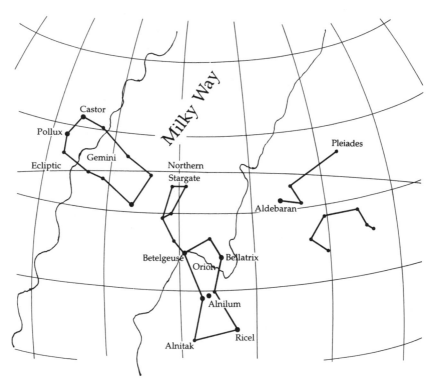

Figure 51   The Gemini 'Star-Gate'

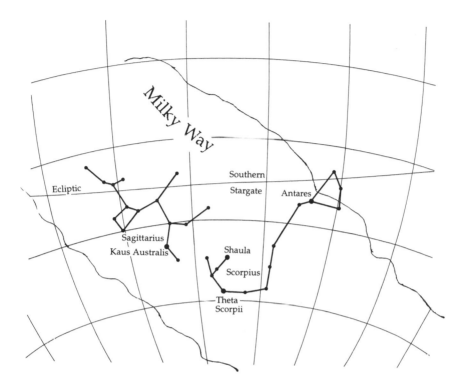

Figure 52   The Scorpio 'Star-Gate'

tradition. In their remarkable essay on precession, *Hamlet's Mill*,
the late American Professor Giorgio de Santillana and his German
colleague Hertha von Dechend followed this tradition on both
sides of the Atlantic. They quote Macrobius[10] who gives a fairly
clear account of the 'gates'. Apparently he, and presumably at
least some other Roman pagans, believed that souls ascend by way
of Capricorn and then, so that they can be reborn, go back down
again through the gate of Cancer. This gate is in fact in Gemini; it
is only because of precessional changes that Macrobius labels it
Cancer.[11] De Santillana and von Dechend go on to draw attention
to Amerindian myths from Honduras and Nicaragua which talk
about their 'Mother Scorpion' dwelling at the end of the Milky
Way, and they equate this with the 'spirit star' (Antares—Alpha

Scorpio). This very bright star lies on the southern junction of the ecliptic and the Milky Way, and marks the southern gate. They point out that the Maya also had an old scorpion goddess, as of course did the Egyptians and Babylonians.[12]

All of these connections and parallels between Old and New World cosmologies may, of course, be purely coincidental, but it does seem more likely that the two traditions have a common origin. The Maya conceived of the Milky Way in two fashions, probably derived from different traditions. On the one hand they saw it as a crocodile, its head at the bottom and body stretching into the sky; and on the other it was a gigantic Ceiba tree which supported the sky like a tent-pole. It would also seem that the Maya, in common with the ancient Egyptians, believed that at least one of their afterlife kingdoms or heavens was near to the Milky Way. Their interest in the risings of the Pleiades star-group, which they associated with their solar rattlesnake cult, indicates that the gate to heaven was believed to be somewhere in the same region of the sky as Taurus and Orion. Could it be that they had, directly or indirectly, learnt about this from the Egyptians? Alternatively, did both civilizations, on opposite sides of the Atlantic, have a common origin? In short, was Brasseur de Bourbourg right when he suggested that the story of Atlantis (thought by many to have given both Egypt and Central America their civilizations) was no myth but the truth? This was a subject that I now wanted to investigate.

8

THE OLMECS AND ATLANTIS

Of basalt heads and bearded men

On our way from Palenque to Merida, my wife Dee and I had made a detour to visit Villahermosa, the capital of Tabasco. This bustling modern city, because of its oil industry, was far more Americanized than any we had so far seen. Today it is very prosperous, but before the discovery of 'black gold', it must have been a desperately hard place to make a living. The area surrounding the city is a flat, boggy swamp into which everything seems eventually to sink, not best suited to farming. Previously, on our way out of the city to Palenque, our coach had been held up for several hours as a bridge was jacked back up to road level. This was apparently a common occurrence, though that knowledge didn't lessen our anxiety as in darkness we gingerly made our crossing over the sleek, dark river some 50 feet below. On this occasion we had no problems, however, and after an uneventful if rather hot journey we arrived in the city in brilliant sunshine. Our goal was not the city itself—which for the approaching Christmas had large Nativity sets on nearly every corner and Christmas trees from Canada filling the sweltering markets—but rather the outskirts. For here, like a little tropical oasis and in defiance of the thundering traffic going past, lies the famous La Venta Park.

I had read about La Venta before leaving England, and very much wanted to see it for myself. Set up in the 1950s by the poet, anthropologist and collector Carlos Pellicer, it preserves in a more or less natural setting 31 of the most extraordinary and oldest sculptures to be seen in the Americas. Their original home, the island of La Venta, is a humid piece of tropical swampland on the Tonalá River. However, between 1200 and 600 BC this unpromising piece of real estate was the capital city of the 'Rubber People' or Olmecs,[1] who once inhabited the Tabasco region, and it features the oldest pyramids so far found in the Americas. The origins of this civilization are lost in the mists of time but go back to at least 3000 BC. The Olmecs are credited with many of the most important cultural developments of Central America, including the first proper cultivation of maize and the invention of the famous ball-game that seems in Classic times to have had as much fascination for ancient Mexicans of all races as soccer does today. Because Olmec pyramids were built out of mud-bricks, little remains of them but mounds of earth, most of which have yet to be excavated. But because they made their sculptures out of basalt—a hard, volcanic stone—these have survived in rather better condition.

The influence of the Olmecs extended throughout much of Central America: to Mayaland in the east and the Oaxaca Valley in the west. Unfortunately, and unknown to them, their capital sat on top of one of the largest oilfields in Mexico. When in 1937, during archaeological excavations, this was revealed, it posed a quandary: how could the site be exploited commercially without destroying it for archaeology? It was realized that little could be done for the site itself if Mexico were to make the most of this new resource. The best that could be achieved was to remove whatever was portable to an area of relative safety. Thus it was that La Venta Park in Villahermosa became the new home of the priceless Olmec statues.

Arriving at the park gates, we made our way through a small zoo to the Lagoon of Illusions where the sculptures stand. The first to greet us was The Walker, a piece of basalt about two feet high displaying a relief of a striding, bearded figure carrying a flag, underneath which were three, barely legible hieroglyphs (*see* Figure 53). To me The Walker looked very much like the Egyptian Orion, except that instead of holding a staff he had a flag. I was therefore not surprised to be told that one of the three symbols represented a star. There was no explanation, however, for why he should have been bearded.

There are quite a number of bearded sculptures by the Olmecs and other early peoples, including some of the 'dancers' of Monte Alban. In that it is a fact of genetics that full-blooded Amerindians do not grow beards, this is a matter that continues to perplex archaeologists. Attempts have been made to explain the beards as deformed jaws, but it is clear to any impartial observer that there really is no explanation that holds water other than that the individuals so represented were not Amerindians. It seemed that right at the start of our jungle trek we were faced with evidence for pre-Columbian contacts.

A little further down the trail we came to the first of the famous Olmec heads (*see* Plate 38). Some 18 of these have been discovered to date, and new ones are regularly being unearthed all over the

Figure 53   Olmec Sculpture 'The Walker'

Tabasco region. Fashioned out of huge blocks of basalt, these heads can be ten feet high and nearly as broad. The ones here in the park were by no means the largest that have been discovered but were nevertheless impressive. The heads have a heavy, lowering presence, like gigantic boxers sunk up to their necks in mud. Like The Walker, it is not known what their true function and purpose was, but it is assumed that they represent either powerful rulers or renowned players of the ubiquitous ball-game[2]. This game, a sort of basketball played with a hard rubber ball on dumbbell-shaped courts with sloping sides, had ritual significance. At Chichen Itza there are shafts radiating from the *Caracol* towards both the stars and the ball-courts below. Because this building is now known to have been used as an observatory for the planet Venus, it has been suggested that this was so that the ritual game could be played in accordance with heavenly phenomena. It is believed that the captain of the winning team was beheaded at the end of the match so that his spirit could take flight and go off to the highest heaven. If this is really the case, maybe the gigantic lumps of basalt somehow represent these now deified basketball captains. Whether or not this is the case, the heads with their thick lips and flat noses look very Afro, again supporting the theory that America was visited by outsiders long before Columbus.

In addition to the heads and The Walker, La Venta Park contains other basalt sculptures from the Olmec period. Foremost among these are several 'altars'. These stand about three feet from the ground and usually have carved on the front of them a 'priest' in semi-lotus position (*see* Plate 39). Looking closely, I could see that some of the figures were wearing rattlesnake insignia and jaguar headdresses, indicating the importance of both these cults even at that early time. Other details were less easy to understand. On one of the altars the priest was holding out a baby as though invoking a blessing upon it. At the sides of the same block were depictions of other adults holding children in a protective manner as though shielding them from something frightening (*see* Plate 40). What this could have been it was impossible to tell, but the youngsters seemed secure with the adults, who probably represented the children's parents, and who once again wore snake and jaguar insignia. Looking at this altar I wondered whether this emphasis on childhood and the need for protection could have some connection with the cataclysmic beginnings of the present age. There was a sense, hard to pin down but nonetheless there, that the adults were protecting the children from the forces of nature. The enigmatic stones remain mute on this point but they do at least give some insight into the strange world of the Rubber People, the earliest known civilization of America.

The Olmecs did not, of course, confine their activities to the Gulf coast; some of them migrated westwards to the Valley of Oaxaca. Here they built the extraordinary city of Monte Alban which so impressed Maurice on his first visit. My wife Dee and I had also visited this mountaintop eyrie before moving on to Palenque, and were able to enjoy its fantastic panoramic view over the surrounding valleys. That it must once have been the most important ceremonial centre in the area is clear from its location, but of equal interest is the skill and labour that went into its construction. Before building the city the Olmecs had first to level the site by removing the top of the mountain. This must have been an extremely arduous task—but was only the prelude to building a complex of pyramidal temples around a central plaza the size of two football fields. At one end of this 'stadium' stands the building where the carved figures of the dancers were found.

The Olmecs seem to have occupied the plateau of Monte Alban from around 800 to 300 BC, before being superseded by the people called the Zapotecs. They built over the older Olmec structures and erected further pyramids, some of which are linked by subterranean passageways. They also built a sophisticated system for collecting precious rainwater—an important consideration when living on top of a mountain—by creating a slight camber to the central plaza so that water was directed into cisterns. However, there are other achievements that have marked out the Zapotecs as particularly advanced in their civilization. The first of these is a narrow vertical shaft found in the temple called Building P by archaeologists. Excavation at the foot of this shaft proved fruitless, and for a long time its purpose remained unknown. Eventually it was realized that its function was astronomical, for twice a year (in May and again in August), when the sun shines directly overhead, it would have illuminated a slab at the bottom of the shaft.

This perhaps rather surprising aspect is explained by the fact that the site lies between the Tropic of Cancer and the equator. Unlike locations in more northerly latitudes, such as Europe and the USA, much of Mexico is subtropical. This means that the sun, instead of reaching its highest point in the sky at the summer solstice, in fact has two zeniths. On these two days in the year the sun blazes directly overhead: at noon a stick placed vertically in the ground casts no shadow. Between these two dates and during the period of midsummer, the sun passes to the north in the sky and at midday would, in fact, illuminate the northern face of a building such as a pyramid, casting a shadow to the south. Throughout Central America the two zenith days were considered the most important times of the year, and it has been suggested that the symbol of the double-headed serpent, as seen on the Aztec Calendar stone for example, represents this understanding. When we visited Monte Alban in December 1994, the guide showing us round was of the opinion that the May zenith was the more important.

Two other Zapotec achievements are connected with another building that lies inside the plaza area and is given the rather unimaginative name of Building J. Unlike all the other structures on the site, this one is not rectangular and neither is it orientated towards the cardinal points.[3] In fact, no two sides or angles of this building are equal, and it is shaped rather like the prow of a ship. The direction in which the 'ship' sails is roughly at 45°—running from the southeast to the northwest. It has been noted by some observers[4] that were a priest to be standing on the steps of this edifice, looking towards the southeast, he would be able to observe the rising of the bright star Capella (Alpha-Aurigae) directly through the doorway of another building. It could be that the earliest appearance of Capella, after its period of invisibility, was used as a time-keeper and herald star for the first zenith passage of the sun, which would have happened later the same day. Again one thinks of the ancient Egyptians and their observation of the dawn rising of Sirius as the start of their year.

It would seem that the Zapotecs began their year with this first zenith return of the sun, and had a double-check on the appropriate day with the star Capella and the narrow shaft in Building P. It has also been suggested that the curious orientation of Building J could be somehow linked with the magnetic north pole because it seems to point in what was the direction of the pole at the time it was built.[5]

The other important find at Building J is a series of pictograms that consist of both dates and hieroglyphs. These have not been fully translated and, in the absence of other examples of Zapotec writing, probably never will be. But this discovery has prompted some archaeologists to say that the Zapotecs were the inventors not only of the sacred calendar but also of New World hieroglyphic writing. Given that there are other untranslated hieroglyphs on some of the Olmec stones at La Venta, it would seem that this assertion is ill-founded. The connection of the Olmecs with Oaxaca and Monte Alban would suggest to any impartial observer that the Zapotecs inherited their calendar and the art of writing from these earlier settlers. Again this points to the advanced nature of the Olmec/proto-Mayan culture. But it still begs the question: from where did the Olmecs get their knowledge? This is a taboo subject as far as orthodox Mayanology is concerned because it has too many cultural or even racist overtones to be discussed in a rational way. Yet, as we have seen, there is persuasive evidence to show that the Olmecs could have come into contact with ancient Egyptian or other mariners. There might, however, be an even stranger, and some might say crazier, answer to the origins of Central American civilization: the lost continent of Atlantis.

Atlantis, the antediluvian myth

As we have seen, a recurrent theme of many of the early books concerning the Maya was their possible connection with the so-called lost civilization of Atlantis. A popular subject among esotericists, the very idea provokes laughs of derision from those who profess to know most about the archaeology of Central

America. But can Atlantis be dismissed as simply a myth, or is there something concrete behind the legend? Feeling there might be, I was prepared to take a fresh look at the evidence.

The earliest written account of Atlantis that we have is that of Plato, who in two of his last books, *Critias* and *Timaeus*, gives a brief outline of the story. This is what he says was told to Solon, the great lawgiver of Athens, when he paid a visit to Saïs in Egypt. Critias, one of Plato's characters, narrates the story to Socrates as told to him by his grandfather, also called Critias. In words very reminiscent of the Mayan belief in periodic destructions of the Earth, an Egyptian priest explains to Solon that they know far more about the history of the world than the Greeks:

> You [the Athenians] remember only one deluge[6] though there have been many ... You and your fellow citizens are descended from the few survivors that remained, but you know nothing about it because so many succeeding generations left no record in writing.[7]

According to Plato's account there was once a great island continent in the middle of what is now the Atlantic Ocean, and it was the Greeks of Athens who checked an invasion of Europe and Africa by people from this island.

> Our records tell how your city [Athens] checked a great power which arrogantly advanced from its base in the Atlantic Ocean to attack the cities of Europe and Asia. For in those days the Atlantic was navigable. There was an island opposite the strait which you call, so you say, the Pillars of Hercules, an island larger than Libya and Asia combined; from it travellers could in those days reach the other islands, and from them the whole opposite continent which surrounds what can truly be called the ocean.[8]

Now what is truly astonishing about this account, which was written around 350 BC, is that it not only presents the earliest known record concerning the existence of Atlantis but indicates that the Egyptians at least knew of the Americas. It states categorically that there is a *whole opposite continent which surrounds what can truly be called the ocean*. Even if one discounts the existence of a former continent of Atlantis, it offers powerful support for pre-Columbian contacts between the Old World and the New, for how else would the Egyptians have known that there was another

continent on the other side of the Atlantic Ocean? Plato's account
goes on:

> On this island of Atlantis had arisen a powerful and remarkable
> dynasty of kings, who ruled the whole island, and many islands as
> well and parts of the continent; in addition it controlled, within the
> strait, Libya up to the borders of Egypt and Europe up as far as
> Tyrrhenia [Tuscany].[9]

It would seem from this that Atlantis was a very powerful naval
empire which ruled over not only western Europe, much of North
Africa and the islands of the Atlantic, but also parts of the continent he has just told us about—ie America. Not content with this
achievement, it would seem that the Atlantean Empire was keen
to push further east and take control of the countries of the eastern
Mediterranean as well, including Greece and Egypt. An alliance
was formed to fight the invaders, but it eventually fell to Athens
alone to repel these seaborne invaders and rescue all the inhabitants of the Mediterranean, east and west, from slavery. Then
Plato tells us:

> At a later time there were earthquakes and floods of extraordinary
> violence, and in a single dreadful day and night all your [Athenian]
> fighting men were swallowed up by the earth, and the island of
> Atlantis was similarly swallowed by the sea and vanished; this is why
> the sea in that area is to this day impassable to navigation, which is
> hindered by mud just below the surface, the remains of the sunken
> island.[10]

In Plato's other account of the myth, *Critias*, he tells us that 9000
years have elapsed since the declaration of war between those who
lived outside and all those who lived inside the Pillars of Hercules.
We do not know how long this war lasted but it is clearly implied
that it began before the Atlanteans took control of Libya and
Europe as far as Tuscany. In that Plato's account was written
c. 350 BC, we must be looking for a date of at least 9500 BC for the
outbreak of this war. Now that is an incredible date, many thousands of years before the accepted beginnings of either Greek or
Egyptian history, and when Europe was only just emerging from
the last Ice Age.

To try to accept Plato's account at face value places enormous and seemingly insuperable problems in front of the investigator; there are so many unanswered questions. If there really had been an island continent the size of Libya and Asia (presumably meaning Asia Minor or Turkey) which sank beneath the waves, why is there no trace of it today? Not only that, but according to Plato the Egyptians of his day still had records in their possession of events that took place in their country at that time. Yet modern Egyptology tells us that to all intents and purposes Egyptian civilization only began around 3100 BC with the First Dynasty. According to modern textbooks, at the time specified by Plato the Egyptians were palaeolithic nomads who spent their time hunting lions, goats, crocodiles and hippos, and had not yet got round to domesticating cattle.[11] Could such people have kept any sort of record concerning a world war on the scale described by Plato?

This is the dichotomy in which we find ourselves. On the one hand we have Plato, a reputable philosopher and student of Socrates, narrating a story that includes important information which he should not have known about (ie the existence of the Americas on the other side of the Atlantic); and on the other there is the evidence of modern science, which gives the lie to the myth of Atlantis. Can there be any way round this impasse? What implications does it have, if any, for our understanding of the founding of Mayan civilization in the Americas? These are the questions that now needed answers.

The Lost Continent

The subject of Atlantis has spawned hundreds of books. Plato's simple account has been twisted in all directions with even the geography of the lost continent called into question. Unravelling all of this was to prove no easy matter. The most bizarre idea— though for some reason currently the archaeologically most acceptable idea—is that the mythical civilization of Atlantis talked of by Plato was really that of Crete. It is now generally believed that Cretan (or Minoan) civilization was brought to an abrupt end when the neighbouring island of Thera (Santorini) exploded in a violent eruption sometime around 1400 BC. The huge tidal waves that resulted from this local catastrophe would have been enough to devastate the coastal regions of Crete, so it is argued, and could have delivered such a blow to Minoan civilization that it never recovered. Given that the Minoans were traditional enemies of the Athenians (as indicated by the story of Theseus and the Cretan Minotaur)[12] we have, according to this theory, the substance of the Atlantis myth put into a manageable local framework.

The only problem with this argument is that Plato states categorically that Atlantis lay beyond the Pillars of Hercules and dominated western Europe and Libya. Nowhere does he suggest a link with Crete, the Minotaur, or any local difficulties with fellow inhabitants of the eastern Mediterranean. To suggest otherwise may be an intriguing and clever idea—and it may also be true that the explosion of Santorini destroyed the power of the Minoan Empire in 1400 BC—but it surely has little to do with Atlantis, mythical or real. To get to the truth we have to dig deeper than this.

Of all the hundreds of books written on the subject of Atlantis, the most influential remains *Atlantis the Ante-diluvian World*. It was written by Ignatius Donnelly, a United States congressman, and immediately became a bestseller. In its revised edition, edited by Egerton Sykes in 1950, it is still widely read and quoted by people interested in the subject. Casting his net widely, Donnelly shifted through thousands of fragmentary pieces of circumstantial evidence in his quest for proof of the existence of the lost continent. As John Michell was to write in 1984:

> Donnelly had compiled an impressive catalogue of similarities between the myths, folklore, anthropology and artefacts, as well as the forms of animal and plant life, of the continents bordering on the Atlantic Ocean. His proof of the reality of Atlantis rested on the cumulative effect of all this evidence rather than any single piece of it.[13]

He was certainly of the view that the continent of Atlantis was where Plato said it should be, beyond the Pillars of Hercules, and sought to find evidence—mythological, geological, religious and linguistic—to prove that this was so. He also, like Brasseur de Bourbourg before him, was of the opinion that Mayan civilization had come from Atlantis, and to prove this he compared names of Mayan cities with those of Armenia. He was on stronger linguistic ground when he compared Atlantis with the Garden of the Hesperides [my italics]:

> According to the traditions of the Phoenicians, the Gardens of the Hesperides were in *the remote west*. Atlas lived in these gardens. Atlas, as we have seen, was king of Atlantis. The Elysian Fields were commonly placed in *the remote west*. . . . Atlas was described in Greek mythology as 'an enormous giant, who stood upon the *western confines of the earth*, and supported the heavens on his shoulders, in a region of the west where the sun continued to shine after he had set upon Greece'.[14]

Donnelly was much taken with the similarity between the names Atlantis and Atlas, following through, with some justification, a possible etymology:

> Plato tells us that Atlantis and the Atlantic Ocean were named after Atlas, the eldest son of Poseidon, the founder of the kingdom.
>
> Upon that part of the African continent nearest to the site of Atlantis we find a chain of mountains, known from the most ancient times as the Atlas Mountains. Whence this name Atlas, if it be not from the name of the great king of Atlantis? And if this be not its origin, how comes it that we find it in the most northwestern corner of Africa? And how does it happen that in the time of Herodotus there dwelt near this mountain-chain a people called *Atlantes*, probably a remnant of a colony from Solon's island?
>
> … Look at it! An 'Atlas' mountain on the shores of Africa; an 'Atlan' town on the shores of America; the 'Atlantes' living along the north and west coast of Africa; and Aztec people from Aztlan, in Central America; an ocean rolling between the two worlds called 'Atlantic'; a mythological deity called 'Atlas' holding the world on his shoulders; and an immemorial tradition of an island of Atlantis. Can all these things be an accident?[15]

Donnelly clearly didn't think so, and spent another 200 pages of his book pushing the point with every possible argument at his disposal. Even so, a doubt remains. How could a high civilization, one that left behind such words as Atlas, Atlantes, Poseidon and others, have so few physical vestiges? Indeed, are there any physical traces of Atlantis?

1 Lithograph by Frederick Catherwood of the Temple-Pyramid of Inscriptions at Palenque

2 Contemporary photograph of the Pyramid of Inscriptions

4 Temple of the Cross group at Palenque

3 Jade death mask of Lord Pacal

5 Man with eagle-headed mask from Palenque

6 Sarcophagus of Pacal with its lid

Above: 7 Door leading to tomb of Pacal

Left: 8 Stairway inside Pyramid of Inscriptions

Below: 9 Meeting of Maya nobles (from a mural by Diego Rivera in Mexico City)

Above: 10 Subjugation of the Maya by Spaniards (from a mural by Diego Rivera in Mexico City)

Below: 11 Indians inscribing Bark Books (from a mural by Diego Rivera in Mexico City)

Above: 12 A surviving Mayan codex in the Museum of Anthropology in Mexico City

Below: 13 Excavated ruins of Old Tenochtitlan

Below: 14 Avenue of the Dead, Teotihuacan

15 Pyramid of the Sun, Teotihuacan

16 Sculptured frieze on the Pyramid of Quetzalcoatl, Teotihuacan

17 Pyramid of the Sorcerer, Uxmal

18 Chaac temple mouth, Uxmal

19 Chaac Masks, Uxmal

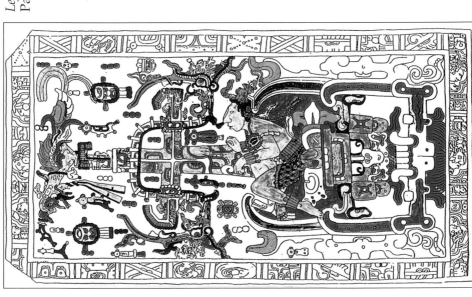

Left: 20 The Lid of Palenque

Right: 21 Four previous cosmogonic ages on the Lid of Palenque

Epoch 2 AIR The second epoch is represented by Ehecatl God of Wind. During this period the human race was destroyed by high winds and hurricanes, and men were converted into monkeys (enabling them to hang on to trees and fight the wind).

Epoch 1 WATER Represented by Chalchiuhtlicue wife of Tlaloc. Destruction came in the form of torrential rains. Men became fish in order not to perish by drowning.

Epoch 3 FIRE Sun God Tonatiuh here representing destruction of the third epoch through fire.

Epoch 4 EARTH (Rain of Lava) The fourth epoch is represented by Tlaloc the God of rain and celestial fire. In this epoch everything was destroyed by a rain of fire and lava, and men were converted into birds to survive the catastrophe.

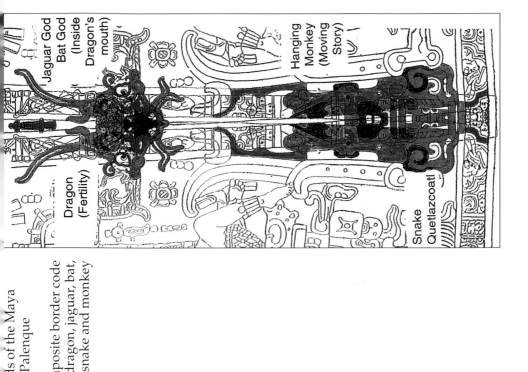

Left: 22 The gods of the Maya from the Lid of Palenque

Right: 22a Composite border code showing the dragon, jaguar, bat, snake and monkey

Jaguar God
Bat God
(Inside Dragon's mouth)

Dragon (Fertility)

Hanging Monkey (Moving Story)

Snake Quetlazcoatl

GODS OF THE MAYA

EHECATL God of Wind

CHALCHIUIHTLICUE Goddess of Water

TONATIUH Sun God

TLALOC God of Celestial Fire and Rain

Above: 23 Bat god overlay with corresponding border code.

Below: 24 Jaguar god overlay

25 Aurorae Borealis (photo © Jim Henderson)

26 The 'Caracol' observatory, Chichen Itza

Above left: 27 Sculptured head of tattooed man, Palenque
Above right: 28 Mayan lord with flattened head, Palenque

29 Ball court at Monte Alban

30 Building 'J' at Monte Alban

Below left: 31 'Dancer' figures at Monte Alban
Below right: 32 'Dancer' at Monte Alban

Left: 33 Lithograph by Frederick Catherwood of the Archway at Uxmal

Below: 34 Lithograph by Frederick Catherwood of the Nunnery at Chichen Itza

35 The Kukulan pyramid-temple at Chichen Itza

Below left: 36 Chac-Moul figure between serpent columns, temple of the Warlords, Chichen Itza

Below right: 37 The Pleiades star group (photo © Jim Henderson)

Top: 38 Olmec head from La Venta Park

Right: 39 Meditating Olmec priest

Below: 40 Olmecs rescuing children

Much of what he wrote would these days be considered racist, for he was keen to prove the origins of different peoples. He writes:

> Without Atlantis, how can we explain the fact that the early Egyptians were depicted by themselves as *red* men on their own monuments? And, on the other hand, how can we account for the representation of Negroes on the monuments of Central America?
>
> Le Plongeon[16] says, 'Besides the sculptures of long-bearded men seen by the explorer at Chichen Itza, there were tall figures of people with small heads, thick lips, and curly short hair or wool, regarded as Negroes. We always see them as standard or parasol bearers, but never engaged in actual warfare'.[17]

Speaking in the language of his time, which was one of European domination over nearly the entire globe, he goes on:

> As the Negroes have never been a seagoing race, the presence of these faces among the antiquities of Central America proves one of two things: either the existence of a land connection between America and Africa *via* Atlantis, as revealed by the deep-sea soundings of the *Challenger*, or commercial relations between America and Africa through the ships of the Atlanteans or some other civilized race, whereby the Negroes were brought to America as slaves at a very remote epoch.[18]

Few people today would agree with his logic that the Negroes themselves were incapable of making such a journey on their own and must therefore have been brought over to the Americas from Africa as slaves. This is, of course, the language of the 19th century. However, he does have a good point that there are many sculptures in the Maya regions of Central America that display Negroid features—not least of these are the Olmec heads which, though they may represent rather round-faced, flat-nosed Indians, could equally well have been black. More tellingly he next quotes from the *Popul Vuh* as evidence for the early appearance of white and black men in the Americas.

> And we find some corroboration of the latter theory in that singular book of the Quichés, the *Popol Vuh*, in which, after describing the creation of the first men '*in the region of the rising sun*' and enumeration of their first generations, we are told, 'All seem to have spoken one

language, and to have lived in great peace, *black men and white men together*. Here they awaited the rising of the sun, and prayed to the Heart of Heaven'.[19]

Donnelly was convinced that Atlantis had been inhabited by both white and black races, and that it was from here, to the east or towards the point of the rising sun as looked at from the North American continent, that civilization had been brought to Mayaland. There was still, however, a big problem with this theory: if Atlantis really had been a large continent situated in the Mid-Atlantic, how is it that today we find no trace of it on the sea-floor? In fact there is quite the opposite. Any searcher scouring the depths of the North Atlantic finds not a continental shelf but some very deep water. True, in the region of the Azores there is the long finger of the North Atlantic Ridge, which in places is only some 200 metres beneath the surface of the ocean. At first sight this is not very hopeful for finding a submerged Atlantis because it marks the site at which two tectonic plates are pulling apart. Closer analysis, however, reveals something more promising.

In his book *The Secret of Atlantis*,[20] a German author, Otto Muck, took up the challenge of finding the lost continent. Unwilling to accept that the theory of continental drift, in its simple form, destroyed all possibility of there ever having been an Atlantis, he looked again at the evidence. He was struck by the fact that whereas the outlines of the continents of South America and Africa fitted together almost perfectly, those that fringed the North Atlantic clearly did not. Not only that, but palaeontological evidence from Europe indicated that the reason that during the last Ice Age an ice-sheet was able to advance as far south as the 52nd parallel (to the outskirts of present-day London, in fact) was that there was no Gulf Stream to oppose it. Had the Gulf Stream brought warm water to the coasts of northern Europe, as it does today, then the ice could not have advanced so far south. He proposed that the reason there had been no Gulf Stream was that until around 10,000 BC it had been blocked by a landmass in the Mid-Atlantic. It was only when this sank (the Atlantis catastrophe) that the Gulf Stream was able to reach the lands flanking the North Atlantic. He overcame the inevitable criticism of his theory—that if this had indeed been the case, where were the remains of the submerged continent?—by going back to basic geological theory. He asserted that whereas continental drift alone could account for the shapes and positioning of the southern continents of Africa and South America, there was a 'hole' in the North Atlantic. It was not possible to make the continents fringing the North Atlantic fit unless an extra 'piece' were added to the jigsaw puzzle. This he believes was Atlantis, the lost continent. As to the reasons for the sudden destruction and submergence of Atlantis, he turned to the heavens. He asserted that it had been brought about by the sudden impact of an asteroid's hitting the Earth in the region of the Atlantic. This catastrophic event, which he believed marked the end of the Quaternary epoch, left behind two large holes in the ocean floor, and brought about the destruction of the lost continent.

Otto Muck's theories, which are not entirely new of course, brought a fresh impetus to Atlantean research in the 1980s. Yet there had for some decades already been another line of research pursued, based on entirely different premises—reincarnation. It was centred on the work of a most unusual man, a Southern State preacher from Hopkinsville, Kentucky.

The sleeping prophet

Born in March 1877 in humble surroundings, Edgar Cayce became, by accident, the most famous clairvoyant of the 20th century. The story goes that at the age of 23 he developed a hoarseness to his voice. None of the physicians his family consulted was of any help, and as the weeks turned into months, he was diagnosed as incurable. It seemed he would never again be able to speak above a whisper. Finally, in desperation he was driven to take up the suggestion of some family friends that he try auto-hypnotism. It was discovered, to the amazement of all present, that while he was soundly asleep, he was able to converse in his normal voice. In this manner he informed them of the causes of his condition and just what was needed to effect a cure. Almost immediately his voice got better and he was able to get on with a normal life. More importantly, he had discovered a technique for tapping into the collective unconscious while asleep and was now able to use this to help others to find cures for their ailments.

For over 40 years he carried on going to sleep, twice a day, and giving people 'readings'. When he woke up he had no idea what he had said until it was read back to him by his stenographer. Doctors, priests and lawyers were confounded. Never before had anything like this been seen—a simple man prescribing often bizarre remedies for patients, many of whom he hadn't even met, while he himself was fast asleep. Yet what silenced the many sceptics was that over and over again he was proved correct. The herbs, folk-remedies and sometimes unknown drugs he recommended were generally effective in curing his patients.

However, the readings that he gave for patients often went far beyond finding physical cures for whatever ailed them. In his sleeping state he was able to diagnose psychological and spiritual problems too. These, it seemed, often sprang not from conditions in the here and now, or even through heredity, but related to past lives. In his sleeping state he disclosed that the soul of each of us is eternal and has usually lived many times upon planet Earth. According to him, the Earth is like a school, and though we may forget past lessons their imprint is left indelibly traced on the fabric of the unconscious mind. It seems that the residue of these past lives affects us in the present in the form of *karma*, for as it says in the Bible, 'As you sow, so shall you reap'. Tapping into the collective unconscious, he found he was able to reveal the faults and strengths of each of his patients and aid them in fulfilling their destiny in their present life.

This was of course important and interesting to the people concerned, but there was a further dimension to Cayce's work. The individual readings he gave to his patients and others were kept and carefully stored. There are some 2500 of these, and they formed the basis for a most unusual research library. Because so many of the readings referred to events in the past lives of individuals—often in graphic detail—it is possible to build up a sort of history of the world based on eye-witness accounts. Many of the readings concerned lives lived in such well-known times and places as ancient Rome and Greece, but a significant number referred to unknown historical events in Plato's mythical realm of

Atlantis. It seems that the mind of the sleeping prophet was able to fill the gap left by the archaeologist's shovel and at last find evidence for the lost continent. By analysing and cross-referencing the Atlantis readings, it is possible to deduce much about this former continent and the causes of its destruction.

Cayce's depiction of Atlantis—or at least what has been gleaned from his sleeping reports—is that of an advanced civilization that fell prey to temptation. In words that seem curiously applicable to the present, he traces the way that a technologically advanced civilization (apparently with aeroplanes, lasers, and other modern machinery) turned its back on God and immersed itself in the delights of materialism. Then, in a series of cataclysms brought on by the Atlanteans' misuse of natural forces, their island paradise erupted and was consigned, as Plato recounts, to the depths of the Atlantic Ocean. This in essence is the story of the destruction of Atlantis as pieced together by researchers on the readings and published by his sons in a little book entitled *Edgar Cayce on Atlantis*.

Yet, as they document in this strange little book, there is another side to all of this: the Noah-like story of the many people who survived the catastrophe. According to the Cayce readings, not all the Atlanteans died when their native lands went under the waves. Many escaped by boats, whereas others—in anticipation of what was to happen—had already moved overseas. As might be expected, they mostly went to the lands bordering the Atlantic: to North Africa (Libya), Spain, Portugal, France and Britain. This, it would seem, was the origin of Plato's great invasion of the Mediterranean. It seems that the Atlantean colonists were not so much intent on establishing fresh outposts for their empire as escaping from what they knew to be a doomed continent. This was not all, however. According to Cayce, Atlantean settlers did go both to Egypt and, significantly, to Central America.

The Lost Continent and the Hall of Records

As we have seen, the whole subject of Atlanteans in Egypt is not new, but the Cayce records add a new twist to the story. If his sleeping reports are to be believed, the time that Atlantis went under the waves (by his reckoning around 10,600 BC) was a period of great turmoil in the world generally. It would seem that Egypt, owing to its geographical location, was one of the few safe places in the world, and it was therefore invaded not only by Atlanteans from the west but also by other peoples from the east. These other newcomers were white-skinned Aryans coming from the region of Mount Ararat in what is now eastern Turkey. Because the native inhabitants of the Nile Valley at that time were Negroes and the Atlanteans were mostly red, Egypt became something of a racial melting-pot. Of the races, the Atlanteans, evidently, were the most culturally advanced, and brought with them some of their technology—including the ability to raise large rocks and build pyramids. However, the invaders from the east, according to Cayce, were the more dominant militarily, and it was they, under their king Osiris, who took charge over the land. It would seem that out of this strange brew arose a new civilization with a new religion: an amalgam of the old animism of the black, indigenous population, the religion of the Atlanteans and that of Osiris and his followers.[21]

Something of this same story seems to have been preserved in the Biblical story of the Flood, though in a rather garbled way. If Moses, the purported author of *Genesis*, was born, raised and schooled in Egypt, it seems likely that it was the Egyptian version of the universal Flood legend he recorded. In *Genesis* it is said that Noah's Ark settled on Mount Ararat and that he had three sons, Shem, Ham and Japheth, the progenitors of three races. If we equate Noah with Osiris (according to Cayce an immigrant from the Mount Ararat region), then his Biblical 'sons' can be seen to be the three founding races of Egypt: the red-skinned Atlanteans, the white Araratians, and the black Egyptians. This accords well with the Cayce account, which records that Osiris ruled over a united, multiracial kingdom.

This, however, was not all that the 'Sleeping Prophet' had to say on the matter of the Atlanteans. In several of his readings he stated that the survivors of the lost continent had brought with them records relating to their earlier history. These, he said, were carefully buried in a secret chamber somewhere near to the Great

Sphinx, which stands guard like a sentinel over the Pyramids of Giza. A second set of these records was taken, he said, by other survivors of the disaster to be buried somewhere in the Yucatan area of Mexico. Cayce claimed that prior to the destruction of Atlantis, a priest called Iltar, with a group of followers from the royal household of Atlan, left Poseidia (the main island), and made his way west to the Yucatan:

> Then, with the leavings of the civilization in Atlantis (in Poseidia, more specifically), Iltar—with a group of followers that had been of the house of Atlan, the followers of the worship of the ONE—with some ten individuals—left this land Poseidia, and came westward, entering what would now be a portion of Yucatan. And there began, with the activities of the peoples there, the development into a civilization that rose much in the same manner as that which had been in the Atlantean land ...[22]
>
> ... The first temples that were erected by Iltar and his followers were destroyed at the period of change physically in the contours of the land. That now being found, and a portion already discovered that has lain in waste for many centuries, was then a combination of those people from Mu, Oz[23] and Atlantis.[24]

This is the closest that I have been able to find to a 'St Patrick' scenario, and it would seem to me that Iltar (to give him his Atlantean name) is the great prophet that the Maya later revered as their teacher Zamna. According to Cayce, besides the records hidden near the Sphinx in Egypt, there were others brought to the Yucatan by Iltar, and a third set still in the heart of Atlantis itself. If we could only lay our hands on these records, then perhaps we would know for certain the truth about the origins of the Mayan civilization and how they came to understand so much about sunspot cycles.

9

THE SUN, ITS ENERGY AND INFLUENCES

The demise of the Maya

At the same time as developing his theories concerning the Lid of Palenque, Cotterell had also been refining his ideas concerning sunspot cycles and their correlation with the Aztec and Mayan calendars. Like the Maya, the Aztecs believed that our present age was preceded by four previous ages. Between each age was a catastrophe in which life was all but destroyed. At the centre of the Aztec Sun Stone, there is a face with its tongue hanging out representing Tonatiuh, the present sun god.[1] He is surrounded by glyphs which at one level of interpretation represent the gods of previous ages.[2] The question now was, how did this all fit with the Mayan Long Count calendar, and more particularly, could it throw any light on the sudden decline of the Maya? To answer this question, Cotterell needed accurate information on how the sun has behaved in the past. This might at first seem impossible to obtain, but fortunately considerable work has been done in this field in relation to dendrochronology.

As we all know, plant growth depends on light. But the sun gives out more than just visible light—it radiates right across the electromagnetic spectrum, including those rays of very short wavelength called cosmic rays. These powerful rays, which would kill all life on Earth were it not for the protective shield of the atmosphere, have the power to transform atoms. Ordinary carbon has an atomic weight of 12, and is very stable. With oxygen as carbon dioxide, it is present throughout the atmosphere and is vital to life. However, the bulk of the atmosphere is made up of nitrogen, which in its ordinary form is comparatively inert. Cosmic rays from the sun cause nuclear reactions in the atmosphere: they can transform nitrogen atoms into a heavy form (isotope) of carbon that has an atomic weight of 14 (C^{14}) instead of the usual 12.[3] These heavy atoms behave just like ordinary carbon and combine readily with oxygen to form carbon dioxide, the big difference being that C^{14}, unlike C^{12}, is radioactive.

All plants, including trees, take in carbon dioxide and use it to make more complex organic compounds, giving back oxygen to the atmosphere in the process. Inevitably a small proportion of the carbon dioxide they absorb contains some heavier C^{14} atoms. All living things (including animals, which directly or indirectly feed off vegetation) thus contain a small amount of C^{14}. When anything dies, it ceases taking in carbon dioxide and contains a ratio of C^{14} to C^{12} that matches the proportions of the two isotopes of carbon in the atmosphere at that time. Because the heavy C^{14} atoms are subject to radioactive decay and break down to give C^{12}, this proportion changes over time.[4] So as a piece of wood, for example, gets older, the percentage of C^{14}—and hence its radioactivity—is reduced. In other words, the less radioactive it is, the older a piece of wood must be. This is the basis of radiocarbon dating—possibly the most important development in archaeology this century.

When it was first introduced into archaeology, radiocarbon dating was greeted with enthusiasm. At last, it seemed, there was a tool available that could provide accurate dates for anything made of wood, cloth, bone or any other organic material. It was not long before it was realized, however, that many of the dates so obtained were inaccurate when compared with other accepted dating techniques, such as the use of pottery. What could be going wrong? Because the decay rate of C^{14} to C^{12} was well known and unchanging, it could not be the cause of the observed anomalies. The answer could only be that the amount of C^{14} in the atmosphere does not stay constant over long periods of time—ie living organisms in the past have not all contained the same proportions of the different carbon isotopes at death that they do today.

At first it seemed like this could be the end of carbon dating as a diagnostic tool for archaeological work, but it was then realized that it might be possible to produce a series of correction tables using another method of dating: dendrochronology. This is based on the simple observation that as trees grow, they lay down a fresh layer of growth each year. If a tree is cut down, it is possible to work out its age by counting the number of rings of growth in its trunk. Individual rings can tell scientists a great deal about the climate at the time the tree was growing, but more importantly they hold a palaeontological record of the balance of C^{14} in the atmosphere at the time the ring was formed. By analysing very old trees and tree-trunks, dendrochronologists have been able to obtain data on atmospheric C^{14} levels as far back as 9000 years ago. This has meant that archaeologists have been able to make the necessary correction to their C^{14} dates. It was quickly realized that the reason C^{14} levels vary in this way is the sun's behaviour—cosmic rays affect otherwise stable nitrogen atoms and turn them into C^{14}. The proportion of C^{14} to C^{12} atoms in archaeological specimens can thus be used as an indicator of high or low solar activity.

Solar radiation is also clearly the most important factor in climatic changes, and Cotterell was able to find a graph correlating radiocarbon levels with solar activity, the European climate, and the advance and retreat of alpine glaciers (*see* Figure 54). The fit was exact—but with one peculiarity: it seemed that high levels of C^{14} corresponded with decreases in solar activity. How could this be? Scientists seemed to have no answer for this, but he surmised that there might be a simple explanation. When the sun is very active it generates a large number of sunspots, and these in turn cause large numbers of charged particles to be thrown into space. This means that there are clouds of charged particles between the sun and the Earth, and there is a thickening of the Van Allen Belts (*see* Figure 55). As a result, the lower atmosphere is effectively

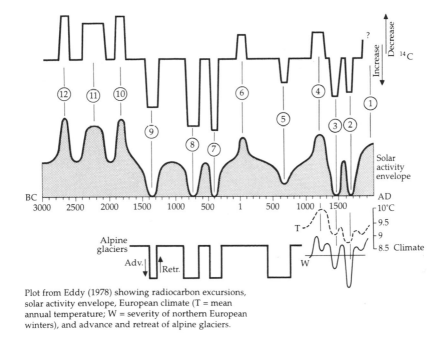

Plot from Eddy (1978) showing radiocarbon excursions, solar activity envelope, European climate (T = mean annual temperature; W = severity of northern European winters), and advance and retreat of alpine glaciers.

Figure 54   The relationship between climate and solar activity

shielded from cosmic radiation and less C^{14} is produced. Conversely, at times of low solar activity, when there are few if any sunspots, there are fewer ions between the atmosphere and the sun to shield out the cosmic rays (*see* Figure 56). More nitrogen is thus converted to C^{14}. What all this means is that there is an inverse correlation between C^{14} levels in the atmosphere and sunspot activity. By consulting the tree-ring record it is therefore possible to see how sunspot behaviour must have varied in the past.

Taking the work a stage further, Cotterell now compared the graphs for solar activity (ie sunspot numbers), temperatures, winter severity, and glaciation against the rise and fall of civilization. Again the correlation was extraordinary (*see* Figure 57). It seemed that high solar activity (ie low levels of C^{14} and therefore, by his hypothesis, large numbers of sunspots) correlated exactly with the growth of powerful, sophisticated civilizations. Low sunspot

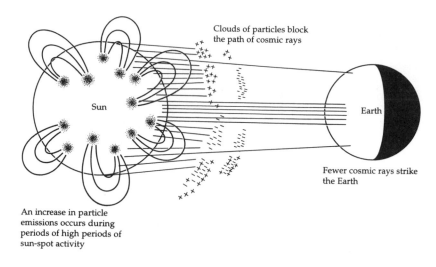

Clouds of particles block
the path of cosmic rays

Sun

Earth

Fewer cosmic rays strike
the Earth

An increase in particle
emissions occurs during
periods of high periods of
sun-spot activity

Figure 55   High sunspot activity reduces cosmic radiation hitting the Earth

activity seemed to be linked with periodic 'Dark Ages', which are
marked by a general decline in the level of cultural achievement
that has coincided with the fall of important civilizations. Because
one of these low periods was experienced between about AD 440
and 814, Cotterell wondered whether this could have had anything to do with the disappearance of the Maya at around the same

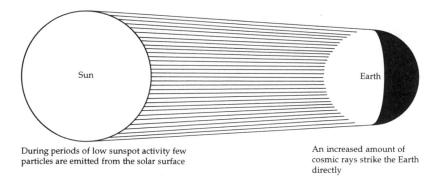

Sun

Earth

During periods of low sunspot activity few
particles are emitted from the solar surface

An increased amount of
cosmic rays strike the Earth
directly

Figure 56   Low sunspot activity increases cosmic radiation hitting the Earth

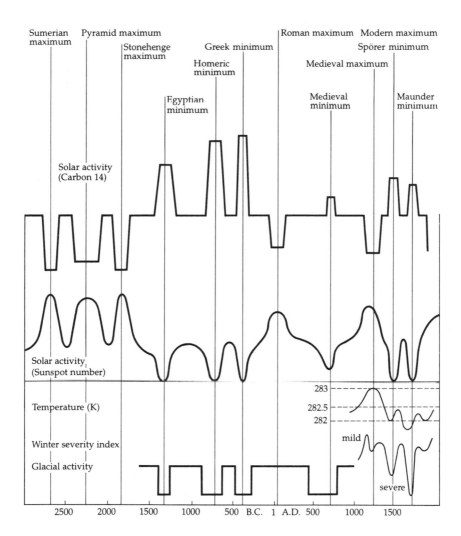

Figure 57   Civilizations and solar activity

time? Clearly the picture was going to be more complicated than this simple correlation implied, but he now felt he was getting near to finding the explanation for the sudden disappearance of not solely the Maya but other peoples of Central America.[5] Elated by this discovery, he turned with fresh resolve back to calendrics and the amazing Maya Long Count.

The Birth and Death of Venus

It is generally agreed that the Long Count began with an event known as the Birth of Venus on 12 August 3114 BC. This event was so important to the Maya that they used it as the basis of their calendar rather in the way we use the Birth of Jesus for our own. Förstemann, the librarian from Dresden, and others had shown that the Maya used cycles of Venus to track long periods of time. They did this in a rather complicated way, but the full cycle as contained in the *Dresden* Tables was 1,366,560 days. This was exactly 5256 of their *tzolkins* and 3744 of their vague (365-day) years. More importantly, when counted forward from the beginning of the Maya calendar, this time-cycle brings us to the year AD 627—the exact centre of the solar magnetic shift and period of low sunspot activity that Cotterell saw as crucial factors in the decline of the Maya. Cotterell knew from his studies of sunspot cycles, however, that there are shorter periods than these great ages which must also have an impact upon human life, and this also connected with another area of study he had worked on—the connection between solar cycles and human fertility.

In his earlier studies, documented in his first book *Astrogenetics*,[6] he put forward a theory concerning the relationship between the solar wind and human hormone production. In this work he also developed the thesis that a person's fundamental astrological type is determined not by the position of the sun at birth in relation to the zodiac but rather to the ambient magnetic field of the Earth at conception. Because solar energy causes variations in this field month by month, so these changes mirror the positions of the sun, sign by sign. According to this theory, the level and polarity of the ambient solar wind also affects levels of the hormone melatonin which is secreted by the pituitary gland and accounts for bio-rhythm regulation and extrovert and introvert behaviour. (See Appendix 3.)

Having discovered the link between the sun's cycle and the production of the hormone melatonin, Cotterell was now anxious to see if it was connected with the secretion of other hormones. Rather surprisingly, he found a further direct correlation with the follicle-stimulating hormone (FSH), also produced by the pituitary gland (which lies at the base of the brain) in response to chemical stimulation by its neighbour, the hypothalamus. There is a direct connection between this hormone and human fertility. In males, FSH controls the development of sperm cells in the testes; in females it determines the maturation and release of ova.

By placing graphs for the solar cycle against the rise and fall of female hormone levels, Cotterell was able to show that there was a direct link between the menstrual cycle and the charge of particles carried on the solar wind. It seemed that in some way these particles, or perhaps the effect they had on the Earth's own magnetic field as they came through the Van Allen Belts, influenced the hypothalamus. This seemed to be the determining mechanism that influenced the production of FSH and hence female fertility.

Once more it seemed to Cotterell that he had made a significant scientific breakthrough, yet it was one with very worrying implications. If the production of FSH could be turned on and off by changes in the magnetic field caused by the switches in polarity of the solar wind, he reasoned that it could also be turned on and off by changes in the solar magnetic neutral sheet. First he noted that the neutral sheet had changed polarity around 3114 BC—the starting date of the Maya calendar—and that it had changed again around AD 627. He concluded that the changing magnetic field at that time had resulted in falling fertility rates and the decline of the Maya.

Taking this a stage further, he conjectured that the current fall in fertility detected in developing countries is not due to changes in lifestyle, chemical pollution, or even effective contraception, but once again to a changing magnetic field. Now, however, the change is not caused by the shifting phase of the solar neutral sheet but by the shifting polarity of the long-term sunspot cycle envelope, which, over the course of the past 50 years, has passed its peak and reversed its trend. But what really intrigued Cotterell about the decline of the Maya was that they seemed to have anticipated the magnetic reversal and consequential decline in fertility, for their magic number corresponds to the 1,366,560 days of the magnetic shift period. Furthermore, when a shift occurs in the Earth's magnetic field more damaging solar radiation enters the Earth's atmosphere, causing genetic mutations and an increase in infant mortality. As Cotterell suggests, the latter provides us with a convincing explanation for the enigmatic carvings of the 'Dancers' at Monte Alban. It could also explain the Mayans' preoccupation with fertility rituals, often involving sacrificial bloodletting from the penis and tongue. Perhaps by punishing themselves in this way (and it does seem to have been voluntary) they hoped to ensure their own fertility as well as that of their land.

This was clearly not the whole story, however. Any decline in human fertility around the 9th century—assuming that it had happened at all—should have been worldwide, but other civilizations had clearly not died out. It seems there must have been more local factors that affected tropical America. One of these was that the solar magnetic reversal may have affected the Earth's magnetosphere, thus allowing an even greater penetration of cosmic rays to take place. Such an increase would be most marked in equatorial regions between 10° and 20° North and South due to the rays' perpendicular incidence on the surface of the Earth in this area. Another factor was that it was becoming drier.[7] Cotterell believes that this too can be attributed to the decline in sunspot activity, for with it came a 'mini-Ice Age' (see Appendix 5) during which there was less evaporation of water from the oceans. This in turn led to a drought. It is noteworthy that the people who survived this catastrophe either moved south to the highlands, where rainfall was more abundant, or north into the Yucatan, where there were underground streams. The Central region, which until very recently was almost entirely covered by tropical rain forest, was then probably quite arid. The great city of Palenque, far from being overwhelmed by the jungle, must have been surrounded by something of a wilderness.

These new ideas of Cotterell's put a fresh cast on the whole mystery of the Maya and their sudden disappearance. Their near obsession with fertility rites and the need to make personal blood offerings to the sun and Earth could be explained both by their declining birth-rate and their concerns over reduced rainfall. It is noteworthy too that throughout pre-Columbian Central America the rain god, whether called Chaac, Tlaloc, or some other name, was always of the greatest importance. This too suggested that fresh water was in short supply.

Following the cycle through to the present time, it would seem that we are already experiencing similar climatic changes and greater desertification of the planetary surface. In Mexico these effects are already pronounced. For the past ten years the valley of Oaxaca has not received its expected rainfall and is rapidly becoming arid. In view of the Mayan calendar's pointing to the date of 22 December 2012 as the end of our present age—when, according to the Maya, we can expect some sort of catastrophe—is this a foretaste of what is to come?

Theories of Catastrophe and Destruction

The Mayan account of the catastrophes that brought each of their four ages to a dramatic end are not unique: the world's mythological traditions are full of similar accounts of disasters of global proportions that serve to explain how the Earth obtained its present form. As Cotterell remarks, the question of whether the Earth's present form was arrived at through chaotic chance or a process of gradual and consistent evolution has been the source of both emotive and rational debate. If indeed the Earth has evolved gradually, as Uniformitarianists would have us believe, geophysicists should be able to measure magnetism or the geological structure of the Earth's surface and extrapolate from it chronological data that enables us to calculate the age of the world and how it came to be as we find it today. The opposite view, that of the Catastrophists, holds that the world as we know it today has been shaped by cataclysmic disaster, with perhaps a measure of uniformitarian activity as well.

Geological and geomagnetic dating techniques have enabled the reconstruction of our planet's geophysical evolution, beginning about 200 million years ago when all of the landmasses we recognize today were part of a single giant continental landmass known as Pangaea (see Appendix 6). Over the ensuing millions of years, this large mass broke up and the individual pieces drifted apart as the large crustal regions of the Earth's surface moved

The Phanerozoic time scale (after the QJGS, 1964, and York and Farquhar, 1972)

	m.y.		m.y.
CENOZOIC		PALAEOZOIC	
Quaternary		*Permian*	
Pleistocene	1.5–2??	Upper	240
Tertiary		Lower	280
Pliocene	*c. 7*	*Carboniferous*	
Miocene	26	Upper	325
Oligocene	37–38	Lower	345??
Eocene	53–54	*Devonian*	
Palaeocene	65	Upper	359
MESOZOIC		Middle	370
Cretaceous		Lower	395?
Upper	100	*Silurian*	430–440??
Lower	136?	*Ordovician*	
Jurassic		Upper	445?
Upper	162	Lower	*c.* 500?
Middle	172	*Cambrian*	
Lower	190–195	Upper	515?
Triassic		Middle	540?
Upper	205	Lower	570?
Middle	215		
Lower	225		

Figure 58   Geological epochs

about the molten inner core of the planet. As a consequence of the vast time-scales involved it has become necessary to subdivide prehistory into periods representing different geological epochs (*see* Figure 58).

While cataloguing the chronological time-scales through the measurement of magnetism in rocks, scientists noticed several anomalies. For example, it was discovered that the Earth's magnetic field, which is generally of a bar magnet orientation around the poles, had repeatedly reversed during the history of the planet. It is now generally accepted that the Earth's magnetic field has reversed on many occasions without any obvious reason or explanation, although theoretical models suggest that a combination of factors representing a worst-case scenario are responsible for

Curves of polar wandering for samples from different continents. Polar movement since the Precambrian, relative to various land masses. Solid curves have been traced where the palaeomagnetic data from three or more levels in geological time follow a fairly consistent sequence. Single pole positions are relative to: ■, China; ●, Greenland; ▲, Madagascar. Letters refer to: (Pε), Precambrian; ε, Cambrian; O, Ordovician; S, Silurian; D, Devonian; C, Carboniferous; P, Permian; Tr, Triassic; J, Jurassic; K, Cretaceous; LT, MT, UT, Lower, Middle, and Upper Tertiary. Polar azimuthal projection of the present Northern Hemisphere. (Garland, 1971.)

Figure 59   Magnetic polar wandering

magnetic inversions or 'flips'.

In addition, the magnetic polar caps are known to have wandered periodically, and in doing so to have changed their geostationary positions. Such events are known as magnetic excursions or apparent polar wander, the cause of which—like the reversals—remains undetermined (*see* Figure 59).

In order to understand these variations and their implications for us, we need first to take a closer look at the Earth's geomagnetic field. It is widely believed that the Earth's magnetic field resembles that of a bar magnet aligned between the two poles. Following a principle similar to that of the dynamo, such a field is thought to be generated within the Earth's core, resulting from the differential rotation of the molten mantle and of the outer crust (*see* Figure 60).

In 1958 Charles Hapgood, an American historian, suggested in his book *The Earth's Shifting Crust* that the Earth's crust had undergone repeated displacements and that the geological concepts of continental drift and sea-floor spreading owed their

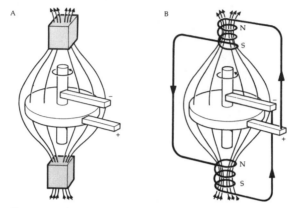

The principle of the dynamo

A simple model of a disc dynamo consists of a metal disc rotating in a magnetic field between two permanent magnets (A). The field produces a force on the free electrons in the disc, pushing them towards the centre. As a result there is a difference in electrical potential between the edge and the centre of the disc, which would produce a current if the circuit is closed. In a self-exciting dynamo (B) this current is used to drive an electromagnetic coil, which replaces the original permanent magnets. The resulting system generates a magnetic field as long as the disc is kept spinning. The model thus demonstrates how mechanical energy may be converted into magnetic energy; some analogous process is thought to be responsible for creating planetary magnetic fields.

Figure 60   The Earth's magnetic field in comparison with the dynamo

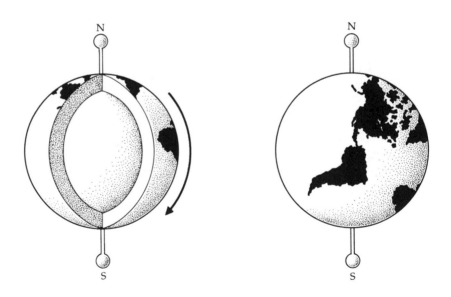

Figure 61   Pole shift, according to Hapgood

secondary livelihoods to the primary nature of crustal shift. According to Hapgood, crustal shift was made possible by a layer of liquid rock situated about 100 miles beneath the surface of the planet. A pole shift would thus displace the Earth's crust in around the inner mantle, resulting in crustal rock's being exposed to magnetic fields of a different direction (*see* Figure 61).

In his bestselling book *Earth in Upheaval*, historian Immanuel Velikovsky gave an account of what might be expected when the Earth tilts on its axis:

> ... At that moment an earthquake would make the globe shudder. Air and water would continue to move through inertia; hurricanes would sweep the Earth, and the seas would rush over continents, carrying gravel and sand and marine animals, and casting them onto land. Heat would be developed, rocks would melt, volcanoes would erupt, lava would flow from fissures in the ruptured ground and cover vast areas. Mountains would spring up from the plains and would climb and travel upon the shoulders of other mountains, causing faults and rifts. Lakes would be tilted and emptied, rivers would change their beds; large land areas with all their inhabitants would slip under the sea. Forests would burn, and the hurricanes and wild seas would wrest them from the ground on which they grew and pile them, branch and root, in huge heaps. Seas would turn into deserts, their waters rolling away.
>
> And if a change in the velocity of the diurnal rotation [slowing the planet down] should accompany the shifting of the axis, the water confined to the equatorial oceans by centrifugal force would retreat to the poles, and high tides and hurricanes would rush from pole to pole, carrying reindeers and seals to the tropics and desert lions to the Arctic, moving from the equator up to the mountain ridges of the Himalayas and down the African jungles; and crumbled rocks torn from splintering mountains would be scattered over large distances; and herds of animals would be washed from the plains of Siberia. The shifting of the axis would change the climate of every place, leaving corals in Newfoundland and elephants in Alaska, fig trees in northern Greenland and luxuriant forests in Antarctica. In the event of a rapid shift of the axis, many species and genera of animals on land and in the sea would be destroyed, and civilizations, if any, would be reduced to ruins.[8]

Velikovsky continues:

... The evidence is overwhelming that the great global catastrophes were either accompanied or caused by shifting of the terrestrial axis or by a disturbance in the diurnal and annual motions of the Earth ... The state of lavas with reversed magnetization, hundreds of times more intensive than the inverted terrestrial magnetic field could impart, reveals the nature of the forces that were in action ... Many world-wide phenomena, for each of which the cause is vainly sought, are explained by a single cause: the sudden changes of climate, transgression of the sea, vast volcanic and seismic activities, formation of ice cover, pluvial crises, emergence of mountains and their dislocation, rising and subsidence of coasts, tilting of lakes, sedimentation, fossilization, the provenience of tropical animals and plants in polar regions, conglomerates of fossil animals of various latitudes and habitats, the extinction of species and genera, the appearance of new species, the reversal of the Earth's magnetic field, and a score of other world-wide phenomena.[9]

In short, Velikovsky suggests that the Earth may be destroyed by fire, water, wind, and volcanic rain, providing us with a scenario that bears a striking resemblance to the end of each of the four ages of Mayan mythology. From his studies of sunspot activity and the Mayan calendar, Cotterell has concluded that the Mayan prophecy for the end of the fifth age concerns a reversal of the Earth's magnetic field. This and its associated cataclysm, he believes, will occur around 2012 AD.

During his lifetime Velikovsky was unfairly pilloried by the scientific establishment which at the time, during the 50s and 60s, still believed in technology as the panacea of all the world's ills. His belief that the world had been closely approached by a comet in Egyptian times was treated with derision, though much of what he said has since turned out to be true. He was, for example, the first to state that comets were not rocky objects but were made largely of hydrocarbons and ice, something we now know to be true. Just recently Jupiter was struck by the remnants of such a renegade comet. The resulting impact features were photographed by astronomers and gave us a graphic demonstration of the vulnerability of planets. It was only after this happened, which could so easily have involved Earth instead of Jupiter, that space scientists at last turned their attention from idle speculation about a possible 'Big Bang', in the deepest recesses of space and time, to the dangers of much smaller bangs closer to home. Subsequent research reveals that there are literally thousands of comets in orbit around the sun, any one of which could be deflected by some random encounter to move into an Earth-threatening trajectory. Though there is probably little they can do about it, scientists are now at last taking seriously Velikovsky's warnings about the danger of collisions with comets. We expect the ideas put forward in this book to meet a similar wall of criticism—if only as a reflex action on the part of the scientific establishments. However, we don't have 40 or 50 years to wait before the risk to the human race of sunspot cycles is recognized. We know that the research done by Maurice Cotterell is only the beginning and not the end of the story. What we ask, and what the public has a right to expect, is that our critics take on the challenge and push this work further. Perhaps we may all then be better prepared to face the challenge of 2012.

10

THE ATLANTEAN CATACLYSM

The History of the Five Ages

After comparing Cayce's accounts of Atlantis with what Don José Diaz Bolio had told me concerning the Yucatan origins of the rattlesnake cult, I now felt in a position to draw some conclusions. I was beginning to understand how the process of cultural transference had occurred in Central America and, more importantly, how the rise and fall of civilizations corresponded with Maurice Cotterell's ages of the sun. I was sure that Maurice was right in seeing the Aztec account of previous ages, as given in the *Leyenda de los soles*,[1] as being more than just a myth. Each of the ages of the sun could be interpreted in terms of historical events—including, it seems, the story of Atlantis. I was now keen to put this all together and produced the following summary of what may have been the sequence of events in Mexico spanning the five ages.

If we accept that there had indeed once been a powerful civilization living on a collection of islands in the Atlantic, then it is not unreasonable to suppose that the location of this Atlantis may have been—at least in part—what we now call the West Indies. Cayce himself asserted that the chief Atlantean island, which he

called Poseidia,[2] had existed in the region of what is now Bimini
Atoll. This small pair of islands stand on the opposite side of the
Florida Straits from Miami. They also lie at the northwest end of
the Great Bahama Bank, an extensive area of shallow waters to the
north of Cuba. If Cayce's account is to be believed, it would seem
that the islands of Bimini are merely mountaintops of what was
once a much more extensive island embracing this bank as well as
other neighbouring islands and shallows. If this is the case,
Poseidia would have been at least as large an island as Cuba is
today (*see* Figure 62).

The fall of Poseidia occurred, according to Cayce, at a date
around 10,500 BC (give or take a few centuries) and, their original
homeland being inundated by the sea,[3] some émigrés made their
way west to the Yucatan region of Mexico. These survivors, he
says, were from the royal house of Atlan and were led by a priest

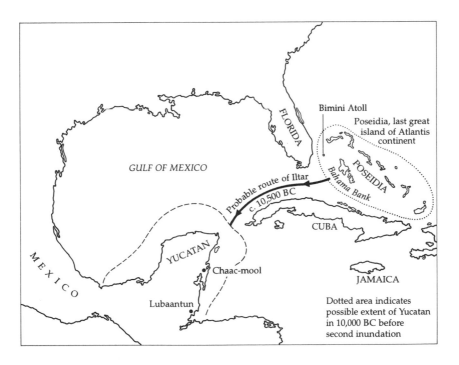

Figure 62   Map of possible 'Poseidia'

called Iltar. Iltar and his followers did not have far to sail to get to the Yucatan—probably stopping at Cuba on the way. They would then have had a choice: either to carry on sailing west into the Bay of Campeche or to go south along the east coast, perhaps landing at either Lubaantun or Thomas Gann's city of Chacmool.

All of this fits well with the Flood story as contained in the *Vatico-Latin Codex* that the first sun (or age) of the water goddess Chalchiuhtlicue was destroyed by a deluge. There is an interesting illustration of the Maya version of this same story on page 74 of the *Dresden Codex* (*see* Figure 63). Here Chac Chel (an aged goddess and clearly the Mayan equivalent of the Aztec Chalchiuhtlicue) pours out a jar of water. Below is a squatting warrior, who may represent the planet Venus. Above her a cosmic Caiman, wearing the insignia of the planets Venus, Mars, Mercury and Jupiter, and itself probably representing the Milky Way, opens its mouth to pour forth a flood. The intention is clear—the world is destroyed by a deluge on the orders of the rain goddess, this destruction having astral significance, perhaps because the planets have completed a grand cycle.

In the Quiché Maya classic the *Popul Vuh*, which as we have seen was first brought back to Europe by Brasseur de Bourbourg, it is said that the first people created by the gods were imperfect. These people were made of mud and quickly lost their shape, ultimately dissolving in water. Though there are obviously some differences in detail between the Yucatan myth as illustrated in the *Dresden* and the Quiché myth contained in the *Popul Vuh*, it is clear that the intention is the same: the first destruction was by water.

The account of how humanity survived the Flood is a little confused in the *Vatico-Latin Codex* but we have to remember that it is written in the language of mythology, not history. It is up to us to get behind the myth and see what it is really all about. First it is said that people were turned into fish and then that either one couple protected by a tree or seven couples hiding in a cave were able to wait until the waters went down. I would suggest that both accounts refer to the escape from Atlantis, that they were not so much 'turned into' fish as able to take to the ocean *in* fish, ie ships. This being the case, they would very likely have taken shelter in

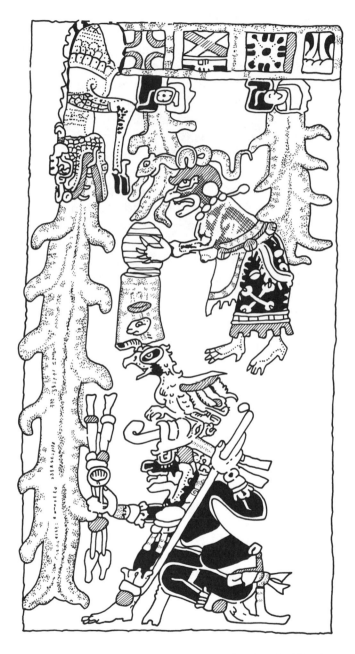

Figure 63 Page 74 of the Dresden Codex *showing the Flood*

a cave when they first arrived in their new home on the Yucatan Peninsula.

It would seem that the immigrants brought with them not only the memory of the destruction of Poseidia but also a great deal of practical knowledge in astronomy, geometry, agriculture and medicine. We can suppose that, like St Patrick in Ireland, Iltar attempted as best he could to impart his advanced Atlantean knowledge to the native proto-Mayan population, and to do this made use of a local rattlesnake, *Crotalus durissus durissus*, to illustrate what he was saying. To the much more backward inhabitants of Yucatan, the Atlanteans would have appeared gods, their leader Iltar being called Zamna by them and revered as the father of the other gods.

The next or second 'sun', which followed the destruction of Atlantis and lasted for some 4000 years, was a golden age. It was, according to the *Leyenda*, ruled over by the god of wind, Ehecatl— an aspect of Quetzalcoatl and symbolized by a Quetzal bird. This suggests a link between Iltar–Zamna and Quetzalcoatl–Kukulcan as gods of civilization. However, all good things come to an end, and like the previous age this sun also perished. How this may have happened is less clear, but according to Cayce the original Yucatan city of Iltar with its temples was destroyed some time after the original sinking of Poseidia. This could be the second destruction referred to in the *Leyenda*, for in this account it is said that this age was brought to an end by winds. Given that the word *hurricane* is derived from the Caribbean name for the wind god, it is clear that hurricane-force winds are what are being talked of. As we now know to our cost, erratic winds as well as rising oceans are a symptom of global warming. The implication is that at that time (probably around 7000 BC) there was another, perhaps more localized, epoch of floods and winds affecting the Yucatan. The statement in the *Leyenda* account that 'man was turned into a monkey, in order to cling to the trees to survive', probably reflects a retreat for a time into the forested areas of Chiapas and Tabasco and away from the more exposed Yucatan Peninsula. Amongst the dense forests of the interior, there would have been some shelter at least from the ferocious winds.

The third age of Tleyquiyahuillo that followed this destruction is also something of a mystery. It seems to have lasted from around 7000 BC to *c.* 3100 BC, and to have preceded that which gave birth to the early Mayan civilization. The third-age people, coming out from the protection of the forest, survived the second destruction and set about rebuilding their shattered world. According to archaeologists, crops were first cultivated in the Teohuacan Valley near Oaxaca around 7000 BC, which would fit in with the imperatives of this age. Because this was before the introduction of corn (maize), the account in the *Leyenda* that at that time people ate something called *tzincoacoc* (similar to almond paste) rather than the wild fruits of the previous age seems to fit. The city of Lubaantun was also built during this age and, according to Cayce, it was constructed with help from other immigrants from Peru. As unorthodox as this idea at first appears, it would at least explain why Lubaantun is unlike any of the later Mayan cities of the region, and also why its walls were built using large unmortared blocks of stone—a building technique typical of Peru.

The third age is said to have been ruled over by the god of fire, and this may be the explanation for the presence of the crystal skull amongst the ruins of Lubaantun. As we have seen earlier, the most likely use for the skull was to act as a highly sophisticated burning-glass; it was, in all probability, looked upon as a magical agent of the sun god himself. The ability of the skull to start fires would have seemed truly awesome to people not instructed in the physics of light.

The later fire ceremonies of the Aztecs and Maya were linked with ideas of regeneration, for the nature of fire is such that it returns organic matter to its primal elements, releasing heat and light in the process. The ancient Mesoamericans clearly looked upon fire in a different way from the way we do, regarding it as the means for regenerating the sun. Hence at the end of a time period, whether 1 year, 52 years or a baktun of 144,000 days, they felt it was necessary to have a ceremony, to burn up the old and make way for the new. In this way, they felt, they were feeding the sun by releasing the life-giving heat trapped in dead matter. It seems likely that this idea originated in the third age of fire.

With the coming of the fourth age, *c.* 3100 BC, we are on more recognizable ground. According to the archaeological record, it was just before the start of this age, at around 3200 BC, that maize was first cultivated. It is also the start of the Mayan Long Count calendar in 3114 BC. The most important event connected with this age is, we are told in the *Leyenda*, the founding, by the 'god' Quetzalcoatl, of the fabled city of Tula which was, by all accounts, a place of great beauty as well as sanctity. Now there has been much archaeological debate and confusion concerning the location of this city. The name is currently applied to the ruins of Tula in Hidalgo, the rather small Toltec capital that was built only in the 9th century AD. This, however, cannot be the full story. A clue to the confusion seems to be that the name Quetzalcoatl was used by pre-Hispanic Mexicans as a title given to certain very holy religious leaders as well as referring to a god who had once lived long ago. Just as in Egypt all living pharaohs were regarded as reincarnations of the god Horus and were given his name, so in Central America the high priests of the Toltecs and Maya were similarly titled Quetzalcoatl (Kukulcan). They were believed to be living embodiments of the god rather as the Dalai Lama is regarded as being a living Buddha by his followers today. However, the evidence suggests that there was one particular individual called by this name who really was outstanding, and who was regarded as being the prophet of the fourth age. It seems likely that the Tula which this man founded was not the Toltec capital uncovered by Charnay but almost certainly the greatest and holiest city of pre-Conquest Mexico, Teotihuacan.[4]

In the *Leyenda* account it is said that after the third age was brought to an end by fire sometime before 3100 BC, some survivors of this catastrophe made their way from the coastal regions of Yucatan and Tabasco to the high plateau. These people, led by a Quetzalcoatl, formed a settlement called Tula, which is probably to be identified with Teotihuacan. By 100 BC this city had grown to perhaps as many as 200,000 inhabitants, and dominated most of southern Mexico. Around AD 100 the Teotihuacanos laid out the main plazas and raised the huge Pyramids of the Sun and Moon. They also built the equally large 'Citadel' containing its smaller Pyramid of Quetzalcoatl. These covered the sites of the earlier, much more modest buildings erected by Quetzalcoatl and his comrades. The city continued to prosper, exerting its influence as far away as Palenque until, at around AD 750, the fourth age came to an end. A reduction in sunspots and an increase in direct solar radiation led to a loss of fertility in people. The catastrophe seems to have been made worse by widespread drought which caused crop failures and famine. The survivors, perhaps realizing that it was the end of a solar age, buried much of the sacred city of Teotihuacan and then set the rest on fire so that the city's energy would be returned to the sun. We can only speculate, but it is tempting to think that at least some of their leaders—perhaps including a sick old man called Nanahuatzin—threw themselves into the flames, believing that through this last, desperate sacrifice the sun god would be fortified and their descendants would prosper. It seems likely that it was this act of self-immolation that was remembered by the later Aztecs as the death of the gods. Certainly the burning of the city was the ultimate fire ceremony and seems to have symbolically terminated the fourth age as far as the Aztecs and Toltecs were concerned.

Out of the ashes of Teotihuacan was born the fifth Aztec 'sun', Nahui Ollin. Survivors from Teotihuacan, reinforced by immigrants from the north and under the leadership of another leader, again with the title Quetzalcoatl, moved to a different valley to set about building a new city. This Tula—in Hidalgo—though much smaller in size, was to become the capital of the Toltecs, and it was these ruins that were discovered by Charnay. According to Aztec and Toltec legends this Quetzalcoatl was tall, fair-skinned, bearded and knowledgeable in all matters spiritual. As king he ruled fairly and justly over the people during what was later seen to have been a golden age. However, his brother and joint ruler at Tula, the war god Tezcatlipoca, became insanely jealous. Quetzalcoatl was forced to leave, accompanied by a large contingent of his friends and supporters. He made his way eastwards to the coast and boarded a raft of snakes. But before sailing away, in the direction of the rising sun, he promised that one day he would return to re-establish the rule of law and enlightenment. It was this prophecy that so frightened the Aztec rulers, for they knew in their hearts that their forefathers had usurped the Toltec empire and they feared Quetzalcoatl's return. Perhaps it was for this reason that they continued to honour him and bury their dead at the ancient site of Teotihuacan, the place of supreme sacrifice. They seem to have been in no doubt of its sanctity as the original city of the benign god Quetzalcoatl, for they had been taught by the Toltecs that it was here that he brought about the birth of the fifth sun. This fourth-age capital, with its pyramids and temples now buried under layers of earth and vegetation, continued to be a great place of pilgrimage for Mesoamericans right up until the coming of the Spanish.

Meanwhile, further east in Chiapas and the Yucatan, a separate Mayan civilization developed in parallel with the rise of Teotihuacan. The early origins of this civilization remain something of a mystery but must have paralleled developments in Teotihuacan. By 1000 BC, as 'Olmecs', the Maya built cities on the coast of Tabasco before spreading west to Oaxaca. They also developed a system of hieroglyphs, which they later taught to the Zapotecs, and the Long Count method of recording dates with reference to the start of the age in 3114 BC.

By AD 600 the Maya of Chiapas were building cities such as Palenque and had developed a highly sophisticated architectural style of their own. As elsewhere in Mesoamerica they built pyramid-temples to serve both as cult centres and tombs for such illustrious rulers as Pacal. They preserved the knowledge of their ancestors and absorbed much from their contacts with far-off Teotihuacan. According to Spanish reports they believed themselves to be descended, in part at least, from people who came from overseas led by a man called Votan. He also was said to have been white-skinned and to have made several return voyages to his old homeland. On one of these he apparently visited a great city with a high tower reaching up to heaven. As the people depicted on the walls of Palenque have large noses and look quite Semitic, it is tempting to think that Votan may have been either an Egyptian or Carthaginian.

Like Teotihuacan, Palenque and the other cities of the Central Mayan area were abandoned by AD 800, due to the same factors that had influenced population decline in western Mexico. The Mayans left their lowland cities and moved to the highland regions, where there was more rainfall. They never returned, and such cities as Palenque, Bonampak and Yaxchilan were quickly swallowed by the jungle. In the northern Yucatan, people fared rather better. By making use of underground reservoirs of water, they were not as dependent on steady rainfall and were able to bring forth a new flowering of Mayan culture at such sites as Uxmal, Chichen Itza and Mayapan. Later the province was invaded by the Toltecs from the second Tula, led by another Quetzalcoatl (the one known as Topilzin), and a new militaristic element was added to what had, until then, been a largely peaceable civilization.

This confused scenario seems to have been the course of history in Central America from the time of Atlantis to the coming of the Spaniards in 1519. How things would have developed had Cortes and his men not made their fateful footfall is anyone's guess. It does seem, however, that the indigenous civilization was already in decline by that time. Incessant warfare, human sacrifice, disease and overworking of the land were all contributory factors to this decline. However, above and beyond all of these was a loss of vision. The lands of Quetzalcoatl–Kukulcan were in need of a fresh input of ideas and energies, for the people had lost their understanding. That this should have happened in such a brutal way as the Spanish Conquest with its attendant Inquisition seems to me to have been one of the great tragedies of history, for it is clear that the expected 'return of Quetzalcoatl' should have been a peaceful event. I was now anxious to explore the deeper, more esoteric side of the Quetzalcoatl tradition and, rather surprisingly, I was to find that it had many resonances with Gnostic Christianity.

Quetzalcoatl, the good god

The involvement of the god Quetzalcoatl in the sacrifice at Teotihuacan is something of an enigma in itself, for it seems that originally the name Quetzalcoatl (or Kukulcan, to give him his Mayan name) was a celestial god. One of the four sons of the primary divine couple Ometeotl (Hunabku in the Mayan tradition), he ruled the sky in the west, his colour being white. This, as one might expect, signified purity, goodness and wisdom. He was also identified with Venus, which is both white and the brightest of all the planets. Quetzalcoatl as Venus was also something of a phoenix, the mythical, self-sacrificing fire-bird. For according to the *Annals of Cuauhtitlan* he immolated himself in the Land of Black and Red (identified as Xicalanco and Acallan on the Maya frontier) and his heart, burning to incandescence, rose to become the planet Venus. We read:

> When they reached the place they were searching for, now again there he [Quetzalcoatl] wept and suffered. In this year 1 Reed (so it is told, so it is said), when he had reached the ocean shore, the edge of the sky-water, he stood up, wept, took his attire and put on his plumes, his precious mask. When he was dressed, of his own accord he burned himself, he gave himself to the fire. So that where Quetzalcoatl burned himself is called the Place of Incineration.
>
> And it is said that when he burned, his ashes rose up and every kind of precious bird appeared and could be seen rising up to the sky ... And after he had become ash the quetzal bird's heart rose up; it could be seen and was known to enter the sky. The old men would say he had become Venus; and it is told that when the star appeared Quetzalcoatl died. From now on he was called the Lord of Dawn.

Once more we see the familiar connection between a fire ceremony and a new birth, the start of a new age. As we have seen, the Birth of Venus has strong calendrical connotations, for it marks the start of the Mayan Long Count calendar in 3114 BC. For the Aztecs this age ended with the destruction of Teotihuacan and the founding of Tula around AD 750. The writer of the *Annals of Cuauhtitlan*, wanting to link the mythical birth of Venus with the start of the fifth age, found his way of linking the Venus myth with the flight of the later Quetzalcoatl–Topilzin. What is also of interest in this story is the stated year of 1 Reed, for it was in such a year that the Aztec empire was rudely invaded not by a benevolent Quetzalcoatl but by Cortes and his knights.

There is, however, very much more to the myth of Quetzalcoatl–Kukulcan than either astronomy or history. As an archetype, he stands for all that a man should aspire to. His depiction as a feathered serpent indicates his dual nature: the feathers symbolize his airy, spiritual nature (the Father) and the serpent his connection with physical creation (the Mother). It was, of course, the statue of Coatlicue, the Aztec earth mother, with her serpentine skirts and head that so disgusted the Spanish authorities that they had it buried. On a deeper, more mystical level, the 'feathered serpent' symbol indicates the way that the enlightened man needs to bring the two opposing aspects of his nature, the spiritual and material, into conjunction.

In the spiritual traditions of the West the serpent (or sometimes dragon), as well as symbolizing the path of the sun through the sky, represents the lower self. According to Gnostic traditions, each one of us is born as a serpent and constrained to a life of crawling in the dust of the earth. Just as a serpent renews itself by casting off its skin and growing a new one, so we ourselves live life after life, dying and being reborn, but still unable to raise ourselves from the earth. In this state of unawareness we are cut off from the higher worlds of spirit and remain the helpless brood of the great Solar Serpent. Thus it is that as the fallen children of Adam and Eve we are imprisoned in our renewable 'skins' and constrained to live life after life and to experience death after death in the material world. This is why Coatlicue, like her Hindu equivalent Kali, has a necklace of skulls and dismembered hands, for the earth mother takes as well as gives life. However, Gnostic traditions also speak of a cosmic destiny, of the possibility inherent in humans as souls of leaving the physical earth to journey to our true home on higher, non-material planes. This is the essence of the spiritual teachings of all the great masters including Jesus, Buddha, Muhammad and, we can presume, the original Quetzalcoatl–Kukulcan.

Yet all of them teach, if we read their words carefully, that to gain freedom requires a transformation of our being. To use another metaphor, the ordinary human lives as a caterpillar on the cabbage-leaf of life. Here he or she can live and die a thousand times without being even aware of the possibility of further development. Yet, just as the caterpillar has within it the potential to be transformed into a beautiful butterfly, so too the human has the possibility of metamorphosing into a higher form. We do not have to remain at the caterpillar stage of life forever: we too can become angels—even while still alive in a physical body.

The practical application of this esoteric philosophy is Yoga and involves raising the 'serpent energy' up the spine and joining it with spiritual 'eagle' forces in the head. To do this requires an act of supreme self-sacrifice as the will of the individual—the serpent—is brought into line with the greater Will of God made manifest by the eagle. The individual has quite literally to 'die' to himself or herself in order to be 'reborn' and be linked to the greater cosmic consciousness. This is not easy, as anyone who has been involved in spiritual work will know. For standing between the would-be initiate and greater destiny is the personal ego, and this is mortally afraid of giving up its illusory identity. It can take years of preparation before an individual is ready to face this supreme test and then, utterly alone, he or she must meet God. If successful in the endeavour, he or she experiences an opening of the heart with the result that the pure energy of unconditional love is able to pour in. This not only fills the individual concerned but flows out to the world which is thereby able to partake of this living sacrifice. The man or woman thus initiated becomes a 'Quetzalcoatl' in the parlance of ancient Mexico, and receives what we who follow the Christian tradition would call the 'gifts of the Holy Spirit'. A tongue of fire has descended, burning away the dross of ordinary life and, like the stars, he or she is resurrected to eternity.

By all accounts Tenoch, who first led the Aztecs to the Valley of Mexico, was what in Native American terms would be called a medicine man. Certainly he made use of dreams for prognostication and he seems to have had at least an inkling of the significance of the eagle–serpent duality. We can imagine that Tenoch himself knew that the mystical marriage of eagle and serpent was the mystic symbol of Quetzalcoatl even if he himself did not achieve such a union. The incorporation of the story of the eagle and serpent in the myth of the founding of Tenochtitlan was probably done deliberately so that this lofty ideal would not be forgotten. Today this supreme symbol of human transformation is used as the emblem of the modern state of Mexico, and is to be found on government buildings, churches, museums and even aircraft.

But long before the coming of Tenoch to the Valley of Mexico, 'Quetzalcoatl' had founded Tula. He was also worshipped at Teotihuacan before that city was put to the flames and as Kukulcan inspired the Maya. Whether the last Quetzalcoatl really was a tall, bearded, white man we will never know. What matters, though, is not the individual but the religious ideas that he represents. This had nothing to do with the superstitious practice of tearing out the living hearts of sacrificial victims. This barbarism was a complete misunderstanding of the true Quetzalcoatl religious tradition which involved sacrifice of the will, not the body—still less the bodies of others; for it is the living heart of a saintly man, one raised from the 'dead' of earthly life and united with the cosmic Will of God, that is the real food of the universe.

The Mayans of Palenque seem to have understood this better than the Toltecs and Aztecs, who mistakenly assumed that sacrificing hostages was a substitute for personal transformation. Though the Mayans were not without their faults and by our standards their society was oppressively rigid, they did at least keep alive the idea of personal sacrifice in the sufferings they inflicted on themselves in the name of religion. Perhaps Pacal himself succeeded in making the great leap of transformation and uniting his serpent-self with the eagle or quetzal bird to become Quetzalcoatl, the highest of gods. The story of this remarkable transformation is depicted in one of Cotterell's decoded images from the Lid of Palenque, entitled 'Lord Pacal Dying'.

Recent excavations at Palenque have unearthed a number of extremely lifelike figurines of people, some of which resemble Pacal. Among these is one of a man with an eagle head (*see* Plate 35), which was possibly sculpted in deference to Pacal's becoming a transformed human being and attaining the status of Quetzalcoatl (Kukulcan). This then could have been the source of the extraordinary knowledge of the Maya. As a transformed man Pacal would have been gifted with second sight and thereby able to make prognostications for the future. He, or others like him, may even have anticipated the rising of Atlantis as the culminating event of our current age.

The Resurrection of Atlantis

The whole question of Atlantis has been a vexed one for archaeologists and explorers alike. As we have seen, the location of the lost continent in the centre of the North Atlantic Ocean is highly problematical. Not only does this disagree with modern theories of continental drift but for the most part the water is very deep here. A more likely position for the sunken landmass seems to be in the region of the West Indies, where in addition to the presence of many islands, the sea is quite shallow. Here at least it is possible to postulate that the 'sinking' of Atlantis was really more of a 'rising' of the sea, brought about by the melting of ice-sheets as the last Ice Age came to an end in *c.* 10,500 BC. The reason we find few, if any, remains of this civilization in the West Indies is because what are today islands were then mountaintops. The lost cities and towns of Atlantis would have been close to the coast and therefore inundated as the waters rose. What is left of these must, after 12,500 years, be deeply covered with sand and mud.

Cayce's sleeping accounts of Atlantis did not end with its destruction, or even with the story of how some people escaped to Egypt and the Yucatan. He prophesied that Atlantis would rise again. This process, he said, would be gradual, beginning in 1968–9. He made this strange prophecy on 28 June 1940:

> … A portion of the temples [of Atlantis] may yet be discovered under the slime of ages of sea water—near what is known as Bimini, off the coast of Florida.[5]

When he died in 1945 he was not to know that this prediction was to be confirmed, for in 1968 some strange submarine ruins were indeed discovered off the coast of Bimini Atoll, in the very area he said they would be.

These curious archaeological remains were discovered by a Dr J Manson Valentine while diving off the coast of Bimini. What he found, at a depth of only about 20 to 30 feet of water, was a long, straight wall consisting of large rectangular blocks. This discovery was confirmed by other divers and immediately the controversy began as to whether or not this was a manmade feature. The sheer size of the blocks (some of them are 10 to 15 feet in length) implies that if they are not natural, then whoever laid them there must have been in possession of some very advanced technology.

It would appear that what Valentine had discovered was the remains of a system of coastal defences against encroachment by the sea. All of this lends support to Cayce's claim that Bimini was part of the ancient island of Poseidia. For it would seem that as the sea level rose, so the Poseidians attempted to hold back the waters with walls—great dikes made of stone blocks. The final cataclysm must have come about when these could no longer hold back the sea and Poseidia itself was overwhelmed. Only the highest mountaintops remained above sea level, and the people—those of them who survived this catastrophe—were forced to migrate elsewhere.

Exciting as the discovery of the underwater wall undoubtedly is, Cayce prophesied something even more remarkable: that, when the time is right, a secret chamber would be found at Bimini. He also predicted that two similar chambers will be found else-where—one near the Sphinx in Egypt, and the other among the ruins of Iltar's temple in the Yucatan. None of these three halls of records have yet come to light—or if they have, they have not been reported—so we can only speculate on what they might contain. However, Cayce was adamant that in all three would be found records relating to the history of Atlantis and its final destruction around 10,500 BC.

Recent research on the Great Sphinx of Egypt indicates that this enigmatic statue may well be over 12,000 years old. From weathering patterns, author John Anthony West and his colleague geologist Dr Robert Schoch have produced strong evidence for believing that the Sphinx itself and its associated Valley Temple must have been carved at a time when Egypt was subject to heavy rainfall. Other geological data indicates that this is consistent with a date of at least 9000 BC.[6] Their work backs up evidence presented by Robert Bauval and myself in *The Orion Mystery*. As we pointed out there, the Egyptians themselves spoke of the founding of their kingdom at some period in the remote past which they called *Tep Zepi*: the First Time. This they regarded as having been a golden age when the gods fraternized with men. Using the SKYGLOBE computer program to recreate the sky as it would have looked around 10,450 BC, Bauval found that the constellation of Orion would then have been at the lowest point of its cycle.[7] What is more, the mirroring of the Orion constellation in the sky with the pyramids of the Memphite Necropolis (the principal theme of *The*

Orion Mystery) seemed to fit best for that date. He concluded that *Tep Zepi* must correspond to the beginning of what we were now to call an Age of Orion.

Returning to the dates given in the *Vatico-Latin Codex*, if we take the beginning of the fourth age (Tzontlilac) as 3114 BC, then it would seem that the first age of the Maya and Aztecs (Matlactili) ended 8091 years earlier—ie 11,205 BC. Significantly, this age is said to have ended with a great flood (Apachiohualiztli) brought on by the goddess Chalchiuhtlicue, wife of Tlaloc. Cayce's psychic accounts of the destruction of Atlantis indicate that this flooding was a gradual process, stretching over many centuries. The first stage of the sinking left many mountainous areas of the former continent of Atlantis poking above sea level as islands. Later, most of these too were inundated. The date of 10,500 BC marks the end of this process. In broad terms there is, therefore, a remarkable correlation between the accounts of a worldwide destruction by flood as given in Plato (*c*. 9500 BC), Cayce (before 10,500 BC) and the *Vatico-Latin Codex* (11,205 BC). It seems likely, then, that this is indeed the epoch when Atlanteans emigrated to both Egypt and the Yucatan.

The Cayce records have more to say about the Yucatan migration of the priest Iltar. In one of his readings he told a client that during a previous life he had lived '… in Atlantean land during a period of egress before final destruction … journeyed to Central America where some of the temples are being uncovered today [1935].'[8]

In this context it is noteworthy that Dr Thomas Gann had carried out his first excavation of the ruins of the city of Lubaantun only 11 years earlier in 1924. The headlines reporting his work in *The Illustrated London News* spoke of Lubaantun as 'A Lost City of America's Oldest Civilization'. Three years later, Mitchell-Hedges—adventurer, theosophist and member of the Maya Committee of the British Museum—had discovered the crystal skull at the same site. However, Lubaantun seems not to be the place Cayce was referring to when he talked about 'temples being uncovered today'. On 10 February 1935, less than three months before the above reading was given, an article by Mitchell-Hedges was published in the *New York American*. This concerned his discovery of some traces of a lost civilization on the Bay Islands off the coast of Honduras. The headline that accompanied the article was *Atlantis Was No Myth but the Cradle Of American Races, Declares Hedges*. It is likely that Cayce saw this article and that it was these discoveries that excited him. If so, it could be here, off the coast of Honduras, that we should start looking for the lost temple of Iltar.

As we approach the doomsday year of 2012 which the ancient Mayans prophesied would be the end of the last age, one can only feel apprehension for the future of our Earth. The start of the last Mayan Age was the Birth of Venus, the Quetzalcoatl star on 12 August 3114 BC. On the last day of the age, 22 December 2012, the cosmic connections between Venus, the sun, the Pleiades, and Orion are once more in evidence. For just as Venus was indeed 'born' on the earlier date, its rising just before the dawn being heralded by the Pleiades at the meridian, so it now symbolically 'dies'. The SKYGLOBE program reveals that just before the sun goes down on 22 December 2012, Venus will sink below the western horizon and at the same time the Pleiades will rise over the eastern. As the sun actually sets, so Orion rises, perhaps signifying the start of a new precessional cycle and symbolically giving birth to a new world age. What this will mean for us physically in terms of the Earth's geology we can only guess—but it might involve the lost continent.

Edgar Cayce not only predicted that Atlantis would rise again but that there would be other significant 'Earth changes' as we approach the millennium. Like Maurice Cotterell he believed there would be a shifting of the magnetic pole giving rise to widescale disruption. Much of this seems to be cyclical in nature in that throughout the Earth's history there have been topographical changes and movements. However, never before has the world been so densely populated, and if his predictions come true, this will be the biggest catastrophe for humanity that we have ever known. He forecasts that large areas along the east and west coasts of America will disappear like Atlantis under the waves of the encroaching sea. At the same time the climate of Europe, a 'continent' suffering similar coastal inundations, will be changed almost instantaneously to become much colder. This could be because the rise of the old continent of Atlantis will disrupt the Gulf Stream and cut off Europe's 'central heating'. The change in the pole will, Cayce says, produce other climatic alterations as what are today polar and tropical regions become more temperate. All of these predictions seem to fit well with the Mayan belief that the present world age would end at roughly the same time: AD 2012. What Cayce didn't say was what the mechanism for such Earth changes might be. Now with the new sunspot theories of Cotterell we have a theory of causation at last. It is the solar magnetic field that produces reversals in the Earth's magnetic field and associated cataclysms. How we approach such events remains to be seen, but we cannot say we haven't been warned.

Modern Mexico is in many ways a microcosm of the world today. It personifies all the anxieties we feel about overpopulation, the destruction of tropical rain forest, pollution, climatic change, political corruption and exploitation. Yet with such huge problems besetting them the Mexicans are a resourceful and cheerful people. More than that, they are deeply religious—in a Catholic rather than Aztec way. Through the relatively recent cult of the Virgin of Guadelupe they have a strong sense of connection with the divine. Though it will take a miracle to bring Mexico through safely to the next millennium, one feels that given their strong faith, such a thing is not an impossibility. This remarkable country that charmed Careri, Brasseur de Bourbourg, Humboldt, Stephens, Catherwood, le Plongeon, and hundreds of other travellers will somehow survive and probably provide a safe haven for other immigrants fleeing their changing world. In the new age that is to come it could well be that Mexico, with her long history of tolerance and cross-cultural fertilization, will play a significant role.

NOTES

Chapter 1

[1] The name Palenque, which means 'fence' in Spanish, is derived from the neighbouring village of Santo Domingo del Palenque. The original Mayan title of the ruined city is unknown but may have been Nachan.

[2] According to a leading Mayanologist, Michael D Coe, it was believed that a Maya lord had an alter-ego called a *uay*. This took the form of an animal (anything from a jaguar to a mouse) which could be contacted through dreams. He also suggests that some of the buildings in Mayan cities may have been sleeping places where Mayan kings could seek out these spirits in a 'vision quest'. See *The Maya* by Michael D Coe, pp.200–201.

[3] These practices included penis-piercing with a ceremonial lance. Such a lance is shown held by King Chan Bahlum on a frieze inside the Temple of the Cross at Palenque. Bloodletting in this way seems to have been a frequent practice in Yucatan also, and is described by Friar Diego de Landa in his book *Rélacion de las Cosas de Yucatan*.

[4] According to Landa, the first Spaniards to land in Yucatan were Geronimo de Aguilar and his companions in 1511. However, John Stephens in his *Incidents of Travel in Yucatan* says that Juan Dias de

Solis with a companion of Columbus himself, Vincent Yanez Pinzon, arrived earlier in 1506. These early expeditions did not succeed, and it was not until 1542 that Don Francisco Montejo was finally able to subjugate the Indians and found Merida.

5 Obsidian is a form of naturally-occurring volcanic glass that can be cut to make sharp instruments such as knives and arrow-heads. It was mined in the Valley of Teotihuacan and exported throughout Mesoamerica. Today it is used for making souvenirs.

6 The name Quetzalcoatl (in Mayan Kukulcan) means 'feathered serpent' and is applied rather confusingly to several different but related conceptions of gods. The Quetzalcoatl who was expected would have been an incarnation of the immortal god bearing the same name, rather as Gautama was an incarnation of the Buddha.

7 Cuahtemoc was taken by Cortes as a hostage to Guatemala where, once he was no longer needed, he was killed. He probably expected nothing else.

8 The most famous of these step-pyramids was the Templo Mayor which, in the unique Aztec style, was crowned with twin temples dedicated to the gods Tlaloc and Huitzilopochtli. There were a number of other pyramids at Tenochtitlan, including one that was elliptical in shape with a round tower.

9 Nahuatl was the lingua franca of the Aztec state and was widely used as a trading language throughout much of southern Mexico at the time of the conquest. The Maya, however, had a number of quite different languages of their own.

10 The Toltecs are thought to have arrived in the Valley of Mexico around AD 850 and have been the dominant power until about AD 1250.

11 The name Quetzalcoatl was used as the title both of a leader and of one of the principal gods.

12 The Aztecs are thought to have entered the Valley of Mexico in the 13th century AD.

13 An incomplete copy of Sahagun's major work, *Historia general de las cosas de Nueva España*, was published in 1840 by Carlos M Bustamente and was translated into English a century later. It is usually referred to as the *Florentine Codex*.

14 The term 'Olmec', though still in general currency, is no longer used in academic circles. The preferred and more accurate term is 'Proto-Mayan'.

15 The Zodiac of Denderah is an astrological sky-map taken from the ceiling of a temple in Upper Egypt. It dates from the late Ptolemaic

period (1st century BC) and portrays the constellations figuratively. It was removed to the *Bibliothèque Nationale* in Paris in 1820, and is now in the Louvre.

16 The Maya are divided into a number of linguistic groups all believed to derive from the same proto-Mayan rootstock. The most important groups are the Yucatecan of the Yucatan Peninsula, the Cholan of the Central Region, and the Quiché mainly further east in Belize and Guatemala.

17 Jacques Louis David (1748–1825) was one of the most important French painters of the Revolution. A fervent revolutionary himself, he painted in the classical manner. Appointed painter to the Emperor Napoleon I, he executed two notable pictures, *The Coronation* (of Josephine) and *The Distribution of the Eagles*. On the return to power of the Bourbons he was exiled, and retired to Brussels.

18 The original Kingdom of Israel, ruled over by King David from Jerusalem, was split in two following the death of Solomon. Led by the tribe of Joseph, ten of the twelve original tribes of Israel formed a breakaway state with its new capital city at Samaria. They were 'lost' after this new Kingdom of Israel (Samaria) was invaded by the Assyrians and its people sent off into exile. They were replaced by non-Israelites, referred to as Samaritans in the Bible. The two remaining tribes of the southern Kingdom of Judaea, Judah and Benjamin, remained to become known as the Jews. The whereabouts of the descendants of the Lost Tribes has been a matter of debate ever since.

19 Peter Tompkins, an American author, is better known for his *Secrets of the Great Pyramid* (1971) and for *The Secret Life of Plants* which he co-authored with Christopher Bird. His *Mysteries of the Mexican Pyramids* (1976) details the history of pyramid research in Mexico and the many, often bizarre, theories put forward to explain them.

20 *Biologia Centrali-Americana, Archaeology*. Text plus four volumes of plates.

Chapter 2

1 The *Description d'Egypte* was published in Paris between 1809 and 1822, running to 9 volumes of text and 11 volumes of illustrations. It was written by Napoleon's *savants* as they were known, the scholars of the *Commission des Sciences et des Arts de l'Armée d'Orient*, who accompanied him on his invasion of Egypt. Monumental in size as

well as scholarship, the *Description* caused a storm throughout Europe, particularly on account of its wonderful illustrations.

2   The Rosetta Stone, which was found near Alexandria in 1799 by an officer in Napoleon's army, proved to be the key in interpreting Egyptian hieroglyphs. This is because it recorded the same piece of text in three languages: Greek, Demotic (a later version of Egyptian writing) and Hieroglyphic. Assuming that the language of ancient Egypt was similar to modern day Coptic, it was possible to make an educated guess at the letters and sounds the hieroglyphs stood for and hence begin the process of decoding ancient Egyptian. The Rosetta Stone is now in the British Museum, London.

3   Possibly as early as 3000 BC.

4   Mayanologists seem to be in two minds about whether the Maya understood that the year was slightly longer than 365 days. On the one hand they talk always about the 'vague year', but on the other they indicate that the Maya were able to make accurate long-term measurements of time. While in Mexico, I was told by a guide that the Maya used to adjust their calendar by 13 days every 52 years, the equivalent of putting in 13 leap days in one go.

5   It should more properly be called a half-century because the Aztecs also used a double 52-year period of 104 years.

6   It is likely that the Long Count was invented by the Olmecs.

7   Sir Eric Thompson, who died in 1975, seems to get a mixed press from his former colleagues. On the one hand he is praised for his work on fixing the dates of the Long Count calendar, but he is also damned for the way he held back research on the deciphering of Mayan hieroglyphs.

8   Roof-combs, as they are known, are a special Mayan device which seem to have had a dual function. On the one hand, by providing vertical pressure a roof-comb would stabilize a corbelled arch, and on the other hand, if holes were cut in it, it could provide a convenient way for observing transiting stars and planets.

9   The Maya were not so much interested in the arrow of time—past, present, future—but in cycles of repetition. The movements of the sun, moon and planets were cyclical, and their mutual relationships formed cycles of longer duration. It was these long-term cycles, expressed numerologically, that formed the core of their astronomical science.

Chapter 3

[1] See, for example, Evan Hadingham, *Early Man and the Cosmos*, pp.226–227.

[2] Jeff Mayo is currently one of the world's leading astrologers and the author of a number of textbooks on the subject.

[3] Professor Hans Eysenck is best known for his work on human intelligence.

[4] Astrologers divide the 12 signs of the zodiac into four groups of three representing the elements fire, air, water and earth, in order of density. Fire and air are considered active elements while water and earth are passive.

[5] There is considerable confusion on this point but in reality it is simple. As the Earth makes its annual pilgrimage around the sun, so the latter appears to spend six months in the northern hemisphere and six in the southern. The date when the sun crosses from south to north is the spring equinox and, regardless of the starry sky, is called 0° Aries.

[6] Not literally. One should never look directly at the sun because it may cause blindness—the sun's image should be projected, using a telescope, onto a piece of white card.

[7] In 1995 we are currently in a period of low sunspot activity.

[8] See *Atlas of the Solar System*, Mitchell Beazley, 1985, p.33.

[9] This theoretical mechanism for solar magnetic behaviour is known as the Babcock-Leighton model.

[10] James Van Allen, a distinguished American scientist.

[11] The sun is largely composed of hydrogen, which in its normal atomic state is composed of one proton and one electron.

[12] *Daily Mail*, 16 December 1986.

[13] BBC radio station for British Forces Posted Overseas.

[14] An independent radio station for London.

[15] These included Professor H J Eysenck, Dr Geoffrey Dean and Dr Michael Ash.

[16] *Early Man and the Cosmos* by Evan Hadingham, William Heinemann Ltd.

[17] The Temple of the Cross is the largest of a group of three pyramid-temples believed to have been raised by Chan Bahlum (Snake Jaguar), the son of Pacal. It gets its name from its principal frieze (the original is now in the Anthropological Museum at Mexico City) which depicts Chan Bahlum and Pacal either side of a large cross.

Chapter 4

[1] The Mexican word *zocalo* is derived from the Castillian *socle*, which means 'base' or 'pedestal'. Prior to its removal following Mexican independence, there was a statue of Charles IV in the square. The base remained for many decades after, bequeathing its name not only to this plaza but to other city squares all over the country.

[2] The steady sinking of churches and other notable buildings is a cause of great alarm and adds to a sense of impermanence in a city also threatened by earthquakes.

[3] Diego Rivera (1886–1957) is the most famous of Mexico's mural artists, an art form that goes back to Mayan times. His masterpieces in the stairwell of the presidential palace depict Mexico's painful history from the foundation of the Aztec empire and the coming of the Spanish, to its revolutionary wars.

[4] This altar stone depicts the Aztec goddess Coyolxauhqui in a dismembered state. It has been suggested that she represents the Milky Way (Karl Taube, *Aztec and Maya Myths*, p.47).

[5] Leopaldo Batres was an ex-militiaman of the dictator Porfirio Diaz. He was also the first Mexican-born archaeologist and combined a professional scientific interest in Mexico's past with his own treasure-hunting. He was among the first to recognize the tourist potential of Teotihuacan and therefore set about its restoration, not always sympathetically.

[6] The Pyramid of the Sun is the second largest in Mexico (exceeded in size only by the Great Pyramid of Cholula). It stands 65 metres high and at one time had a temple on its summit making the total height 75 metres. Its square base has sides of 225 metres—almost the same as the Great Pyramid of Giza in Egypt, which has sides of 230.

[7] The 'feathered serpents' actually have rather jaguarish heads with large teeth, so perhaps snake-jaguar would be a better description.

[8] See Karl Taube, *Aztec and Maya Myths*, pp.41–44.

[9] *Ibid.*, p.44.

[10] Pronounced *Wahaca*, with three short vowel sounds.

[11] Cortes was given the title Marquess of the Oaxaca Valley by the King of Spain.

[12] Ball-courts are to be found all over Central America and even in the southern states of the USA. The rules of the ball-game are not clear but it seems to have involved striking a rubber ball with elbows and hips through a horizontally mounted stone ring. In later times, if not

earlier, the game ended with the ritual beheading of some of the players as a sacrifice to the sun god.

13 When Stephens and Catherwood visited the site in 1840, much of the stucco work was still intact. Unfortunately time, vandals and souvenir-hunters have done their worst, so that today little remains by way of decoration.

14 The name Pacal means 'shield' and was one of the first hieroglyphs to be translated. His full title is Makin Pacal, which means 'Great Sun Shield'. See Michael D Coe, *Breaking the Maya Code*, pp.188–191, Penguin Books, 1994.

15 The remains of Pacal look like those of a tall well-built man who died at around the age of 40. Yet according to hieroglyphic evidence he lived to the ripe old age of 80 years and 158 days. His apparent youthfulness is another puzzle for archaeology.

16 Possibly the goddess Chac Chel.

17 Dennis Tedlock (trans.), *Popol Vuh*, Touchstone, 1986, p.23.

18 Probably two of those sent back to London by Maudsley at the turn of the century and deposited in the Victoria and Albert Museum.

19 The Maya, living in a jungle area, practised a system of slash-and-burn crop rotation. This involves clearing an area of jungle, farming it for two or three years, and then leaving it fallow for another 20 years or so. It is now being realized that, far from being primitive, this is the only way to farm these areas of high tropical rainfall without permanently destroying the fertility of the land.

Chapter 5

1 On our second day in Mexico City there was a mild tremor measuring about 5.2 on the Richter scale.

2 The Zapotista rebellion seems to be only one aspect of a much wider cycle of discontent in Mexico at the present time focused on political corruption.

3 The meridian is an imaginary line drawn in the sky that runs from north to south. As the Earth turns, so all celestial bodies appear to rise in the east and set in the west. They reach their highest declination as they cross the meridian.

4 How Cortes and his few hundred Spaniards managed to defeat thousands of Aztecs, themselves skilled warriors, is one of the mysteries of history. Though he did have allies from other tribes, it seems the Aztecs were already resigned to their fate, and this greatly aided him.

[5] *Feng-shui*, literally 'Wind and water', is the Chinese science of geomancy that determines where and how to site buildings. In the Far East, practitioners of this art are called in as consultants by architects and other clients to give advice concerning decor and even the positioning of furniture. At its root is the underlying Taoist philosophy of *yin* and *yang*.

[6] See Evan Hadingham, *Early Man and the Cosmos*, pp.214–15 for a discussion on this point.

[7] The frescoes in the Cross Group Temples seem to be mainly concerned with Chan Bahlum's rights of succession as the son of Pacal.

[8] Waldeck spent over a year at Palenque, part of it living in a hut with a mestizo mistress. During this time he made a number of drawings which he eventually published in London along with an accompanying text.

[9] John L Stephens, *Incidents of Travel in Yucatan*, Dover Publications, 1963, p.97.

[10] According to Michael D Coe this period runs from AD 800 to 925. *The Maya*, p.9.

[11] The Itzas were another race who invaded the Yucatan, and are believed to have been Mexicanized Maya from the Tabasco region. They arrived in the contemporarily dilapidated city of Chichen around AD 1224. Because they were also led by a leader called Kukulcan (Quetzalcoatl), there is some confusion between their influence and that of the Toltecs.

[12] Friar Diego Landa, *Yucatan Before and After the Conquest*, translated by William Gates, Dover Publications, 1978, p.10.

[13] *Ibid.*, p.11.

[14] *Ibid.*, p.89.

[15] *Ibid.*, p.60.

[16] In subtropical latitudes there are two zenith days in the year, one when the sun is travelling north and the other when returning south.

[17] José Diaz Bolio, *The Rattlesnake School*, p.20.

Chapter 6

[1] In fact he was wrong on this score. As everywhere else it is invisible for some 70 days every year owing to the proximity of the sun. What he should have said is that in equatorial regions Orion passes almost directly overhead.

[2] The Pleiades, or Seven Sisters, are part of the Taurus constellation and precede Orion in their rising. A telescope reveals that there are many more of them than seven.

[3] José Diaz Bolio, *Why the Rattlesnake in Mayan Civilization*, Area Maya, 1988, pp.52–3.

[4] According to Coe, Mayapan was founded by the Itzas between AD 1263 and 1283. It was a fortified city in the west central region of Yucatan. After 1283 it became the dominant city of Yucatan until in around 1441–61 it was destroyed following a revolt by subservient Maya. *The Maya*, Michael D Coe, pp.155–6.

[5] Friar Diego Landa, *Yucatan Before and After the Conquest*, pp.73–4.

[6] *Ibid.*, p.74.

[7] *Ibid.*, p.59.

[8] '… Itzamna, the Great Initiator, in a way corresponding to Osiris.' *Ibid.*, p.143.

[9] See R Bauval and A Gilbert, *The Orion Mystery* for a full discussion of this matter.

[10] K Taube, *Aztec and Maya Myths*, p.73.

[11] José Diaz Bolio, *Guide to the Ruins of Chichen Itza*, p.17.

[12] *Ibid.*, p.38.

[13] *Why the Rattlesnake in Mayan Civilization*, p.54.

[14] David H Childress, *Lost Cities of North and Central America*, p.139.

[15] K Taube, *Aztec and Maya Myths*, pp.39, 42.

[16] According to Childress it is not clear that Mitchell-Hedges actually found the skull at Lubaantun; it may have been a cover-story to hide its real origins. Some writers have suggested that it is really a 12,000-year-old relic of Atlantis.

Chapter 7

[1] The site of this burial was discovered in 1993 and pointed out to Adrian Gilbert by a tour guide in December 1994. The tall man's legs had been broken and there is reason for suspecting that he died a violent death.

[2] A small island in the South Pacific, famous for its strange megalithic statues of staring, tight-lipped gods.

[3] Barry Fell, *America B.C.*, pp.318, 320.

[4] *Ibid.*, p.319.

[5] *Ibid.*, p.320.

[6] *Ibid.*, p.100.

[7] *Ibid.*, pp.316–17.

[8] *Ibid.*, p.272.

[9] The reader is advised to consult *The Orion Mystery* for a detailed discussion of all these matters.

[10] Ambrosius Theodosius Macrobius, grammarian, philosopher, proconsul of Africa and later Lord Chamberlain. He flourished during the reigns of Honorius and Arcadius (AD 395–423) and wrote a number of books, mostly on Virgil and the Roman calendar. He also wrote two books of commentaries on the *Somnium Scipionis* as contained in Virgil's *De republica*.

[11] G Santillana and H von Dechend, *Hamlet's Mill*, p.243.

[12] *Ibid.*, p.244.

Chapter 8

[1] The term Olmec is really a misnomer. It would be better to call this culture proto-Mayan.

[2] Following his decoding of the Lid of Palenque, Cotterell believes that the heads represent Quetzalcoatl or are at least associated with him.

[3] See José Diaz Bolio, *The Geometry of the Maya*, pp.55–61.

[4] See Evan Hadingham, *Early Man and the Cosmos*, p.179.

[5] I was told this by the guide who showed me around the ruins in 1994.

[6] The Greeks, like many other people, had a Flood myth. Their Noah-equivalent was called Deucalion.

[7] *Timaeus*, Penguin edition, p.36.

[8] *Ibid.*, p.37.

[9] *Ibid.*, pp.37–8.

[10] *Ibid.*, p.38.

[11] Eg A Rosalie David, *The Egyptian Kingdoms*, Elsevier/Phaidon.

[12] Theseus was the hero who slew the Minotaur, a fearsome beast that was half man half bull, and lived within the Labyrinth on the island of Crete.

[13] John Michell, *Eccentric Lives and Peculiar Notions*, Thames & Hudson, p.204.

[14] Ignatius Donnelly, *Atlantis the Ante-diluvian World*, revised by Egerton Sykes, Sidgwick & Jackson, 1970, p.153.

[15] *Ibid.*, pp.132–7.

[16] The discoverer of the first Chacmool figure at Chichen Itza and another keen Atlantean.

[17] *Ibid.*, p.134.
[18] *Ibid.*, p.134.
[19] *Ibid.*, p.134.
[20] Otto Muck, *The Secret of Atlantis*, William Collins, 1978.
[21] See *Edgar Cayce on Atlantis*.
[22] *Ibid.*, p.114.
[23] It seems that the people of Mu and Oz came from Mexico and Peru respectively.
[24] *Ibid.*, p.118.

Chapter 9

[1] Nahui Ollin, the current sun of motion, who was believed to have been born at Teotihuacan.
[2] The four glyphs also represent days in the *tonalamatl*: 4 Ehecatl, 4 Quihuitl, 4 Atl, 4 Ocelotl. They clearly relate to the four directions, four colours, four elements, and other related concepts linked with the idea of the quincunx.
[3] C^{14} is produced by the transformation of N^{14}.
[4] The half-life of C^{14} (the period taken for half of the original amount to decay) is 5568 years ($\pm$30 years).
[5] A number of cities, such as Teotihuacan and Monte Alban, show signs of having been abandoned, their pyramids and other sacred buildings deliberately buried under mounds of earth.
[6] Published in 1988.
[7] At the time the Aztecs' Lake Texcoco was still full of water. Today there is hardly anything left of this once large body of water and Mexico City sprawls over its bed.
[8] Immanuel Velikovsky, *Earth in Upheaval*, Pocket Books, New York, 1977, pp.124–5.
[9] *Ibid.*, pp.239–40.

Chapter 10

[1] See Chapter 4.
[2] Plato ascribes the founding of the Atlantean civilization to Poseidon, the Greek god of the sea. His eldest son by Cleito, a human woman, was Atlas who became the first ruler, giving his name to Atlantis, the

Atlantic Ocean and the Atlas Mountains. (See Plato's *Critias* dialogue, Penguin classics, pp.136–7.)

[3] The cause of the inundation may have been a rising of the sea level as the polar ice-caps retreated at the end of the last Ice Age, low-lying coastlands being flooded. On a smaller scale, global warming today is threatening the same thing for many Pacific islands.

[4] It should be noted that the root word *huacan* (pronounced *wacan*) means 'Holy' in the sense of being blessed with occult power. *Teo-ti-huacan* means 'Holy city of the god'.

[5] *Edgar Cayce on Atlantis*, p.90.

[6] John Anthony West, *Serpent in the Sky*, and television documentary *The Mystery of the Sphinx*.

[7] Because of the Earth's precessional movement, all stars appear to go through a 26,000-year cycle, oscillating between an extreme northerly and southerly position in the sky. To go from one extreme to the other thus takes roughly 13,000 years.

[8] *Edgar Cayce on Atlantis*, p.111.

Appendices

by **Maurice Cotterell**

Note: The start of the Mayan Long Count Calendar is usually taken as 3114 BC. This is because astronomers and others do not recognize the date '0' BC/AD, but go straight from 1 BC to 1 AD. Some authorities, however, prefer to take the year 0 into account and present BC dates as one digit lower. Thus 3114 BC becomes 3113 BC. There is also not 100% agreement as to whether the starting day of the Long Count, 4 AHAU 8 RUMHU, is 12 August or 10 August.

Appendix 1: Astrogenetics

Astrogenetics—the scientific study of how astronomical forces influence biological rhythms and genetic factors—pulls together a number of scientifically established facts to prove that solar particles can affect the personalities of individual humans from the moment of conception (*see* Chapter Three, pp. 52–4).

Specifically, it has been discovered that changes in the weak magnetic field of the Earth cause genetic mutation in cells that are in the process of mitosis—a method of cell division that occurs at conception. Experiments performed under the direction of Dr A R Lieboff of the Naval Medical Research Institute, Bethesda, Maryland in 1984, on human cells called fibroblasts, showed that variations in environmental magnetic fields affected the synthesis of DNA in the cells. This means that the cells could undergo mutation when subjected to varying magnetic fields at strengths below that of the Earth's own magnetic field.

It has been established since 1927—through the work of Dr Johannes Lange in his studies on identical (one-egg) and non-identical (two-egg) twins—that personality (the overall aspect of 'character') is fundamentally related to genetic makeup. Genetic change, as through mutation by variation of local magnetic field strength, may thus be responsible for unexpected personality traits. Or, to put it another way, your personality depends on the local magnetic field composition and strength at the moment of your conception.

This conclusion is confirmed by the extroversion/introversion studies undertaken by astrologer Jeff Mayo and Professor H J Eysenck which resulted in the fascinating personality distribution graph linked to zodiacal birth-dates (*see* Figure 11, page 42). The conclusion also forms the basis of the theory of Astrogenetics, which I first made public in 1988.

Elements of the theory are amplified in Appendix 2a.

Appendix 2a: Astrogenetics and the Twelve Astrological Types

Investigation into the radiation emitted by the sun shows that it changes every month. It also shows that there are four different types of radiation, which follow each other in a net sequence a month at a time. This sequence of solar radiation corresponds in many ways with the millennia-old cosmological view that there are four primary 'elements'—Fire, Earth, Air and Water—which somehow hold sway over people's dispositions and moods on a monthly basis throughout the year, corresponding to the twelve zodiacal personalities distinguished by astrologers.

The evidence for the 'monthly' fluctuation in solar radiation is complex, but not difficult to understand.

The rotational period of the sun at its equator is the equivalent of 26 Earth-days. During this 26-'day' duration the Earth moves approximately

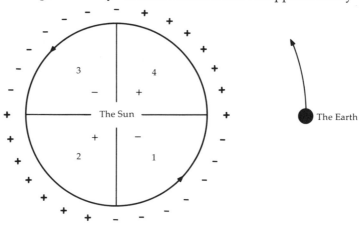

The sun rotates, sending out positive and negative magnetic radiation towards the Earth, which receives the radiation over a 28-day period (because it is itself moving while the sun actually rotates over 26 Earth-days. Each field thus bathes the Earth for a week at a time).

Figure A1

26 degrees through its annual orbit around the sun, and because it does so, from a point of reference on the Earth's surface the sun's rotation actually appears to take 28 Earth-days.

If the four different types of solar equatorial magnetic field are numbered 1 to 4, and 1 and 3 are said to be negative, and 2 and 4 positive, it means that all four fields are exposed to the Earth's surface for an equal time every 28 days—that is, the Earth is showered with solar particles of a polarity that alternates between negative and positive every 7 days.

But the polar regions of the sun rotate much more slowly—every 37 days, on the solar surface. This means that an observer standing on earth sees the polar field sweep through 90 degrees of the equatorial field every month.

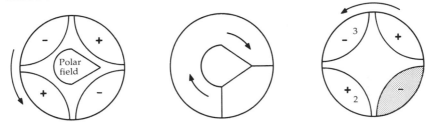

Plan view of the sun showing the Equatorial magnetic field and the polar magnetic field. Both fields rotate, though the polar field rotates more slowly. The effect of this is that the polar field sweeps through one Equatorial field every month.

Figures A2, A3, A4   Equatorial and polar magnetic fields

As the pole impinges upon the equatorial field it disturbs both the field and the particle emissions from that field. Every month the next equatorial field is affected. If we number the four fields (as above), we can keep track of the resulting interaction.

During the first month, field number 1 is neutralized, so we observe only the remaining fields.

Possible fields observed from Earth

1^-	2^+	3^-	4^+	
/////	2^+	3^-	4^+	Actual solar output month 1
1^-	/////	3^-	4^+	2
1^-	2^+	/////	4^+	3
1^-	2^+	3^-	/////	4

Figure A5

The result is that during the first month field number 1 is neutralized. This means that during month 1 we observe field number 2 (which is positive), field number 3 (which is negative), and field number 4 (which is positive). On Earth, therefore, more positive particles than negative particles are recovered from the sun during the first month. We can say that during the first month the sun's radiation overall is positive. The next month's radiation is negative because field number 2 is neutralized—and so on. Each month's radiation alternates in polarity, and each month is punctuated by a particular coded radiation sequence (either 234, 134, 124, or 123). Thereafter the radiation pattern repeats. This can be tabulated for a 12-month period thus:

Month number					
1		2	3	4	+
2	1		3	4	−
3	1	2		4	+
4	1	2	3		−
this then repeats 5		2	3	4	+
6	1		3	4	−
7	1	2		4	+
8	1	2	3		−
and again 9		2	3	4	+
10	1		3	4	−
11	1	2		4	+
12	1	2	3		−

Figure A6

And illustrated thus:

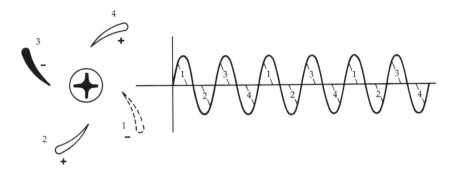

During the first month number 1 is neutralised and hence the radiation leaving the sun is positive.
The second month field number 1 is neutralised and the radiation leaving the sun is negative etc.

Figure A7   Net monthly radiation output

This distribution agrees with the claims of astrologers that astrological elements/'personalities' corresponding to the first four months of the zodiac are thereafter repeated in sequence over the rest of the year.

	Aries	Fire
	Taurus	Earth
	Gemini	Air
	Cancer	Water
	Leo code	F
	Virgo	E
	Libra	A
	Scorpio	W
and again	Sagittarius	F
	Capricorn	E
	Aquarius	A
	Pisces	W

This of course can be represented diagrammatically:

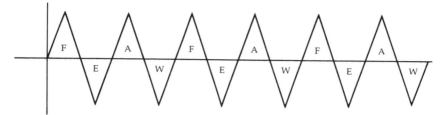

Figure A8

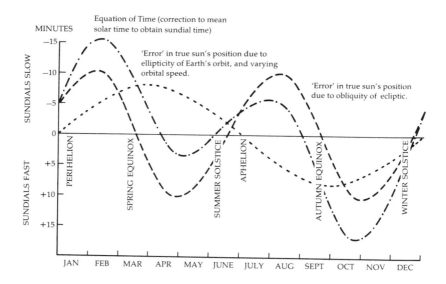

Curves showing the time gained and lost by the sun compared with the uniform motion around the celestial equator of the fictitious 'mean sun', due to: (1) the non-uniform motion of the Earth (the Earth's orbit is an ellipse, not a circle); and (2) the obliquity of the ecliptic (see above). When these two factors are added together the curve of the equation of time results; this is the correction that must be made to mean time to give apparent (ie sundial, or true) time.

Figure A9

Although the overall distribution is correct, the amplitude of the waveform does not agree with the Mayo-Eysenck data because radiation leaving the sun is not necessarily that radiation which impinges upon the Earth. The difference results from the Earth's non-uniform motion around the sun, and because the Earth is tilted on its axis. Both of these 'errors' may be reconciled by the 'sundial equation of time' correction necessary to accommodate fluctuations in arriving particles emitted by the sun.

Correcting the graph according to the idealized solar radiation output we see this:

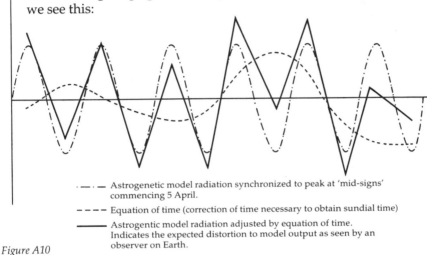

.—.— Astrogenetic model radiation synchronized to peak at 'mid-signs' commencing 5 April.

– – – – Equation of time (correction of time necessary to obtain sundial time)

——— Astrogentic model radiation adjusted by equation of time. Indicates the expected distortion to model output as seen by an observer on Earth.

Figure A10

From this we can extrapolate the radiation pattern impinging upon the Earth's magnetosphere:

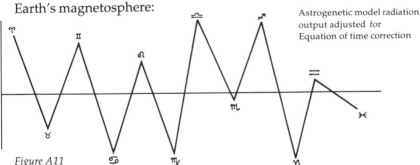

Astrogenetic model radiation output adjusted for Equation of time correction

Figure A11

This correlates very closely with the data from the Mayo-Eysenck personality tests (see Chapter Three, pp. 41–2).

DETERMINATION OF PERSONALITY

THE ASTROGENETIC THEORY

This suggests that personality is a function of genetic mutation caused by modulated magnetic fields acting upon the foetus (egg/Zygote) at conception. These modulations are in turn caused by solar particle interaction with the Earth.

THE SUN

Solar radiation output

SOLAR WIND

Charged solar wind particles enter the Van Allen belts, spiral from N pole to S pole

Van Allen Belts

The varying magnetic field affects the manufacture of DNA at conception causing genetic mutations to occur

The terrestrial magnetic field varies at ground level

Net monthly radiation output (as seen on Earth)

These are four sequential codes of radiation that leave the sun

Extroverted

Introverted

Mean

- - - First study (1795 samples)
——— Second study (2324 samples)

FIRE   AIR   FIRE   AIR   FIRE   AIR   FIRE   AIR
EARTH   WATER   EARTH   WATER   EARTH   WATER   EARTH   WATER

Sun-signs and Extroversion/Introversion Tendencies

Genetic mutations lead to variations in personality

Appendix 2b: A Scientific Rationalization of Astrology

Personality types that share the same solar radiation code have an affinity with each other, whereas those with opposite codes respond unfavourably. Fluctuations in solar radiation patterns nonetheless cause people of opposite zodiacal signs to be attracted to each other.

The solar radiation sequence determines the natural moment of birth in babies born at full term (after 275 days' gestation), and does the same also for those who are in fact born prematurely or late.

A further influence on personality, though in a minor way only, is the position of the planets at the moment of conception. The position of the planets may in addition affect the moment of birth.

As we saw in Appendix 2a (Figures A2, A3 and A4), the equatorial magnetic field of the sun rotates at a greater speed than the sun's polar magnetic field, a fact that holds great significance for the reception of solar radiation upon the Earth. This can be shown diagrammatically (let us label the polar magnetic field of the sun P, the equatorial field E, the receiving Earth W, and let us say that all begin at a moment of alignment corresponding to time zero A):

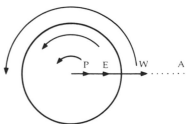

P, E and W all rotate counterclockwise.

P takes 37 days to complete one revolution of 360°.

E takes 26 days to complete one revolution of 360°.

W takes 365.25 days to complete one revolution around the sun.

Figure A12   P, E and W all commence rotation at point A at time zero

Because astrology relates to 'Calendar months', our interest must focus on the period of 30.4375 days (365.25 divided by 12).

E moves 360 divided by 26 degrees per day, ie 13.8461° per day.
P moves 360 divided by 37 degrees per day, ie 9.7297° per day.
W moves 360 divided by 365.25 degrees per day, ie 0.9856° per day.

After 30.4375 days, therefore,
E has moved 1 revolution plus 61.4423°.
P has moved only 296.1486°.
W has moved 30°.
All movements are from their initial starting point, marked by the letter 'A', (0/360°).

After 30.4375 days (1 month):
E has moved 360+61.44°
P has moved 296.148°
W has moved 30°

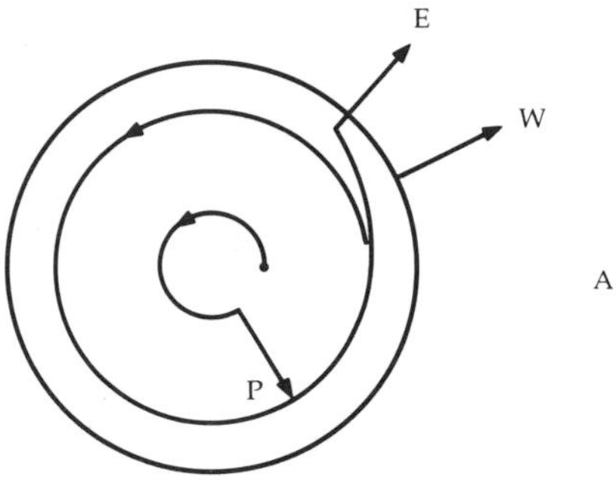

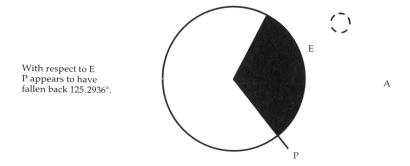

Figure A13

With respect to point A, P appears to have 'fallen back' 63.8513°. But with respect to E, P has fallen back by 61.4423° + 63.8513°, ie 125.2936°.

With respect to E
P appears to have
fallen back 125.2936°.

Figure A14

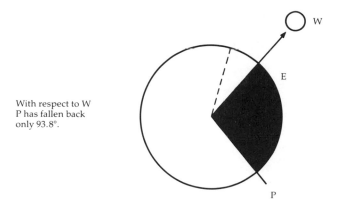

With respect to W
P has fallen back
only 93.8°.

Figure A15

With respect to W (Fig. A15) P appears to have fallen back or 'scanned'
only 93.8° of E. It is this effect that interests us. An observer stationed on
the Earth would see P scan through 93.8° of E every calendar month.

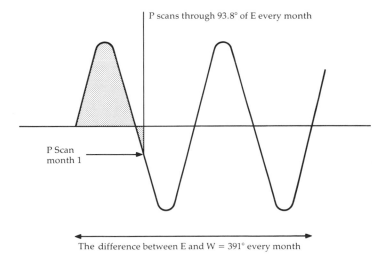

Figure A16

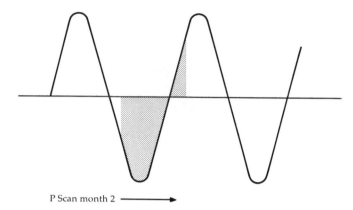

P Scan month 2 ⟶

Figure A17

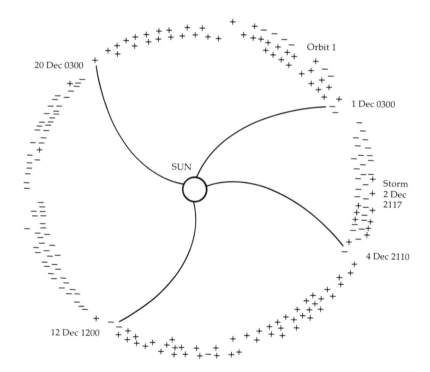

The sectored structure of the solar
wind (Actual snapshot 1-IMP 1963)

Figure A18

The total monthly E scan with respect to W is 391.437°. Each E field quadrant equates to 90°. So 4.349 E fields scan W in one month. Each E field therefore takes 7 days, exactly, to scan W.

Compare this with Figure A18 which shows the sectored structure of the solar wind, as discovered by the Mariner II spacecraft in 1962, and later redefined by Interplanctary Spacecraft IMP1 in 1963.

The effects of P on the duration of the E field quadrants are now evident. We clearly see that every 7.5 days the sun emits particles. Each 7.5 days, with respect to W, the polarity of particles switches. We can see, on 1–4 December, the reduced E quadrant caused by the mixing of P and E. By the end of December this reduced sector has slid counterclockwise, as we would expect, through the E field. (In the next month, January, this adjacent quadrant will be reduced in duration.)

In the foregoing calculations, the sun and Earth's declinations have been omitted to simplify the explanation. Variation in the velocity of the Earth around the sun has likewise been excluded. (Because the Earth's orbit is an ellipse, its speed varies as a function of proximity to the Earth, as stated in Kepler's laws.) These omissions have produced the .5-day error between calculation and observation (Figure A18), *at one moment in time*. Over a long period, however, the average quadrant duration is 7 days.

Let us label the columns of alternating emissions thus:

+	-	+	-		
4	**3**	**2**	**1**	and tabulate the results	
4	3	2	.	= month 1 Aries	+
4	3	.	1	= month 2 Taurus	−
4	.	2	1	= month 3 Gemini	+
.	3	2	1	= month 4 Cancer	−
4	3	2	.	= month 5 Leo	+
4	3	.	1	= month 6 Virgo	−
4	.	2	1	= month 7 Libra	+
.	3	2	1	= month 8 Scorpio	−
4	3	2	.	= month 9 Sagittarius	+
4	3	.	1	= month 10 Capricorn	−
4	.	2	1	= month 11 Aquarius	+
.	3	2	1	= month 12 Pisces	−

Figure A19

Three signs share the solar emission code 234 (Fire). Three signs share the solar emission code 134 (Earth). Three signs share the solar emission code 124 (Air). Three signs share the solar emission code 123 (Water).

Fire and Air are both positive and harmonise together. Earth and Water are both negative and harmonise together. Positives and negatives are subject to opposite polarity solar radiations and hence have an opposite effect.

The dispersion of signs on a month-by-month basis accords to the Mayo-Eysenck astro-personality study (*see* Chapter Three, pp. 41–3).

Let us now analyse P (the position of the sun's magnetic pole), E (the position of the sun's equator), and W (the position of the Earth) over a 12-month period of time, from the point of view of human procreation. First imagine that a sperm enters an ovum on day 1, as shown:

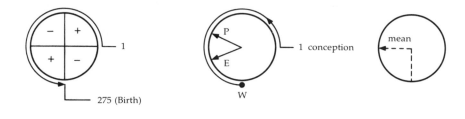

| 12 month period of radiation output | Relative positions of P, E and W after 9 months | After 9 months the average combined position of P and E is 90 degrees displaced from W; 90 degrees displacement indicates that a change of field polarity occurs between the 1st day and 275th day of gestation. |

Figure A20

For three months the fetus will feel comfortable within the womb (because it will be under the influence of a positive emission sequence having been conceived during a positive emission sequence). For months 4, 5 and 6 the fetus will be bombarded by negative solar radiation, which gives rise to fetal anxiety, stress and discomfort. But the fetus is still in the early stages of its development. Its glandular system and brain (the hypothalamus region) are not yet able to function as systems.

During months 7, 8 and 9 the fetus is comforted by positive radiation. On the 275th day—calculated from the time of release of the ovum from the ovary, and including the seven-day period before the ovum attaches to the uterine wall—the bombardment of solar radiation again switches to a negative sequence. The child again feels discomfort, anxiety and stress. This time the fetus reacts by producing hormones which are carried through the bloodstream causing the onset of labour to commence in the mother. Shortly after, the mother gives birth to a 'positive' offspring.

In effect the fetus chooses its own moment of birth. This is ideally when the radiation pattern that was instrumental in its creation at the time of conception (and which is repeated during months 6 to 9) ceases. The moment of birth is thus related to the moment of conception. And in this way personality traits ostensibly determined, say astrologers, by events at the moment of birth can be seen to correlate with events at the moment of conception, and to have arisen due partly or wholly to genetic mutations attendant at that time.

Do the planets influence the fetus in any way at birth?
We have seen how the fetus 'selects' its own moment of birth. That moment coincides with the first onslaught of 'alien' particles once the fetus has reached maturity. The child actually reaches maturity 266 days after womb implantation, ie $266 + 7 = 273$ days. Birth therefore coincides to within seven days of this time, dependant on solar emissions. However, if a substantial solar flare or 'prominence' occurs on the sun's surface, a short burst of alien radiation may cause premature or delayed triggering of birth. Consider Figure A18, and note the magnetic storm that begins on 2 December at 21.17 hours and lasts until 4 December 21.10 hours. This is the type of storm that could cause premature or delayed triggering of labour due to the release of a radiation burst of 'inappropriate' polarity.

Such bursts are associated with solar flares and prominences. The question then arises: can the gravitational pull of the planets cause disturbances in solar activity so as to cause the eruption of solar flares and/or the occurrence of prominences?

Contemporary science provides no answer to this question. Furthermore, if a correlation can be found between planetary aspects and solar disturbances, it ought also to be possible to predict a storm sequence, and hence, a disruptive burst of radiation that is likely to adversely affect a particular offspring.

It is not totally outside the bounds of conjecture that, if a more intelligent civilization once lived on Earth, any such correlations were once known and handed down in the form of astrology.

Role of the Planets at the time of conception

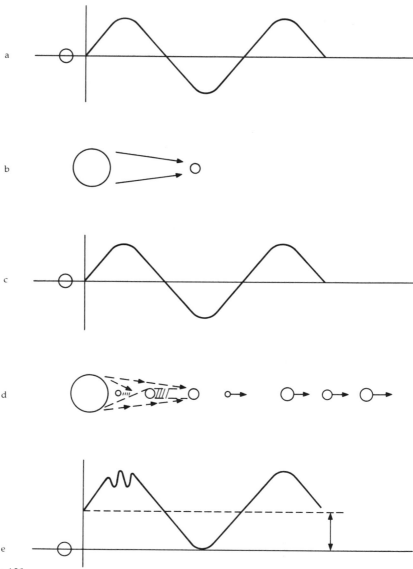

Figure A21

A degree of personality variance may result from the effects of planetary activity at the moment of conception. In Figure A21 the 'ideal' solar wave (a) is shown at one moment in time. Without any planets in the model (b), this same wave (c) interacts with the Earth. In the case of a planetary configuration (d) the inner planets adjust the focal plane of the beam (in much the same way as electrodes are deflected in a cathode-ray tube): the outer planets have the ability to accelerate the particles in the beam, thus increasing kinetic energy carried by the particles. So, as the particles impinge upon the magnetosphere, the degree of modulation (the 'absolute bias') must also vary. The resulting waveshape (e) shows the wave modulated in amplitude and the overall bias level increased.

Figure A22 shows another configuration with the beam magnitude attenuated. This would mean that planetary aspects could fine-tune the solar wave pattern (b), creating a 'unique' pattern that leads to a degree of personality variance within each sign of the zodiac.

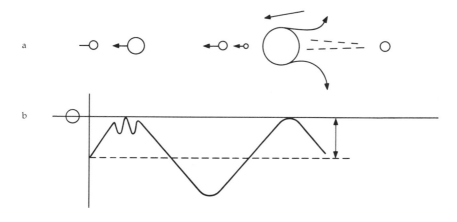

Figure A22

Appendix 3: Solar Radiation and Hormone Production in Humans

The Maya worshipped the sun as the god of fertility. Here we show how solar radiation affects the manufacture of fertility hormones, and to such a degree that leads us to the conclusion that human fertility is in fact dependent on solar radiation.

Evidence exists that serves to illustrate that female humans, deprived of solar radiation for a length of time, experience disruptive changes in their endocrine systems. Such disruption in turn severely affects the production of the 'timing' hormone melatonin and the fertility hormones oestrogen (estrogen) and progesterone.

Among such evidence is a report in the *New Scientist* of June 1989, which illustrates endocrine dependence upon solar radiation. Stefania Follini, an Italian interior designer, spent four months in a cave in New Mexico. Italian scientists watched how she responded to the isolation because of its implications for space travel. Her waking days lasted 35 hours and were punctuated by sleeping periods of about 10 hours. She lost 17 pounds (7.7 kilograms) and her menstrual cycle stopped. Follini believed she had spent two months underground, not four.

Such effects should be no surprise to us now, for we have seen (in Appendix 2) how the sun's radiation is responsible for the mutation of cells at the moment of conception. Let us now consider how the sun's radiation would likewise directly affect the endocrine system.

Dr Ross Adey of Loma Linda Hospital, California, has undertaken more than 15 years' research into the effects of magnetic fields on living cells. In a scientific paper published in 1987, 'Cell membranes, Electromagnetic fields and Intercellular Communication', he explains how the combined effect of two magnetic fields, one static and another oscillating (similar to the Earth's and the sun's fields), cause changes in the 'timing hormones' of various living creatures:

About 20% of pineal cells in pigeons, guinea-pigs, and rats, respond to changes in both direction and intensity of the Earth's magnetic field (Semm, 1983). Experimental inversion of the horizontal component of the Earth's magnetic field significantly decreases synthesis and secretion of the peptide hormone melatonin, which powerfully influences circadian rhythms and also reduces activity in its synthesizing enzymes (Walker et al., 1983).

Adey's results suggest that the sun's radiation is responsible for biorhythmic regulation of organisms at all times after conception.

This in turn suggests that the sun's 28-day radiation sequence is responsible for the 28-day biorhythm cycle as disposed by the effect of modulating magnetic signals on the peptide hormone melatonin.

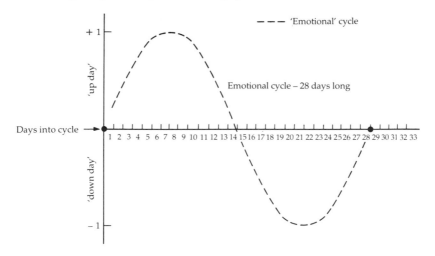

The emotive inputs of the biorhythm cycle on a given day may be expressed as a value between –1 and 1.

Figure A23

Any hypothesis relating to emotional—or indeed biorhythmic—causes and effects requires rigorous testing. But such data is very difficult to collect and/or monitor.

In that we are searching for links between the sun's 28-day radiation sequence and hormonal activity we could select another group of hormones—those responsible for fertility and menstruation—with which to test our hypothesis. These are much more defined, predictable, and understood.

Mechanisms of fertility hormone production

The hypothalamus, a tiny structure at the base of the brain, sends chemical signals via blood vessels that connect it to the so-called 'master gland', the pituitary. The pituitary responds by manufacturing and releasing into the bloodstream two protein hormones: LH, the luteinizing hormone, and FSH, the follicle-stimulating hormone, both of which are essential for the release of spermatozoa or eggs from the gonads—the testes in the male and the ovaries in the female, respectively. The gonads in turn stimulate production of other sex hormones. These are steroids, corresponding in the male to testosterone, and in the female to oestrogen (estrogen) and progesterone. Steroid production is part of a process involving the hypothalamus and the pituitary gland that is a closed loop. The gonads monitor the overall level of hormone and shut off production, via the pituitary and hypothalamus, when adequate levels have been produced.

This is illustrated opposite:

Hormonal production is a three-stage process in males and females. (A) Summary of hormonal control of the testicular function. The hypothalmus sends chemical signals to the pituitary, which responds by producing FSH and LH, which stimulate the release of spermatozoa and testosterone. When the amount of testosterone reaches a certain level, the hypothalmus and pituitary stop production of FSH and LH. (B) Summary of hormonal control of ovum development and oestrogen secretion, which follows the same pattern as the male.

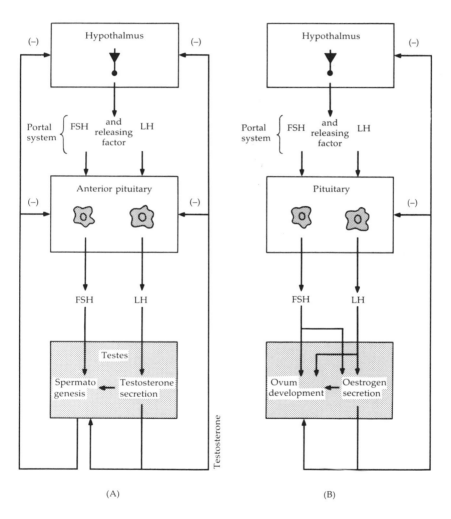

(A)   (B)

Figure A24

In the 28-day human menstrual cycle it takes 14 days to make an egg available for fertilization, while during the next 14 days the reproductive tract is prepared for implantation and growth of the fertilized ovum. If solar radiations affect the female cycle we should be able to show a) some sort of correlation between hormone generation and solar activity, and b) that menstruation is disrupted in the case of disrupted solar radiation.

Figure A25 shows the production of FSH, LH, oestrogen (estrogen) and progesterone during a menstrual cycle in which fertilization does not occur.

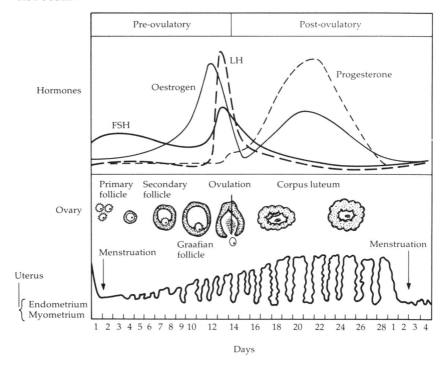

A menstrual cycle in which fertilization does not occur. The events that take place within the pituitary, ovary, and uterus are precisely synchronized.

Figure A25

Upon first examination the levels of production of the fertility hormones appear to have little in common in relation to a 28-day cycle. What

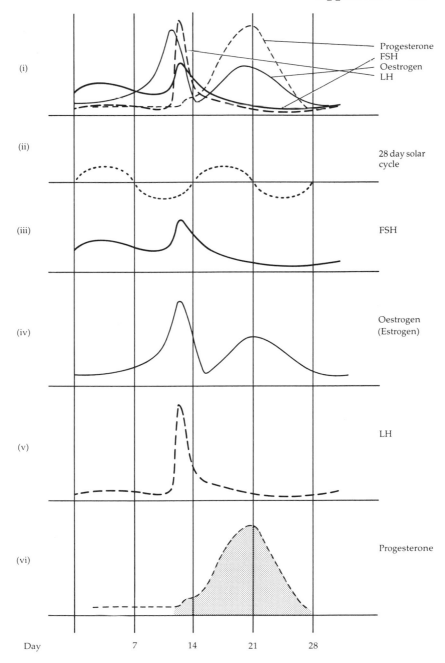

Figure A26 Function-by-function analysis of hormonal activity

we must remember is that although solar radiation may trigger the process, the process itself may lag in time before triggering other biological functions. This 'hysteresis' or time delay does not help analysis. In addition, the effects of one process do not necessarily give rise to another; they may for example have an inverse relationship and lead to suppression. Further triggers may be a result of two previous triggers which do not necessarily have recognizable signatures. One may lag behind not only in time but also in periodicity. A much more separational analysis of events is shown in Figure A26.

The production of FSH may be plotted against the solar radiation cycle:

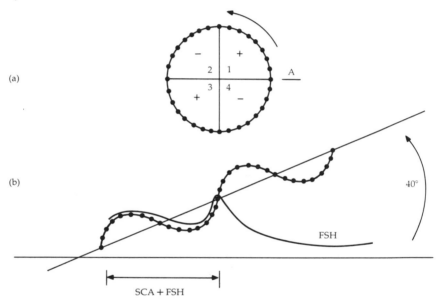

Figure A27   FSH rises and falls with the solar cycle

In figure A27, the waveform (b) shows that when the solar cycle is laid 40 degrees tangential to FSH production, a correlation can be clearly seen during the first two quadrants of the solar cycle. It appears that FSH production is triggered by solar cycle activity but that it takes two days or so actually to start. Once FSH production begins, it appears to 'track' the solar cycle until the end of the second quadrant before switching off and decaying exponentially.

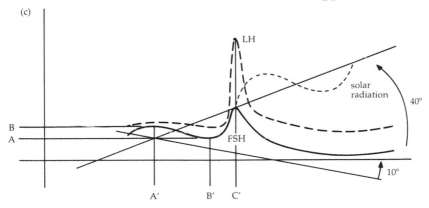

Figure A28 LH production against solar cycle radiation

In figure A28, FSH plus solar radiation from quadrants 1 and 2 become additive between points A' and B'. At A' solar radiation begins to fall, as does FSH against the *y* axis. Because *both* FSH and solar radiation are falling, this gives rise to a falling LH from B to A, between A' and B'. At B' both FSH and solar radiation are rising, against the *y* axis. This leads to an increase in LH. LH rises rapidly at point C' and peaks at 14 days, switching off and decaying exponentially at the end of quadrant 2.

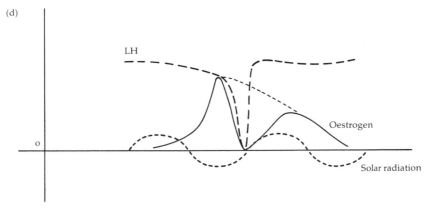

Figure A29 Oestrogen (estrogen) production against solar cycle radiation

Although solar radiation triggers an exponential growth in oestrogen at commencement of the cycle, the massive pulse of LH suppresses oestrogen production for its duration and oestrogen production recovers only gradually after suppression.

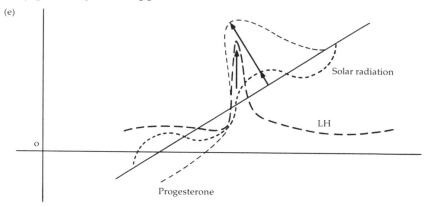

Figure A30   Progesterone production against solar cycle radiation

Meanwhile progesterone, inhibited by the increase of oestrogen on day 1, is now allowed itself to increase, triggered by solar radiation and in the absence of oestrogen through the effect of LH on day 14. Progesterone increases with solar activity, peaks with the solar radiation peak, and tracks the decay of solar radiation before falling exponentially to zero.

Altogether a very complex interaction occurs which translates solar cycle activity into hormonal activity. These hormones determine fertility levels. Any disruption in solar radiation thus likewise disrupts fertility.

One obvious objection to this mechanism questions why all females do not menstruate at the same time in response to a common radiation stimulus from the sun. It is of course because all females were not conceived at the same time. The biorhythm and fertility clocks commence at the moment of conception. Those females who are conceived at the same time may be expected to menstruate at the same time, subject to environmental modifying factors.

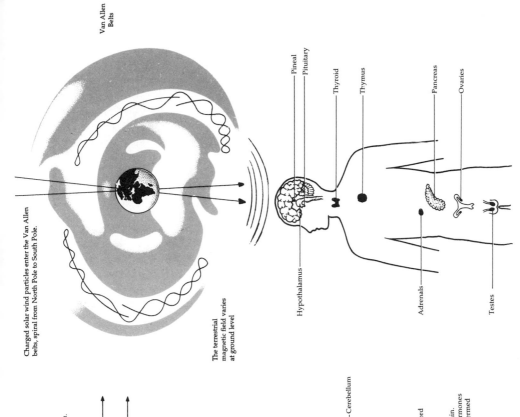

Van Allen Belts

Charged solar wind particles enter the Van Allen belts, spiral from North Pole to South Pole.

The terrestrial magnetic field varies at ground level

Pineal
Pituitary
Thyroid
Thymus
Hypothalamus
Pancreas
Ovaries
Adrenals
Testes

THE SOLAR HORMONE THEORY

This suggests that the human organism is bio-regulated by solar particle induced magnetic modulations after conception. Changes in melatonin affect bio-rhythms. Changes in oestrogen and projesterone affect fertility.

SOLAR WIND

This 'Magnetic to Chemical' conversion process is termed 'Electrochemical Transduction' (Astrogenetics 1988)

THE SUN

Solar radiation output

Cerebral hemisphere
Corpus callosum
Thalamus
Hypothalamus
Cerebellum
Spinal cord
Medulla
Midbrain
Pons
Brain stem

The Pineal Gland converts magnetic fields into the Bio-rhythm hormone Melatonin. The Pituitary and Hypothalamus affect the Manufacture and release of fertility hormones Oestrogen and Projesterone. This 'magnetic-to-chemical' conversion process is termed 'Electrochemical Transduction' (Astrogenetics 1988).

Appendix 4: The Sunspot Cycle

The sun's surface is punctuated from time to time by tiny black spots, the number of which fluctuate in a cyclic pattern lasting somewhere around 11.5 Earth years. The spots are symptomatic of the electromagnetic activity that is constantly taking place deep within the sun.

Analysis of the spots shows that the sun's magnetic field, and its effects in local space (the 'neutral sheet'), reverses about every 3,750 years, so that five magnetic reversals take place every 18,139 years, and each reversal takes 374 years to accomplish from start to finish.

In 1943, R Woolf was the first Western observer to suggest the existence of a cyclic pattern in the appearance and disappearance of sunspots on the sun's surface. He established an average period of about 11.1 years.

It is the different rate of rotation of the sun's outer layers, specifically the difference between the rotation rates of the polar and equatorial magnetic fields, that are mainly responsible for the sunspot cycle. As shown in Chapter Three (pp. 45–7), the polar field gradually becomes 'wound up' to form a toroidal field that varies in strength with latitude. Magnetic lines of force get 'tangled up' with turbulent gases beneath the sun's surface, and burst through the photosphere, forming a pair of sunspots (*see* Figure A31 d and e).

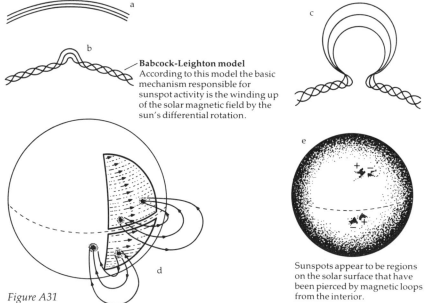

a

b

Babcock-Leighton model
According to this model the basic mechanism responsible for sunspot activity is the winding up of the solar magnetic field by the sun's differential rotation.

c

e

d

Figure A31

Sunspots appear to be regions on the solar surface that have been pierced by magnetic loops from the interior.

Year	No.	Year	No.	Year	No.	Year	No.	Year	No.
1851	64.5	1877	12.3	1903	24.4	1929	65.0	1955	38.0
1852	54.2	1878	3.4	1904	42.0	1930	35.7	1956	141.7
1853	39.0	1879	6.0	1905	63.5	1931	21.2	1957	190.2
1854	20.6	1880	32.3	1906	53.8	1932	11.1	1958	184.6
1855	6.7	1881	54.3	1907	62.0	1933	5.6	1959	159.0
1856	4.3	1882	59.7	1908	48.5	1934	8.7	1960	112.3
1857	22.8	1883	63.7	1909	43.9	1935	36.0	1961	53.9
1858	54.8	1884	63.5	1910	18.6	1936	79.7	1962	37.5
1859	93.8	1885	52.2	1911	5.7	1937	114.4	1963	27.9
1860	95.7	1886	25.4	1912	3.6	1938	109.6	1964	10.2
1861	77.2	1887	13.1	1913	1.4	1939	88.8	1965	15.1
1862	59.1	1888	6.8	1914	9.6	1940	67.8	1966	47.0
1863	44.0	1889	6.3	1915	47.4	1941	47.5	1967	93.8
1864	47.0	1890	7.1	1916	57.1	1942	30.6	1968	105.9
1865	30.5	1891	35.6	1917	103.9	1943	16.3	1969	105.5
1866	16.3	1892	73.0	1918	80.6	1944	9.6	1970	104.5
1867	7.3	1893	84.9	1919	63.6	1945	33.1	1971	66.6
1868	37.3	1894	78.0	1920	37.6	1946	92.5	1972	68.9
1869	73.9	1895	64.0	1921	26.1	1947	151.5	1973	38.0
1870	139.1	1896	41.8	1922	14.2	1948	136.2	1974	34.5
1871	111.12	1897	26.2	1923	5.8	1949	134.7	1975	15.5
1872	101.7	1898	26.7	1924	16.7	1950	83.9	1976	12.6
1873	66.3	1899	12.1	1925	44.3	1951	69.4	1977	27.5
1874	44.7	1900	9.5	1926	63.9	1952	31.5	1978	92.5
1875	17.1	1901	2.7	1927	69.0	1953	13.9	1979	155.4
1876	11.3	1902	5.0	1928	77.8	1954	4.4	1980	154.6

Figure A32 *Zürich yearly means of daily relative sunspot numbers*

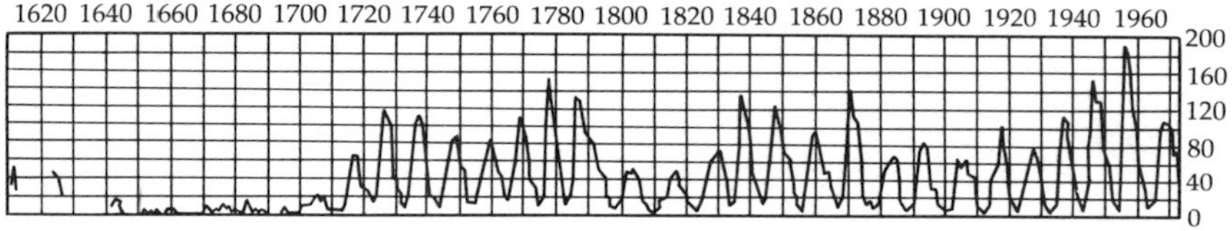

Figure A33 *The numbers and latitudes of sunspots have varied over eight complete cycles between 1874 and 1976*

The number of spots visually counted on the sun's surface has varied yearly, but a sunspot cycle can be clearly detected amongst the data. The cycle peaks approximately every 11.1 years. The longest peak-to-peak cycle was 17.1 years (1788–1805), and the shortest interval 7.3 years (1829.9–1837). From 1645 to 1715, no sunspots at all were recorded (the 'Maunder minimum').

It is often said that we cannot ask the question 'What is the angular difference between the sun's magnetic field and the Earth' because we are, on the face of it, unable to quantify the differentially rotating fields in relation to the Earth's position.

But there *is* a method of achieving this, one that I have termed 'rotational differentiation'. It may be explained as follows:

P (the polar magnetic field) rotates once every 37 days; E (the equatorial magnetic field) rotates once every 26 days. There comes a time (after 87.454545 days) when E 'laps' or begins to overtake P.

We are therefore in a position to examine the solar field in relation to the Earth provided we take measurements only every 87.4545 days. By doing this we are comparing only *two* variables at any one time; the combined position of P and E against the position of W.

We can now feed the following numbers into a computer program— 37 (P), 26 (E) and 365.25 (W)—and ask the program to calculate the positions of these every 87.4545 days. Clearly, as we have just mentioned, P and E will always be together every 87.4545 days. When we have plotted the graph of P and E at 87.4545-day intervals and also plotted the graph of W at 87.4545-day intervals we can subtract one graph from the other, which gives us the difference between the sun's magnetic field and the Earth. It looks like this:

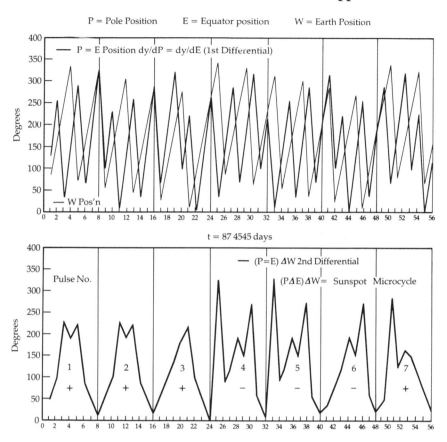

Figure A34   The first seven microcycles of the 187-year cycle

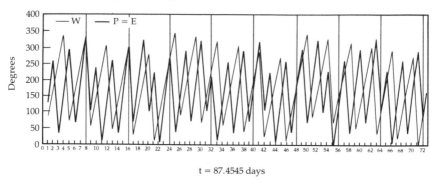

t = 87.4545 days

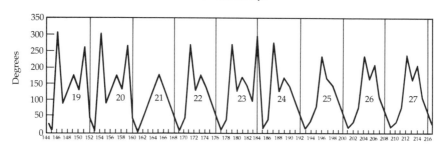

t = 87.4545 days

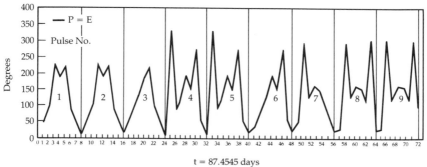

t = 87.4545 days

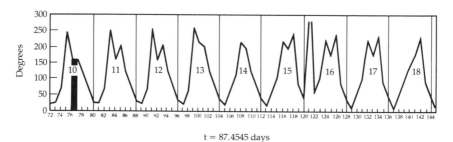

t = 87.4545 days

Figure A35   One complete 187-year (97 microcycle) cycle

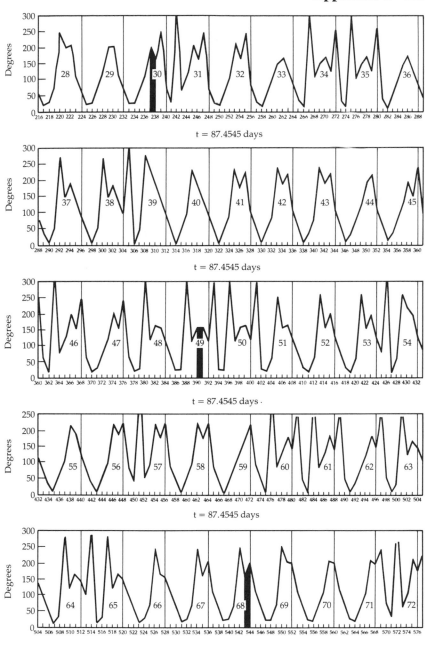

Figure A35 continued

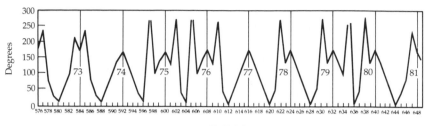

t = 87.4545 days

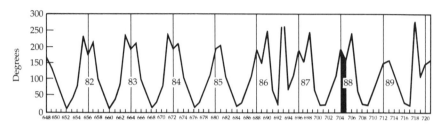

t = 87.4545 days

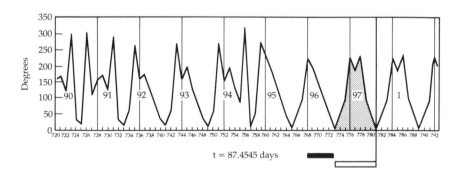

t = 87.4545 days

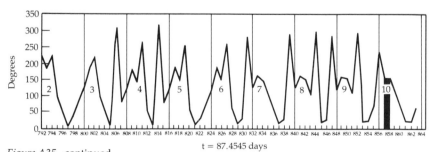

t = 87.4545 days

Figure A35 continued

Analysing the resultant waveforms we can observe that 97 different cycles occur which take 781 periods (bits) of time; 781 bits of time is $781 \times 87.4545 = 68{,}302$ days (187 years). This is one sunspot cycle. The waveshapes after bit 781 are simply repeats of the shapes that occurred at the beginning of the 187-year cycle.

We have already noted, from empirical observation, that the average sunspot cycle amounts to approximately 11.1 years. We note that 6 microcycles each of 8 bits' duration amount to 11.49299 years ($48 \times 87.454545 = 11.4929$ years). Given that 6 microcycles correspond most closely to the average, we can hypothesize that 6 microcycles amount to one 'fundamental' (11.1 year average) sunspot cycle.

Superimposing these fundamental 11.4929-year cycles along the 187-year sunspot cycle we derive this (microcycles have been polarized to accommodate the hypothesized fundamental cycle):

Hypothesized fundamental cycle
of 6 microcycles = 11.4929 years.

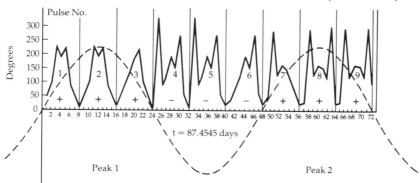

Figure A36

The peak–peak cycle therefore equates to 48 bits—ie 48×87.454545 days = 11.492999 years. This is the hypothesized idealized fundamental solar cycle period.

Next, careful observation of the 97 microcycles shows that 92 of these cycles are indeed 8 microcycles in duration, but microcycles numbers 10, 30, 49, 68, and 88 are of 9 bits duration, (examine Figure A34). These microcycles contain an extra 'shift bit'. The positions of the shift bits may be marked along the 187-year sunspot cycle:

Figure A37   Shift bits

These shift bits, which appear five times during the 187-year cycle, have the effect of shunting, or 'shifting', all following microcycles forward along the cycle (*see* page 260). This suggests that the true cycle is only 768 bits long but is pushed forward by 5 bits during the 187-year interval, to bit 773.

The shift bit positions correspond with the intersections of the sun's neutral sheet (*see* Chapter Three, pp. 54–5).

The neutral sheet shifts by 8 bits (one microcycle) each 187-year period. The shift bits hence shunt along the microcycle sequence. For one single shift bit to shift through 97 microcycles will take 97 × 187 years = 18,139 years.

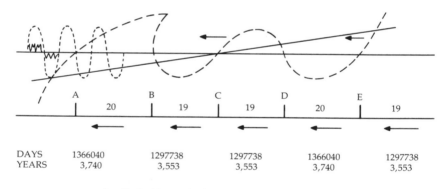

| DAYS | 1366040 | 1297738 | 1297738 | 1366040 | 1297738 |
| YEARS | 3,740 | 3,553 | 3,553 | 3,740 | 3,553 |

It will take 19 periods of 187 years for bit A to shift to bit E
It will take 20 periods of 187 years for bit E to shift to bit D
It will take 19 periods of 187 years for bit D to shift to bit C
It will take 19 periods of 187 years for bit C to shift to bit B
It will take 20 periods of 187 years for bit B to shift to bit A

Total   97 microcycles

Figure A38

At these times the magnetic field direction, as read off the neutral warp waveform, shifts from its initial direction, as shown.

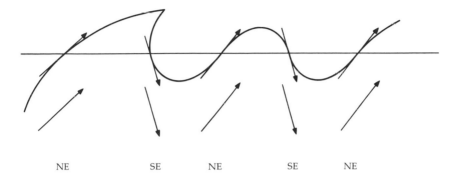

Figure A39   Neutral sheet showing field direction

In Figure A39, the neutral sheet field direction is shown on the neutral sheet. Underneath, to illustrate the initial direction, arrows freeze the field direction for comparison purposes. We can now compare the shifting neutral sheet to its original direction.

We have just seen how it takes 20 shift bits for shift bit E to collide with shift bit D. During this 1,366,040-day period (3740 years) the neutral sheet completely reverses its field in comparison with its initial position. This is illustrated by comparing waveforms at the two different times and by observing the shift in the frozen field arrow orientation.

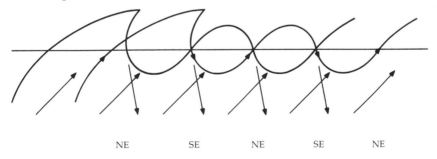

The neutral sheet shifts with respect to the fundamental cycle every 187 years. Shift bits hence shift along the 97-microcycle sequence. As shift bits collide the sun's neutral sheet effectively shifts direction compared with its initial field direction *(indicated by arrows)*.

Figure A40

This means that the neutral sheet intersections reverse (shift direction) five times during every 18,139-year grand cycle. The sun's magnetic field shifts after 3740 years, again after 3553 years, again after 3553 years, again after 3740 years, and finally for the fifth time after 3553 years during the grand cycle.

The observed Sun Spot cycle will hence rise and fall, carried on top of the neutral sheet waveform, and may be observed thus:

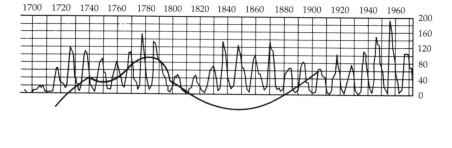

Figure A41   Idealized neutral sheet during one 187-year cycle

Before we move on, we need to understand how the sun's field reverses (or more precisely shifts from NE to SE).

After 1,366,040 days, shift bit A moves to a new position where shift bit B once was. Does this mean that at midnight on the 1,366,040 day the field will invert or 'flip over'? The answer to this is no.

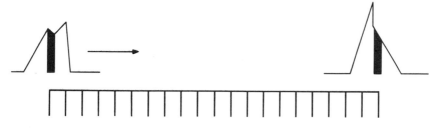

Original position
of microcycle
that contains
shift bit A

Original position
of microcycle that
contains shift bit B

Each division represents one microcycle

Figure A42

Both the microcycle that contains shift bit A and the microcycle that
contains shift bit B shift one microcycle every 187 years (68,302 days).
From the moment the microcycle that contains shift bit A 'touches' the
microcycle that contains shift bit B the fields effectively begin to mesh.
The microcycle containing shift bit A begins to mesh with the previous
position of the microcycle that contained shift bit B.

Figure A43

It takes 187 years from when these two microcycles first 'touch' for them to completely rest on top of each other. It will then take a further 187 years after this time for them to completely clear each other. The transitional flip-time must therefore be 2 × 187 years = 374 years. Any field reversal therefore bottoms out after 187 years from the start of field inversion.

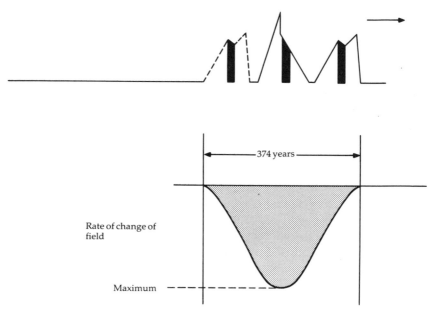

Figure A44

Appendix 5: The Decline of the Maya

Both the sun's magnetic field and the magnetic field from the sunspots reversed at around the time that the Maya disappeared. The combined magnetic disturbance led to infertility and genetic mutation on Earth, the effects of which were most severe in equatorial regions. Sunspot activity caused a mini-Ice-Age, in which the ensuing reduction in the water that evaporated from the oceans led directly to a drought in the Maya homelands (*see* Chapter Nine, pp. 186–7). This was the root cause of the decline of the Maya.

The Effect of the Mini-Ice-Age on the Maya

Brooks cites the decline of the Maya as an example of evidence for wide variation in the overall moisture of climates prevailing in tropical latitudes between AD 600 and 1100 (*Climate, Past, Present and Future*, H H Lamb). Certainly it was demonstrated during the 1970s that the zone of the northern latitudes between 10 and 20 degrees is particularly susceptible to sharp fluctuations in climatic moisture.

Other authors have similarly suspected that the Mayan civilization was subjected to drought between AD 790 and 810, notably Dr Sherret S Chase of the Botanical Museum, Harvard University. He discerned a Mayan preoccupation with rainfall (in the form of the worship of the rain god Chaac). It has been suggested that the lack of rainfall in this region, in especially dry periods, results either from a failure of the equatorial rain system (the inter-tropical convergence zone) to reach the area in the course of its normal seasonal migration north and south (ie a monsoon failure), or from its making only a curtailed sojourn so far north of the equator.

The Effects of Increased Cosmic Ray Bombardment

Implicit in the statistics presented in Appendix 4 was the fact that the sun's magnetic field reversed (in relation to its direction for the previous

3740 years) between AD 440 and 814, and that cosmic ray bombardment of the Earth's magnetosphere during this change-over period—as against earlier and subsequent activity—was greatly increased. Cosmic rays are generally harmful to life on Earth; an increase in rays corresponds to an increase in the harm caused to organisms.

Ionizing radiations have the ability to eject electrons from atoms in matter through which they pass, leaving in their wake positively- or negatively-charged atoms. These radiations may be absorbed by the body through the lungs (the air we breathe), through the bones, through the isotropic element strontium absorbed in food, or directly from gamma rays or X-rays. When these radiations pass through matter, the atoms in their path become excited in sympathy with the radiation frequency. Electrons may be so disturbed as to eject from a normally stable orbit further from the nucleus or, in the extreme, to eject from the atom leaving behind an ionized atom. Ionized atoms are known to be extremely chemically reactive.

Molecules within a living cell exposed to ionizing radiations are thus subject to chemical change, and such changes occur very quickly in the genetic material DNA after energy absorption, leading to genetic mutation and potential physical deformity.

Now any increased bombardment by cosmic rays occurs with particular effect in the equatorial regions between 10 and 20 degrees north and south because of the perpendicular incidence of rays at this point with the surface of the Earth. At the same time the sun's magnetic field reversed for the first time in 3740 years, and this may have affected the Earth's magnetosphere, allowing even more penetration by cosmic rays (*Royal Astronomical Atlas*: ... 'When the Earth's magnetic field undergoes reversal, the absence of a magnetosphere may allow cosmic rays to enter the atmosphere unchecked ...').

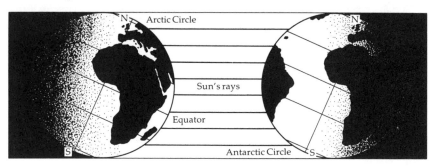

Figure A45   Cosmic ray bombardment affects equatorial regions more than polar regions

The Dancers
In Monte Alban, near Oaxaca (about 200 miles from Palenque), there is a series of carvings named 'The Dancers' because archaeologists imagined that the strange depiction of 'deformed' human positions related to bodily contortions through movement and dance. Upon closer inspections one can see that the series of carvings depicts various deformations in humans, many occurring during childbirth. (*See* Figure A46.)

Mayan prediction
What is intriguing about the Maya decline, as against all the others, is that the Maya seemed to have been expecting a solar magnetic reversal during the period of decline, and they seem to have anticipated the effects of the reversal—increased bombardment from solar rays, and consequent increased infant mortality and ultimately extinction.

In 1880 a librarian in the library of Dresden, Ernst Förstemann, announced the results of many years' investigation into the meaning of one of the oldest surviving Maya bark books, the *Dresden Codex* (named after the library where it was deposited). At the core of the astronomical texts, suggested Förstemann, was the Maya preoccupation with the 260-day cycle. Some have commented that 'this endlessly repeating chain of days bears no correspondence with any celestial rhythm'. However, we have noted that this cycle relates to the sun's overlapping polar and equatorial magnetic fields, as was pointed out in Appendix 4. But recognition of this cycle was only made possible using the most modern of astronomical observations that have resulted directly from space travel and space-age observations over the past few years. So how could the Maya have possibly understood the importance, or existence, of this cycle which itself can be used to calculate, it seems, the timing of (for the Maya) the next solar magnetic reversal?

Förstemann noted that at least 'five' full pages in the *Dresden Codex* are concerned with the positions of the planet Venus. Others have commented that the most curious feature of the Venus tables is the number 1,366,560 days, referred to as 'the Birthdate of Venus', which is set at 10 August 3113 BC. Elsewhere we note that this 1,366,560-day period may be easily calculated by using the 260-day cycle, and curiously—and more importantly—if we count 1,366,560 days forward from the beginning of the Maya calendar we arrive at AD 627—the exact centre of the solar magnetic shift that caused the Maya decline.

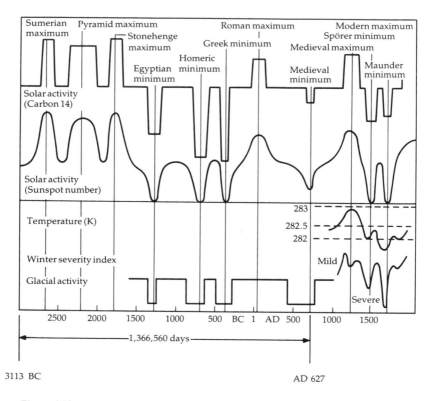

Figure A46

The decoding of the Maya numbers (*see* Chapter Two) shows that the planet Venus was monitored in order to keep track of sunspot cycles, because it was after 20 of these cycles that the Maya expected the reversal to materialize as it did.

The Maya number system has been investigated by many scholars to date and has mystified them all. As we have seen, however, the numbering system can be broken by insertion of the 'missing' 260-day cycle. It is by drawing attention to the exception that one is able to recognize the rule. By so doing we note that 9 of each of the Maya cycles amounts to the Venus, or magnetic reversal, number 1,366,560 days. Similarly, there are 620 inscriptions carved into the Temple of Inscriptions in Palenque (the burial place of Lord Pacal). How are we to interpret this? After all, it is the number 260 which is the all important number. Moreover, the decoding of the Maya numbering system reveals that the Mayan system—like the Babylonian—was based upon 360 (and from this we learn that the Maya used not only the decimal base 10 system but also that the unit of measure for angular measurement was exactly the same as our own is today: 360). So if we subtract 260 from 620 what are we left with? 620 − 260 = 360: the Maya base for the numbering system. So again if we 'correct' the mistake (an intentional anagram) showing 620 (instead of 260) the Maya were indicating that only a person who understands the importance of 260—together with the necessary sciences of astronomy, astrology, biology and genetic engineering—could decode the message of the Maya, encoded in their architecture, their numbering system and their art.

And even more mysteriously, they encoded all of the information contained in this book into one single picture—the amazing Lid of Palenque.

Appendix 6: Catastrophe and Destruction

When the sun's magnetic field shifts direction, it tends to twist the Earth off its axis. The tilting Earth is subjected to earthquakes, floods, conflagrations and volcanic eruptions.

The sun's magnetic field shifts five times every long cosmic cycle. This would seem to be the reason that the Maya and others believed that the Earth has been destroyed four times in the past, and that destruction at the beginning of the 21st century in this, the fifth age of the sun, will follow in the same way.

Around 200 million years ago, all of the continental landmasses recognizable today were part of a single giant continental landmass now called Pangaea. This is a fundamental concept of what is now well known as the continental drift theory, a theory that was first advanced by Antonio Snider in 1858. But its most important single advocate was

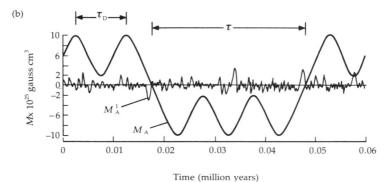

Time (million years)

Model for reversals used to derive the distribution function for reversals, τ_D is the period of the dipole field and τ is the length of a polarity interval. A reversal occurs whenever the quantity M'_A, which is a measure of the non-dipole field, becomes sufficiently large relative to the dipole movement M_A. (*see* Olsson, 1970).

Figure A47

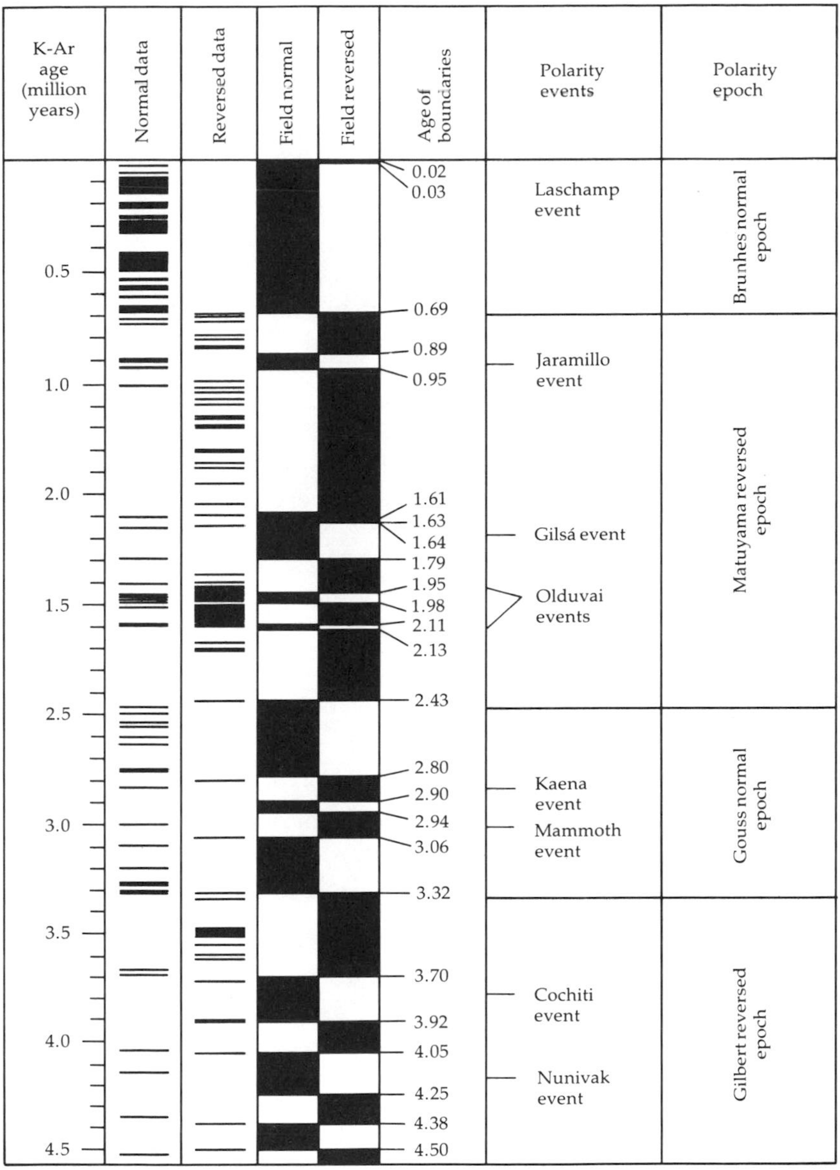

Timescale for geomagnetic reversals. Each short horizontal line shows the age as determined by potassium-argon dating. Normal polarity intervals are represented by the solid portions of the 'field normal' column, and reversed polarity intervals by the solid parts of the 'field reversed' column. (Cox, 1969).

Figure A48

probably Alfred Wegener who, in 1915, published evidence from geology, climatology and biology. His conclusions were very similar to those reached by current research—although he was wrong about the speed of events.

After 20 million years, the single great landmass had itself begun to split into two giant supercontinents, Laurasia (comprising most of what is now North America, Europe and Asia, less the Indian subcontinent) and Gondwanaland (comprising South America, Africa, Antarctica, Australasia and the subcontinent of India).

In addition to these strictly physical changes to the Earth's surface, it is well established that the Earth's magnetic field has reversed on many occasions. Theoretical models suggest that a combination of factors (representing what some call a 'worst-case scenario') are responsible for such magnetic inversions.

Appendix 7: Maya Numbers and Counting Systems

It has been suggested that the Maya used a Vi-gesimal (base 20) counting system where each operand level exceeded the next level by a factor of 20:

Baktun	Katun	Tun	Uinal	Kin
144,000	7,200	360	20	1
Days	Days	Days	Days	Days

Figure A49

But the Maya cycle count periods, as shown above, are *not* vigesimally related; 360 is not 20 times the Uinal figure of 20, as this would be 400.

Similarly the Maya Calendar Round of 52 'years', ostensibly reconciles the 260-day Maya calendar with the 365-day Solar year, which it would if the Solar year were 365 days in length, but it is not. It is 365.25 days in duration. So, the calendar round, then, does not mesh every 52 years but every 52 years minus $52 \times .25$ day periods *ie* the calendar round amounts to 18,980 days and not 18,993 days of 52 Solar years.

Notwithstanding: Maya hieroglyphs can be translated accurately, and correctly, using Baktuns, Katuns, Tuns, Uinals and Kins. But such translations defy a logical rationale. It has been suggested that the Maya were of a low intellect, and that although they made use of zero, they were otherwise numerically and mathematically unexceptional. But can this be the case? Could the Maya approach to numbers actually have been a simplified method of today's decimal (base 10) system?

Let us examine this possibility:

1 Time periods used by the Maya

i)   The Maya system favoured a *Month* consisting of *20 days* where each day had its own name, for example 'Imix'.

ii) Each day also carried a *Prefix Number* ranging from *1–13*, for example 6 Imix.

iii) The choice of these two sequences meant that any particular day number/name combination could not recur until the 260 day number/name combinations (13×20) had each in turn subsisted and passed.

The Maya name for this *260-Day Period* was Tzolkin, however the Aztec referred to it as the *Tonalamatl*; the 'Sacred Year'.

It is hereby noted that although this 260-day period was of the greatest importance, in regard to the prophesying of events and omens for the Maya, (especially in the Codex) it is rarely represented in the inscriptions in the recordings of long periods of time; Baktuns, Katuns, Tuns, Uinals and Kins being preferred instead. The scientific importance follows on p 284, where we note that 260 days is the most important solar period; a product of the rotational solar variables of 37 and 26 days.

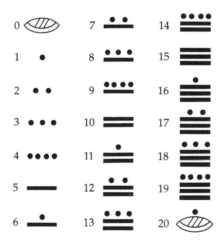

Figure A50   Maya Numbers: a dot represented a unit of 1, a bar represented a unit of 5

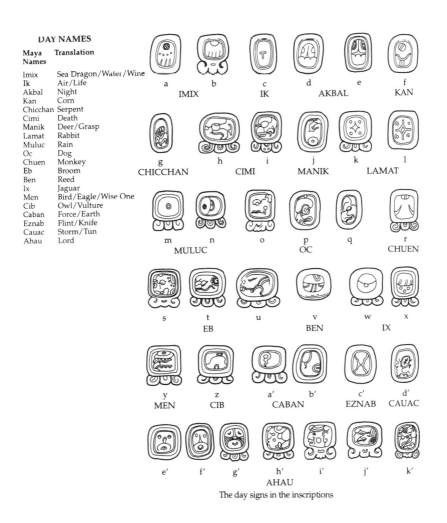

DAY NAMES

Maya Names	Translation
Imix	Sea Dragon/Water/Wine
Ik	Air/Life
Akbal	Night
Kan	Corn
Chicchan	Serpent
Cimi	Death
Manik	Deer/Grasp
Lamat	Rabbit
Muluc	Rain
Oc	Dog
Chuen	Monkey
Eb	Broom
Ben	Reed
Ix	Jaguar
Men	Bird/Eagle/Wise One
Cib	Owl/Vulture
Caban	Force/Earth
Eznab	Flint/Knife
Cauac	Storm/Tun
Ahau	Lord

a   b   c   d   e   f
IMIX   IK   AKBAL   KAN

g   h   i   j   k   l
CHICCHAN   CIMI   MANIK   LAMAT

m   n   o   p   q   r
MULUC   OC   CHUEN

s   t   u   v   w   x
EB   BEN   IX

y   z   a′   b′   c′   d′
MEN   CIB   CABAN   EZNAB   CAUAC

e′   f′   g′   h′   i′   j′   k′
AHAU

The day signs in the inscriptions

Figure A51

2-MANIK, 67th day of the 260-day cycle which begins I-IMIX

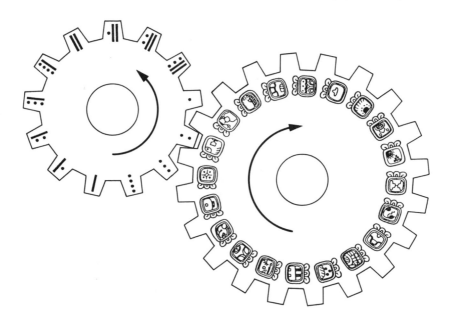

Figure A52

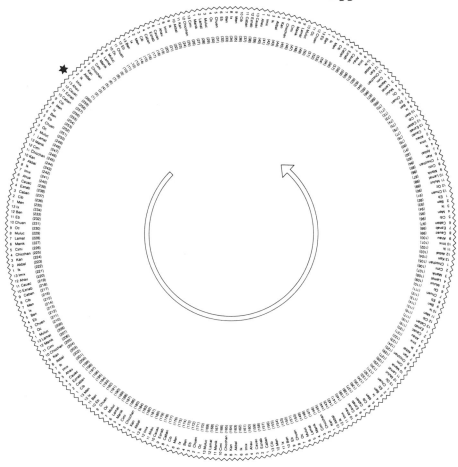

Figure A53 Tonalamatl Wheel, showing sequence of the 260 differently named days

Month names always had their own coefficient numbers, such as 4 Muan, 9 Pop, etc. The numbers ran from Zero, or 'Seating' of the month, to 19.

Month Numbers

8 . . . 9 . . . 10 . . . 11 . . . 12 . . . 13 . . . 14 . . . 15 . . . 16 . . . 17 . . . 18 . . . 19 . . .
0 . . . 1 . . . 2 . . . 3 . . . 4 . . . 5 . . . 6 . . . 7 . . . 8 . . .

HAAB

The 365-day year, or *haab* was composed of 18 months (*uinals*) of 20 days each, to make a year of 360 days (18 x 20 = 360). Five 'unlucky' days, called Uayeb, were added to bring the year to 365 days.

The month names were:

1	Pop	11	Zac
2	Uo	12	Ceh
3	Zip	13	Mac
4	Zotz	14	Kankin
5	Tzec	15	Muan
6	Xul	16	Pax
7	Yaxkin	17	Kayab
8	Mol	18	Cumhu
9	Chen	19	Uayeb (5 days)
10	Yax		

Each had 20 days except the last which had only 5.

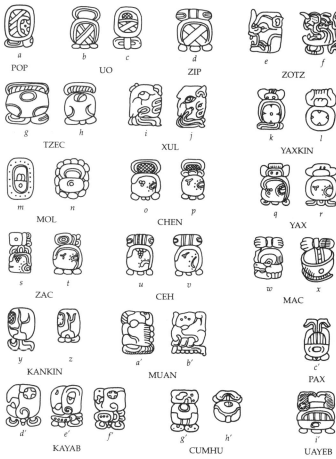

Figure A54

The month signs in the inscriptions

2 The Haab
The Haab was the 365-day period of time for the Maya which came closest to our modern Solar Year of 365.25 days.

The Haab was made up of two distinct periods:

The Tun	=	360 Days
The Xma Kaba Kin	=	5 Days (unlucky 'days with no name')
	Maya	365 Day Haab

Today we add one day to our month of February every four years in order to maintain our time recording with a true solar year period. These 'Leap years' therefore accommodate the $4 \times .25$ yearly discrepancies that accumulate between each 'Leap' adjustment. No such Leap adjustment (intercalary adjustment) is known to have been used by the Maya.

The 360-day Tun at least facilitated division into 18 Maya (20-day) months. And this meant that every 361st day began with the same day name. Unlucky named days in one 360-day period therefore carried the same name during the next 360-day period *ie* some names were always lucky and some always unlucky—unlike our modern calendar, for example, where a birthday may fall on Tuesday this year, Monday last year and Wednesday next year—it was 'fortune' and 'adversity' that interested the Maya.

3 The Calendar Round: 18,980 day period
Clearly the 260-day 'sacred year' period and the 365-day Haab would sequentially iterate. We could say with confidence that they would recommence at their initial starting positions every 260×365 days (more than 95,000 days) after they began. But they will actually recommence at their starting positions *before* this time. When this correspondence occurs may be found as follows:

Because each 20-day period was 'named', and 20 divides into 360, we can safely say that every 361st day has the same name as in the 360th day period preceding it (as we mentioned earlier). But the Haab was 365 days long. We can therefore safely say that the 366th day will carry a name 5 places different than the preceding 365-day period. Now, 20 is also divisible by 5 ($4 \times 5 = 20$). It can be shown, that because of this, any 365-day period can only begin with one of *four* of the *twenty* named available days.

We must also remember that 260 can also be divided by the number 5, and so can 365. To find the shortest period of rotational correspondence between the 260- and 365-day periods, we need to find the lowest common multiple:

$$\frac{260}{5} \times \frac{365}{5} \times \frac{5}{1} = 52 \times 73 \times 5 = 18,980 \text{ days}$$

Every 18,980 days the 260-day and 365-day periods restart together. This is the *Calendar Round*.

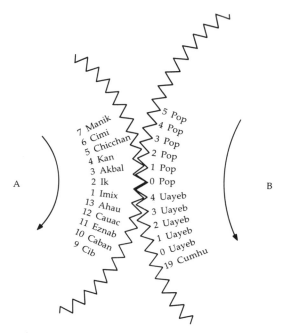

Diagram showing engagement of tonalamatl wheel of 260 days (A), and haab wheel of 365 positions (B); the combination of the two giving the Calendar Round, or 52-year period.

Figure A55   The Calendar Round: 18,980 day period

Which direction to read the glyphs

Mayan dates *usually* read across and down, in columns of two. In the following figure, we read A1, then B1, then go to the next line, A2, B2, etc.

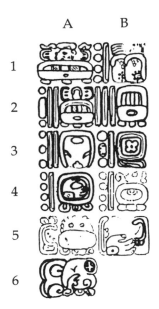

1

2

3

4

5

6

Figure A56

Figure A57 overleaf shows multiples of Calendar Round periods. The first period is 18,980 days. Subsequent Calendar Rounds are listed below this. In the column next to this is the same date as the one which can be found on carvings and stelae of the Maya.

For example, one Calendar Round may be factorized into:

Zero Baktuns	2 Katuns	12 Tuns	13 Uinals	and	Zero Kins
ie (0 × 144,000)	(2 × 7,200)	(12 × 360)	(13 × 20)		(0 × 1)
ie 0	2	12	13		0

This is written as 2.12.13.0. Would any intelligent civilization have used such a cumbersome and illogical system of notation?

My calculations show that the sunspot cycle duration is 68,302 days, and that after 20 periods of time (20 × 68,302 = 1,366,040 days) the sun's neutral sheet magnetic field tilts. The Earth's magnetic field attempts to re-align its magnetic axis with that of the sun, and the Earth tilts on its axis. At this time the Earth's magnetic poles shift their geostationary position. Cataclysmic destruction takes place on Earth through violent

BUREAU OF AMERICAN ETHNOLOGY

80 CALENDAR ROUNDS EXPRESSED IN
ARABIC AND MAYA NOTATION

Calendar Rounds	Days	Cycles, etc.	Calendar Rounds	Days	Cycles, etc.
1	18,980	2. 12. 13. 0	41	778,180	5. 8. 1. 11. 0
2	37,960	5. 5. 8. 0	42	797, 160	5. 10. 14. 6. 0
3	56,940	7. 18. 3. 0	43	816,140	5. 13. 7. 1. 0
4	75,920	10. 10. 16. 0	44	835,120	5. 15. 19. 14. 0
5	94,900	13. 3. 11. 0	45	854,100	5. 18. 12. 9. 0
6	113,880	15. 16. 6. 0	46	873,080	6. 1. 5. 4. 0
7	132,860	18. 9. 1. 0	47	892,060	6. 3. 17. 17. 0
8	151,840	1. 1. 1. 14. 0	48	911,040	6. 6. 10. 12. 0
9	170,820	1. 3. 14. 9. 0	49	930,020	6. 9. 3. 7. 0
10	189,800	1. 6. 7. 4. 0	50	949,000	6. 11. 16. 2. 0
11	208,780	1. 8. 19. 17. 0	51	967,980	6. 14. 8. 15. 0
12	227,760	1. 11. 12. 12. 0	52	986,960	6. 17. 1. 10. 0
13	246,740	1. 14. 5. 7. 0	53	1,005,940	6. 19. 14. 5. 0
14	265,720	1. 16. 18. 2. 0	54	1,024,920	7. 2. 7. 0. 0
15	284,700	1. 19. 10. 15. 0	55	1,043,900	7. 4. 19. 13. 0
16	303,680	2. 2. 3. 10. 0	56	1,062,880	7. 7. 12. 8. 0
17	322,660	2. 4. 16. 5. 0	57	1,081,860	7. 10. 5. 3. 0
18	341,640	2. 7. 9. 0. 0	58	1,100,840	7. 12. 17. 16. 0
19	360,620	2. 10. 1. 13. 0	59	1,119,820	7. 15. 10. 11. 0
20	379,600	2. 12. 14. 8. 0	60	1,138,800	7. 18. 3. 6. 0
21	398,580	2. 15. 7. 3. 0	61	1,157,780	8. 0. 16. 1. 0
22	417,560	2. 17. 19. 16. 0	62	1,176,760	8. 3. 8. 14. 0
23	436,540	3. 0. 12. 11. 0	63	1,195,740	8. 6. 1. 9. 0
24	455,520	3. 3. 5. 6. 0	64	1,214,720	8. 8. 14. 4. 0
25	474,500	3. 5. 18. 1. 0	65	1,233,700	8. 11. 6. 17. 0
26	493,480	3. 8. 10. 14. 0	66	1,252,680	8. 13. 19. 12. 0
27	512,460	3. 11. 3. 9. 0	67	1,271,660	8. 16. 12. 7. 0
28	531,440	3. 13. 16. 4. 0	68	1,290,640	8. 19. 5. 2. 0
29	550,420	3. 16. 8. 17. 0	69	1,309,620	9. 1. 17. 15. 0
30	569,400	3. 19. 1. 12. 0	70	1,328,600	9. 4. 10. 10. 0
31	588,380	4. 1. 14. 7. 0	71	1,347,580	9. 7. 3. 5. 0
32	607,360	4. 4. 7. 2. 0	72	1,366,560	9. 9. 16. 0. 0
33	626,340	4. 6. 19. 15. 0	73	1,385,540	9. 12. 8. 13. 0
34	645,320	4. 9. 12. 10. 0	74	1,404,520	9. 15. 1. 8. 0
35	664,300	4. 12. 5. 5. 0	75	1,423,500	9. 17. 14. 3. 0
36	683,280	4. 14. 18. 0. 0	76	1,442,480	10. 0. 6. 16. 0
37	702,260	4. 17. 10. 13. 0	77	1,461,460	10. 2. 19. 11. 0
38	721,240	5. 0. 3. 8. 0	78	1,480,440	10. 5. 12. 6. 0
39	740,220	5. 2. 16. 3. 0	79	1,499,420	10. 8. 5. 1. 0
40	759,200	5. 5. 8. 16. 0	80	1,518,400	10. 10. 17. 14. 0

Figure A57   Calendar Rounds expressed in Arabic and Maya Notation

tectonic activity, volcanic eruptions, floods and hurricanes, as is clearly told in stories on the Lid of Palenque. It was therefore important for the Maya to monitor the progress of this 68,302-day period because after 20 of these periods destruction would follow. But the counting of such a long period of time, without a judicious counting (and calibration) system is unlikely to be successful. Moreover, no observable astronomical calibrator was available for use to monitor these periods exactly. The closest astronomical calibrator is Venus, whose sidereal rotational period amounts to 584 days. 117 passes of Venus in the sky (117 × 584) amount to 68,328 days—which, though not exactly amounting to 1 sunspot cycle of 68,302 days, is very close. (Of course the extra 26 days added to the correct figure of 68,302 would need to be monitored, stored, anticipated and used for correcting the total period of calculation. The total period, for example, would amount to 1,366,560 instead of 1,366,040 days.) So it was vital to watch Venus.

So, for the Maya, the sunspot cycle was 68,302 + Venus calibrator (26) = 68,328 × 20 = 1,366,560 days. I have discovered that the 1,366,560-day period may be calculated in several ways:

1 By computer
2 By using the 260-day period in conjunction with the Calendar Round 18,980
3 By using the system of Maya cycles, Katun, Baktun, Uinal, Tun and Tonalamatl and monitoring the Venus interval

Calculating the Cataclysmic Period Duration using the 260-day figure and calendar round (method 2)—see Figure A58
The Sun's polar regions rotate every 37 days.

The Sun's equatorial region rotates every 26 days.

This is known as 'The differential rotation of the Sun's Polar and Equatorial magnetic fields'.

P moves 360/37 (9.729729) degrees per day.

E moves 360/26 (13.84615) degrees per day.

After 260 Days P has made 7.027027 revolutions. It rests at 9.729729 degrees in front of where it started (b).

After 260 days E has completed 10 solar revolutions, and rests at zero degrees (b).

The second 260-day period begins with P leading E by 9.729729729 degrees (b).

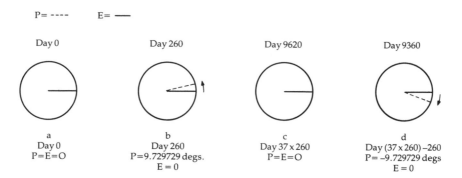

Figure A58

We can make use of this 260-day P:E error:
9.729729 is 1/37th of a circle. We know therefore that after 37 errors (37 × 260) P and E must again be together at zero. So P = E = O after 37 × 260 days ie 9,620 days (c).

We could subtract 260 days from this figure and be 9.729729 degrees behind E, eg 9620 − 260 = 9360, E lies at zero, P *lags* E by 9.729729 degrees (d).

We could double this figure (e) and know that P lags E by 2 × 9.729729 degrees eg after 2 × 9,360 days (18,720) E = O P = − 2 × 9.729729 degrees (e).

We could now add 260 days to this new figure 18,720 + 260 (18,980) and know that E = O, and P rests only 1 × 9.729729 degrees behind E.

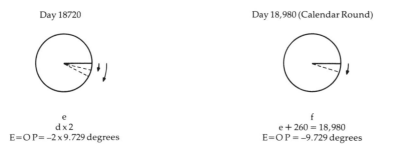

Figure A59

Figure A59 gives us the Calendar Round using only two figures; the solar pole 37 and the solar equator 26.

Now we have this situation:

g
f x 36 (68,3280) degrees
E=O P = 9.729

h
g x 2 (1,366,560) degrees
E = O
P= 2 x 9.729729 degrees

Figure A60

This method must contain a 520-day error because of the means of calculation, and this is illustrated as:

2 × 9.729729 degrees for P leading E. 2 × 260 = 520. 1,366,560 − 520
= 36,920P
52,540E
3,740 (Earth)

(Remember that the 520 excess facilitates the use of Venus as a calibrator.)

i
(g x 2) – (2 x 260)
1,366,040
Period of Destruction

Figure A61

Requirements of a system to monitor the Sunspot cycle using Maya cycles (method 3)

i)a   sunspot cycle = 68,302 days
                  20 of these 68,302 = 1,366,040 = destruction
i)b 117 Venus intervals of 584 days = 68,328 days (26 days too many)
                  20 of these 68,328 = 1,366,560 (520 too many)

Therefore monitor Venus for 117×20 periods of 584 days, remembering to subtract 520 days ie destruction will come during the last pass of Venus in this series.

ii)a In order to calibrate with Venus we must ensure that 117 appears as a factor in any counting system.
ii)b In order to ensure synchronization to solar variables we must include 260 in any counting system (260 days is the most important astronomical cycle, P/E).
ii)c In order to calculate the moment of destruction we must count up to 20 sunspot periods.
iii) In order to satisfy ii)a, ii)b:
          'Raise' (Multiply) 117 (passes of Venus) by 2.22222 = 260
      Places Venus in terms of Tonalamatls
iv) In order to satisfy ii)c, and accommodate iii:
          Instead of multiplying by 20 (to obtain 20 periods) we must now remember to multiply *only* by 20/2.22222 = 9.

	Baktun	Katun	Tun	Tonalamatl	Uinal	Kin
days	144,000	7,200	360	260	20	1

Figure A62 Determination of Maya Cycle durations

Dates inscribed on monuments are known to have been illustrated with reference to the Baktun, Katun, Tun and Uinal, and also the Kin. (The Tonalamatl, the most important, was purposely omitted.)

We need to monitor the period 1,366,560 days. A system of counting is required to simplify and accommodate this.

The Maya chose a 360-base system, as this relates to angular degrees and facilitates recognition of the revolving variables. Venus, the Solar Pole (P), Equator (E) and the World (W).

$$\frac{68,328}{360} \times 360 \qquad\qquad\qquad = 68,328$$

$$\frac{68,328}{360} \times 360 \times 20 \qquad\qquad = 1,366,560 = \text{destruction}$$

$$189.8 \times 360 \times 20 \qquad\qquad\qquad = 1,366,560$$

Calendar	Base/Tun	Numbering
Round Factor	Factor	System

$$189.8 \quad\times\quad 360 \quad\times\quad (2.2222 \times 9) = 1,366,560$$

$$(189.8 \times 2.2222 = 421.77) \times 360 \times 9 \qquad = 1,366,560$$

This means 421.77777 cycles of 360 days will be one ninth of the required destruction figure: this may be tabulated thus:

$(\underline{400} \times 360)$	$(\underline{20} \times 360)$	$(\underline{1} \times 360)$	$(.\underline{777777} \times 360)$ *i.e.* 421.777×360		
= 144,000	7,200	360	280		
Baktun	Katun	Tun	Tonalamatl	Uinal	
= 144,000	7,200	360	260	20	Days
1	1	1	1	1	= 151,840
2	2	2	2	2	= 303,680
3	3	3	3	3	= 455,520
4	4	4	4	4	= 607,360
5	5	5	5	5	= 759,200
6	6	6	6	6	= 911,040
7	7	7	7	7	= 1,062,880
8	8	8	8	8	= 1,214,720
9	9	9	9	9	= **1,366,560 = 9**
= 400 × 360 × 9	20 × 360 × 9	360 × 9	.7222 × 360 × 9	.0555 × 360 × 9	
= 360 × (400)	(20)	(1)	(.7777) × (9)		= 1,366,560
= 360 ×	421.777777777		× 9		= 1,366,560

Figure A63

To check: subtract 520. 1,366,560 − 520 = 1,366,040 =
a complete cycle for 52540 revolutions of E
                      36920 revolutions of P
                    3,740 revolutions of W (The Earth)

This is why the number 9 was worshipped by the Maya. Nine 'Lords of the Night' are painted on the tomb walls in the Temple of Inscriptions, similarly nine codes appear along each side of the Lid of Palenque. But why was the period of 260 days never shown on the inscriptions? It is quite clear that the table above must contain 260 days in order to make sense of the Maya cycles. What we learn from the Lid of Palenque is this:

The most important thing on the lid is the missing corners (see Appendix 8); without first 'finding' the missing corners the Lid cannot be decoded.

The most important number in the Maya cycle system (260) is missing from dated monuments (and the Calendar Round notation expressed herein, Figure A57). We note, moreover, that without the 260-day period presence the counting system makes no sense.

By not realizing this, those who translated the Maya cycles at face value, as shown on pp 281–2, misunderstood the Maya intellect. Such a misunderstanding implies that the Maya were less intellectually developed than ourselves. Only when we become as intellectually developed as the Maya, therefore, can we ever begin to understand just how advanced they were.

The Long Count
A Long Count extending to 136,656,000 (over 374,000) years has been deciphered and we need to ask how the Maya could distinguish any particular date in this period.

So far I haven't mentioned that the Maya used even longer cycles than the Baktun and Katun; for example, they used the Calabtun of 57,600,000 days and the Kinchiltun of 1,152,000,000. This raises the interesting question: 'Why did the Maya wish to refer to periods of time greater than the day of destruction?' How could it be important, if the World had ended?

This is another fine illustration of the Mayan intelligence and humour, and leads to another intellectual enigma: what we find is that the mechanics of our 360-base counting system does not accommodate cycle durations longer than 144,000 days, and yet the Calabtun and Kinchiltun have been noted.

We would expect these to 'fit' like this:

Kinchilitun	Calabtun	Pictun	Baktun	Katun	Tun	Ton.	Ui.
1,152,000,000	57,600,000	2,880,000	144,000	7,200	360	260	20

But here our numbering system appears to grind to a halt. It appears to fail to iterate after 1,366,560 has been reached. Before we proceed we need to look a little closer at the qualities of the number 9.

1/9 = .111111111111	also	10/9 = 1.111111111111
2/9 = .222222222222		20/9 = 2.222222222222
3/9 = .333333333333		30/9 = 3.333333333333
4/9 = .444444444444		40/9 = 4.444444444444
5/9 = .555555555555		50/9 = 5.555555555555
6/9 = .666666666666		60/9 = 6.666666666666
7/9 = .777777777777		70/9 = 7.777777777777
8/9 = .888888888888		80/9 = 8.888888888888
9/9 = .999999999999		90/9 = 9.999999999999

Figure A64

Note that the number 9.999999999999 uses only *one* digit, namely 9.

Note that the number 10 uses *two* digits, namely 1 and 0, twice as many digits as the 9.

Could the Maya have actually been using a 9-based decimal system that was *half* as complex as today's 10-based decimal system? We will examine this question, but first let's see what happens when we pursue the Maya cycle numbering system beyond 1,366,560. If we increase our cycle size of 144,000 by 20 our counting system breaks down, for example:

2,880,000	144,000	7,200	360	260	20	
1	1	1	1	1	1	1 = 3,031,840.
.	.	.	.	.	.	
.	.	.	.	.	.	
9	9	9	9	9	9	9 = 27,286,560

Figure A65

In no way can this lead to the Long Count of 100 periods of destruction, ie 136,656,000 days. So what must we do to obtain the Long Count using only cycles smaller than 144,000 to progress the count? (Cycles of longer duration may be used to denote a particular 'bunch' of days but not to progress time periods.)

as before

144,000	7,200	360	260	20		
1	1	1	1	1	=	151,840
2	2	2	2	2	=	303,680
3	3	3	3	3		.
4	4	4	4	4		
5	5	5	5	5		.
6	6	6	6	6		
7	7	7	7	7		.
8	8	8	8	8		.
9	9	9	9	9	=	1,366,560
now . . . 10	10	10	10	10	=	1,518,400
and . . . 20	20	20	20	20	=	3,036,800
30	30	30	30	30		.
40	40	40	40	40		.
50	50	50	50	50		.
60	60	60	60	60		.
70	70	70	70	70		.
80	80	80	80	80		.
90	90	90	90	90	=	13,665,600
now . . . 100	100	100	100	100	=	15,184,000
and . . . 200	200	200	200	200	=	30,368,000
300	300	300	300	300		.
.	.	.	.	.		.
etc .	.	.	.	.		.
900	900	900	900	900	=	136,656,000

Figure A66

Notice that, in the vertical columns, we go from 9, 10 straight to 20, 30. This allows us to 'skip' 11, maintaining a 9-based system. The same thing happens again later: 90, 100 to 200, 300 again 'skipping' 110, maintaining a 9-based vertical sequence whilst maintaining our number processing system up to, and beyond, if necessary, the Long Count. Only by introducing this 'skip and leap' can the numbering system remain useful beyond amounts of 1,366,560. But of course the Maya did not use the number 10 or the number 100, so what were they trying to tell us?

In the above table substitute 9.999999 for 10 and substitute

$$2 \times 9.999999 \text{ for } 20$$
$$3 \times 9.999999 \text{ for } 30 \text{ etc}$$

similarly substitute   99.999999 for 100 and substitute

2 × 99.999999 for 200
3 × 99.999999 for 300 etc

By doing this we overcome the need for 10 and 100 respectively. But what we see is that *the decimal point begins to move along the 9's*. Hence, by referring to cycles of lengths *greater* than those that are required the Maya were leaving us a coded message:

The Maya used the decimal point

In what other way could you tell another civilization that you actually *used* a decimal point, because unless you know what a decimal point *is* the concept remains meaningless. So, the Maya were the first civilization to use the decimal point arithmetical system *and to tell us about it*. But they went to great pains *not* to use decimal notation on monuments—lest we did not have the intelligence to understand. And the message of the Maya was too important not to understand, hence an 'unrequired' Long Count of 100 periods of destruction.

Numbering system summary

The Maya wished to communicate the following messages to later civilizations:

i) The sunspot cycle duration is 68,302 days and may be calculated using the 260-day cycle which itself is derived from the solar rotational variables P (Pole) 37 days and E (Equator) 26 days.

ii) This cycle may be monitored using the planet Venus as a calibrator: 117 sidereal passes of Venus (117 × 584) = 68,328 days.

iii) After 20 of these periods the sun's neutral sheet warp magnetic field shifts direction. The Earth's magnetic field attempts to realign with this new magnetic orientation. Cataclysmic destruction frequents the Earth.

iv) The fact that the Maya were intellectually more advanced than generations to come needed to be conveyed.

v) The fact that the Maya used a decimal counting system must be conveyed. This would satisfy iv) above.

vi) A 'counting system', ostensibly irrational and illogical may be used to convey these facts:
   a) The counting system should be 'cyclical' permitting reference to

the cyclical periodicity of the variables in question (Venus, Earth, Solar Pole and Solar Equator) and therefore based upon 360 (degrees).

b) The system should contain the number of Venus passes: 117.

c) The system should contain the 260-day cycle.

d) The system *must* break down after the important 1,366,560 day figure has been reached (in order to emphasize the importance of this period).

e) Attempts to rationalize the system beyond 1,366,560 must make reference to cycles that are not required for the purpose of 'monitoring' (Pictun, Calabtun, Kinchilitun etc) and durations (Long Count of 136,656,000) which are irrelevant (because any period after destruction is irrelevant).

f) Such a contradiction, as espoused in e) above, should call for (demand) an intellectual leap that requires the use of a decimal system—indicating that they were aware of such a decimal system.

Hence the choice of Maya cycle durations of 144,000, 7,200, 360, 260, and 20-day periods, and the choice of counting systems discussed herein. Numbers transcend all tongues.

Angular measurement of the Maya
Did the Maya divide a circle into 360 segments for measurement purposes, as we do today? The Maya counting system as we have seen employs 421.77 such circles for its foundation. Clearly if we can provide other indicators to substantiate this then the 360 degree premise will be supported.

The Nunnery at Uxmal
In 1980, a team from Colgate University, USA, led by astronomer Anthony Aveni and architect Horst Hartung, carried out an architectural survey of Uxmal, in the Northern Yucatan.

The Nunnery, so called because the four detached buildings face inwards to a common courtyard (similar to what might be found inside a Spanish convent), is one of the more perplexing arrangements of buildings at Uxmal. Each occupies a different level, on separate platforms, and each has a different number of doors. (*See* Plates A1 and A2 in the Appendix Plate section.)

Hartung's survey revealed an almost 'illogical' juxtaposition of the

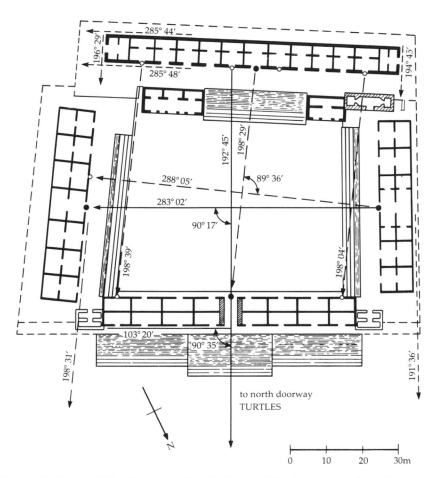

Figure A67 Survey of 'The Nunnery' at Uxmal by Hartung. Note the geometric relationships between buildings.

buildings. He noted that the lines connecting certain doorways form a double set of axes which cross at almost perfect right angles near the centre of the courtyard. He also noted that the wall on the east wing of the Nunnery displayed a complex pattern of crosses and counting these, for the first time it seems, Hartung arrived at the number of 584 crosses: the Venus interval period. But beyond these scholarly enquiries little progress on the interpretation of these elaborate architectural relationships has been made, until now.

So far, our enquiries into the Maya have contained the instruction 'make perfect that which is imperfect'. The corners of the Lid of Palenque, for example, were imperfect (*see* Appendix 8). The inferred instruction is therefore 'make perfect that which is imperfect', or 'find the missing corners'. By looking for the corners we are able to decode the Lid of Palenque. Similarly the period of 260 days was 'missing' from dates inscribed on monuments. Again we need to 'make perfect that which is imperfect', and by inserting the missing 260-day cycle into the counting system, we are able to rationalize the meaning of why the Maya chose to use the cycles that they did.

Once again we are handed perplexing information, this time in the architecture of the Nunnery at Uxmal. As Horst Hartung noted, '. . . lines connecting certain doorways form a double set of axes that cross at *almost perfect* right angles . . .'

Firstly, (*see* Figure A67) we need to 'interpret' the degrees and minute measurements as *decimal* measurements, then we can subtract the 192.45 degree measurement from the 198.29 degree measurement to arrive at 5.84 degrees (perfect agreement with the 584 crosses on the wall (Figure A69), that relate to the important Venus interval—displaced by two decimal places). But the axes of the crosses do not cross at 'perfect' right angles. Making perfect that which is imperfect we must swing the 283.02 degree measurement down by 0.17 degrees. This then forms a 'perfect' right angle, (X), to its neighbour, (*see* Figure A68).

Next we have to swing the 288.05 degree measurement upwards by 0.64 degrees so that this line now forms a right angle with (Y), its neighbour. The resulting difference now between the 288.69 (288.05 + 0.64) and 282.85 (283.02 − 0.17) = 5.84. This makes perfect the two right angles that separate the axes between the buildings and tells us that i) the number 584 is important, ii) the Maya used the decimal system and iii) the Maya used a 360 degree system for the measurement of angles.

So we see that the architecture, as well as the numbering system (117 intervals of Venus 584 = 68,328 = 1 sunspot cycle) and the sculpture (the Lid of Palenque) of the Maya all provide the same message and each supports the other, providing unequivocal support to the decoded interpretations of each.

The 1,872,000 Cycle
The Baktun cycle lasts for 144,000 days. Thirteen of these cycles amount to 1,872,000 days, after which, if the prophecies of the Maya priests are correct, the cycle will end as cataclysmic destruction frequents the Earth. So we need to ask just how such a catastrophe may come about, and what

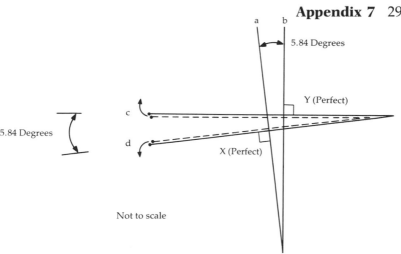

The survey by Hartung shows that the difference between a) and b) is 5.84 degres. But the difference between c) and d) is only 5.03 degrees. But note that the axes between the two sets of measurements are not pefectly 90 degrees. By making angle X 90 degrees and by making angle Y 90 degrees the difference between the two odd measurements c) and d) now becomes the desired 5.84 degrees, as with a) and b). In order for the Maya to arrange this they must have used a 360-degree system. It was this 360 degree system upon which the Maya counting system was based where 421.7777777777 cycles of 360 = 1/9th of the destruction period of 1,366,560 days. And it was the number 9 that was worshipped by the Maya.

Figure A68

the significance of the 1,872,000 period is, in terms of sunspot cycles and concomitant magnetic solar/Earth activity. The section on catastrophism versus uniformitarianism (Appendix 6) juxtaposes previous catastrophist theory with that of mythological belief of the Maya and other civilizations. Here, then, we are concerned with whether or not a change in the sun's magnetic field direction affects in any way the direction or intensity of the Earth's geomagnetic field. If it does, is the 1,872,000 period of any cataclysmic significance?

Our sunspot cycle activity model in Appendix 4 suggested that after 1,366,040 days the sun's magnetic field shifts, as against the orientation 1,366,040 days earlier. We noted that the shift represents 20 shift cycles of the 68,302 sunspot period.

In *Maya Numbers*, we noted that the Maya actually used cycles of 68,328 days, (instead of 68,302) which could conveniently be monitored by 117 revolutions of the planet Venus ($117 \times 584 = 68,328$) and that 20 of these cycles amounted to the Maya super number of 1,366,560 (as against 1,366,040). Further, we note that the Maya calendar commenced in 3113 BC and that the shift occurred around 627 AD +/− 187 years (*see* Appendix 4).

We can examine the Earth's geomagnetic field and Figure A69 clearly shows that the Earth's magnetic field (a) changes in sympathy with that of the sun and (b) suggests that the intensity of the Earth's field is directly affected by that of the sun's neutral sheet.

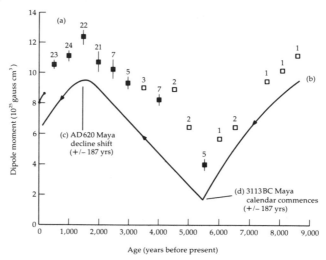

(a) Variations in the geomagnetic dipole moment. Changes during the past 130 years, as determined from observatory measurements, are shown by the slanting bar at left. Other values were determined palemagnetically. The number of measurements that were averaged is shown above each point, and the standard error of the mean is indicated by the vertical lines.

Figure A69   (b) Shows the changing direction of the sun's neutral magnetic sheet. The changing field direction correlates significantly with geomagnetic field intensities over the same period suggesting changes in the Earth's field are influenced by the direction of the sun's field.

Source: *Climate and Evolution*, Pearson from Cox

Our analysis of the solar neutral sheet shows that calculations covering the last 3,740 years indicate a reversal of the neutral sheet direction between 3,113 BC and 627 AD (both periods +/– 187 years). Note: 'Before Present' is usually interpreted as 'before 1952'.

The 8,000-year Cox/Bucha geomagnetic intensity cycle means that two reversals take place, during the 8,000-year period, as against a theoretical double reversal of the solar neutral sheet time period of 2 × (3,740 +/– 187 years), or 7,854 years, which, given the confidence level of the geomagnetic and Carbon 14 data means that a near perfect correlation exists between the calculated solar neutral sheet and geomagnetic intensity variations during a near perfect chronological historical period.

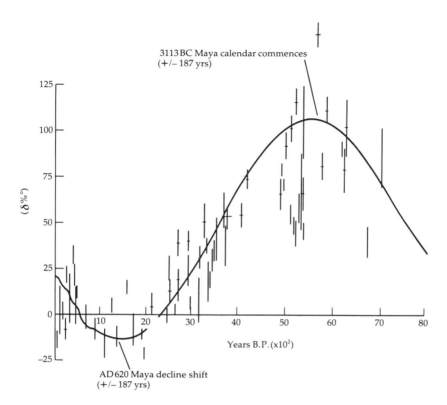

3113 BC Maya calendar commences
(+/– 187 yrs)

AD 620 Maya decline shift
(+/– 187 yrs)

δ (%) plotted against tree-ring age. The theoretical curve assumes a
sinusoidal geomagnetic field intensity with a period of 8,000 years (Bucha, 1970)

Figure A70   Supporting evidence from Bucha, 1970

Significance of the 1,872,000 day period

Maya number	1,872,000
Maya magnetic shift number	−1,366,560
	505,440 days

505,440 days ÷ 68,302 (actual sunspot number) = 7.40 sunspot cycles.

Immediately, this suggests that the 1,872,000 number is a fraction of a
larger cycle, because there is an incomplete number of actual sunspots
in the period and therefore it cannot represent a solar cycle activity
period.

   In order to overcome this the remainder, of .4 (contained in the
number 7.4) must be multiplied by 5: $5 \times 7.4 = 37$ sunspot cycles.

37 of course is a solar prime number (the Polar cycle amounts to 37 days).

Multiplying 1,872,000 by 5 (in order to dispense with the fraction) gives:

$$1,872,000 \times 5 = 9,360,000 \text{ days}$$

Is this a cycle? Examination of the numbers shows that at this time P = −9.729729 degrees. E = 0, and the Earth is not coincident with either. From *Maya Numbers* we know that if we add 260 days we can add 9.729729 degrees to any number of days, hence:

9,360,000 + 260 = 9,360,260

$$P = 0$$
$$E = 0$$
$$W = 0$$

This period, then, is another longer Grand cycle of Solar activity; of 25,627 years.

9,360,260-day precession period
This amounts to 137.0 Sunspot cycles. Referring to our Neutral warp diagram (Figure A71) we can observe the following:
Note: during the first 68,302 day cycle (1 cycle of 187 years) the shift bits are generated and take up residence within the cycle. Thereafter, 20 shift bit movements (20 × 68,302 = 1,366,040) result in shift bit collision and solar magnetic shift.
Again, from above, 9,360,260 days = 137.0 Shifts
$$\underline{-97} \text{ Max shifts possible}$$
40 Shifts

In other words, if we count 20 shifts, the shift bits collide. If we count 97 shifts, the shift bits complete one circuit and return to their initial shift positions. Counting 40 more shifts we arrive at the central warp shift bit position (1 + 97 + 39 = 137). By flagging the number of 1,366,560 the Maya introduce us to the shifting nature of the neutral warp and solar magnetic reversals. So by flagging the number 1,872,000 the Maya draw attention to:

i) The precession cycle
ii) That the moment of seven collisions (5 during 97 shifts, followed by two during the next 39 shifts) following cycle commencement, is in some way significant, in collision terms.

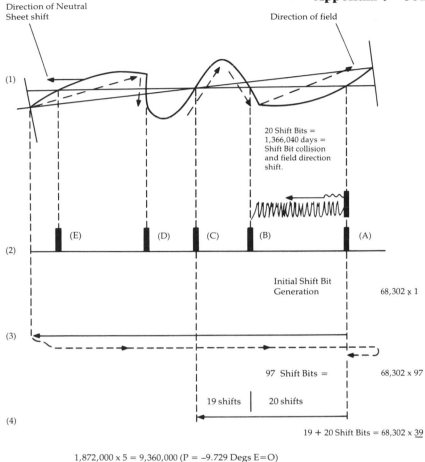

Direction of Neutral Sheet shift

Direction of field

(1)

20 Shift Bits = 1,366,040 days = Shift Bit collision and field direction shift.

(E)   (D)   (C)   (B)   (A)

(2)

Initial Shift Bit Generation   68,302 x 1

(3)

97 Shift Bits =   68,302 x 97

19 shifts | 20 shifts

(4)

19 + 20 Shift Bits = 68,302 x 39

$$1,872,000 \times 5 = 9,360,000 \ (P = -9.729 \ \text{Degs} \ E=O)$$
$$\frac{260}{9,360,260} \ (P = O, E=O, W=O) \longrightarrow \text{Total} \quad 137$$

Plot (1) shows the 'Neutral Sheet' 'Direction of Shift' and 'Direction of Field'.

Plot (2) shows the positions of shift bits caused by Neutral Sheet interaction with the fundamental cycles.

The sequence of Shift Bits are generated (appear) during the first 68,302 day cycle. For Shift Bit (A) to shift to the position of Shift Bit (B) will take 20 shifts. At this time the field direction shifts relative to its direction 1,366,040 days earlier.

Plot (3): For Shift Bit (A) to shift through (B), (C), (D) and (E) positions and return back to its original (A) position will take 97 shifts. For Shift Bit (A) to CONTINUE shifting (Plot 4), will take 20 shifts to collide with (B) and a further 19 shifts to collide with (C). This total of 137 shifts (1 original) + 97 + 37) amounts to 9,360,260 days ((5 x 1,872,000) + 260 days). At this time P=E=W=O degrees = 25,627 years. One master cycle therefore amounts to the cycle of Precession.

Figure A71

Precession of the Equinoxes
The Earth spins on its axis as it orbits the sun. As it does so the poles describe an arc in relation to the stars. This behaviour is known as 'precession', and takes around 26,000 years to complete one cycle. The exact figure is very difficult to obtain because the motion is believed to result from a combination of influences; the gravitational influences of the sun and the moon having the greatest effect. It is generally thought to last for between 25,800 and 26,000 years, but few sources agree on the duration, for example:

Astronomy in Colour Lancaster	25,800 years
Guinness Book of Astronomy	25,920
The Earth's Changing Climate Milne	25,780
The Book of Time Wilson (Ed)	'about 26,000'
Atlas of Solar System (Roy. As. Soc.)	No Mention

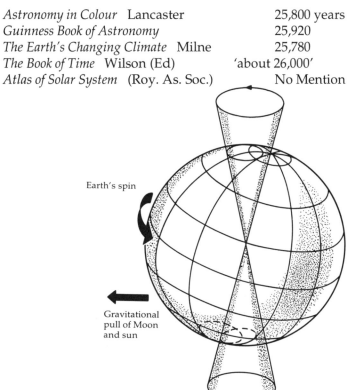

Figure A72   Precession of the axis. The Earth spins at an angle to the plane of its orbit around the sun; its axis is tilted nearly 23.5°. The gravitational pull of the sun and the moon cause a slow wobble. The north and south poles take nearly 26,000 years to complete a circle.

Earth's spin

Gravitational pull of Moon and sun

A Maya mystery
Could the Maya, given their preoccupation for cataclysmic destruction, have been indicating that the seventh collision which occurs after 25,627

years is, in some way, more significant than others? Or could the message have been much simpler?

When decoding the Maya numbering system we noted that the system itself raises many questions. By answering those questions we eventually realize that the only way to overcome the enigma is to use a 'decimal point' system. By asking ourselves questions we generate answers which lead to the awareness that 'there is no other way to describe what a decimal point is—to *someone who does not know what a decimal point is'*, the final message thus being 'the Maya used a decimal point system'.

Similarly, it would be difficult to convey the concept of a polar shift. We need to remind ourselves that orthodox science was only beginning to suggest that the Earth rotated on an axis as recently as the 16th century in Europe. So perhaps the whole point of the 1,872,000 cycle is to convey the message of pole shift or *the earth tilts on its axis.*

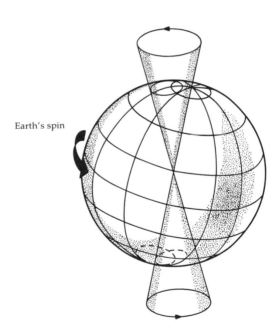

Earth's spin

Pole Shift
or
'The Earth tilts on its axis'

Figure A73

Could the other collisions simply shift the Earth's magnetic field resulting in infertility and mutational cycles, whilst the 25,627-year collision results in a pole shift, denoted by a 'reversal' of the neutral sheet at that time? Or was the message 'the next 1,366,040-day cycle will be followed by a pole shift?', and if so, when?

Given that the accounts of the Vatico-Latin codex and Aztec Sunstone Calendar, and others, speak of the five periods amounting to somewhere between 23,000 and 25,000 years, could the end of the 25,627-year cycle have actually occurred in 627 AD? If it did occur in 627 AD, is the Earth's molten core now slowly remagnetizing to a new neutral sheet direction and can we, as a consequence, expect a pole shift in the year 2012?

The 1,872,000 cycle and the Maya numbering system
Previously we noted that the 1,872,000 cycle comprised of 5 Baktun cycles ($5 \times 144,000$). An alternative view is that the 1,872,000 cycle comprises of $360 \times 260 \times 20 = 1,872,000$, and this fits in with the Maya numbering system of cycles previously covered. The precession cycle, we noted, amounts to 5 of these 1,872,000 cycles ie $360 \times 260 \times 100 = 9,360,000$ days. The 260-day figure, multiplied by the number of degrees contained in one hundred circles *must* therefore amount to a value of *a complete grand cycle* $+/- 9.729729$ degrees, and of course it does.

After 9,360,000 days P = 252972.9729729, the polar region of the sun has made 252,972 revolutions and .9729729 of a revolution, ie it rests at 350.27027027 degrees, (– 9.729729 degrees) as predicted. By adding 260 days to this figure, the P resting position advances by 9.729729 degrees meaning that after 9,360,260 days P completes 252,980 revolutions exactly. Similarly E makes 360,010 revolutions exactly and W, the World, makes 25,626,995 revolutions (25,627 revolutions exactly). This is the closest the three variables will be, compared with the 68,302 day fundamental sunspot cycle period; there are 137.0 sunspot cycle periods during this time. This is to say that P = E = W = Neutral sheet every 25,627 years: the Maya grand cycle of time. Working backwards this can be obtained from the Maya numbering base system.

$360 \times 260 \times 100 = 360 \times 26,000 = 9,360,000 \ (+ 260) = 9,360,260$

From above:
P; $252,980 \times 37$ = 9,360,260
E; $360,010 \times 26$ = 9,360,260
W; $25,626.995 \times 365.25$ = 9,360,260

Divide throughout by Maya numbering system base; 360
P; $\dfrac{252,980 \times 37}{360}$ = 26,000

$$E; \quad \frac{360,010 \times 26}{360} = 26,000$$

$$W; \quad \frac{25,627 \times 365.25}{360} = 26,000$$

Hence the Maya base number 360
Hence the Maya year number 260
Hence the Maya numbering system $360 \times 260 \times 20$
Hence the Maya precession calculation $360 \times 260 \times 20 \times 5$

The Maya number 1,359,540 days
The foundation date carved into the Temple of the Cross in Palenque is 1,359,540. What does this number mean?

Maya Super Number	=	1,366,560
Temple of Cross Number	=	1,359,540
Difference	=	7,020

This number means little in itself so we need to operate upon it by 260, the Maya important number:

$$27 \times 260 \text{ (days)} = 7,020 \text{ days}$$

and we know that after 260 days P = 9.729729 degrees.

Changing the days into degrees:

$$27 \times 9.729 \text{ (degrees)} = 262.7 \text{ degrees}$$

This number means little in itself so we need to operate on it by 260, the Maya important number: changing degrees into days:

$$262.7 \times 260 = 68,302 = 1 \text{ True Sunspot Cycle}$$

This clarifies the fact that the super number of 1,366,560 (Maya solar magnetic collision figure) amounts to 20 Maya sunspot cycles of 68,328 days, where 68,328 is derived using Venus as a calibrator. The 1,359,540 figure *corrects* this to reveal the true calculated figure of 68,302 days, and (after 20 of these, 1,366,040 days), the true solar magnetic collision figure.

1,359,540 also conveys the message 'change the days into degrees and change the degrees into days'; and thus by doing 'nothing' (changing from days to degrees and then degrees back to days—one step forward, one step backwards) we observe that we achieve the solution. If we remember, the decoding of the Lid of Palenque was made possible by finding the corners that were not missing. Such is the enigma of the Maya.

Maya numbers—summary
9 = Magic number of the Maya. All relevant numbers compound to 9 (except the special number 260).

260 = Solar pole: equator differential operator and Maya 'year'. After 260 days P = 9.729 degrees E = 0 degrees.

360 = Maya numbering system base.

144,000 7,200 360 260 20 = Maya cycles that comprise the numbering system.

68,302 = Sunspot cycle as calculated by computer.

68,328 = Sunspot cycle as tracked by the Maya and calibrated using Venus.

1,366,040 = 20 sunspot cycles = 1 solar magnetic collision/shift (computer calculated).

1,366,560 = 20 Maya sunspot cycles = 1 Maya solar magnetic collision/shift. Calculated by multiplying each numbering system number by 9. This is the 'Super-Number' of the Dresden Codex.

1,359,540 = Carved on the Temple of the Cross, Palenque. This number reconciles the Venus calibrated periods of 68,328 and 1,366,560 with the 68,302 and 1,366,040 computer calculated versions.

1,152,000 and 57,600,000 = used to 'over-drive' and 'break-down' the numbering system.

136,656,000 = 100 sunspot collisions/catastrophe periods. Modifies, and in so doing, extends the Maya numbering system to accommodate the handling of larger numbers (136,656,000) and in so doing overcomes the system breakdown when used for cycles larger than 144,000. This is achieved with recourse to a modified numbering system based upon the number 9 and the decimal point. This indicates that the Maya used the decimal point system.

1,872,000 = 360 × 260 × 20. 1,872,000 − 1,366,560 (Super Number) = 505,440 = 7.4 sunspot cycles. This indicates that 1,872,000 represents only 1/5th of a greater time period.

9,360,000 = 5 × 1,872,000 = 9.729729 degrees short of a Maya Grand Cycle.

9,360,260 = P = E = W = Neutral Warp = 1 Grand Maya Cycle = Cycle of Precession. Precession is indicative of Earth wobble/tilt or pole shift.

Appendix 8: The Amazing Lid of Palenque

Although a book of *The Amazing Lid of Palenque* has been published separately it is important to understand how the decoding was achieved in the first place, because this decoding logic, which pervades all that the Maya believed, led to all of the other discoveries about the Maya.

The first thing one notes about the Lid is the complexity and the beauty of the carved picture. The second is the plethora of unknown and confounding symbols and shapes littered around the more easily recognizable designs and motifs. Given that many interpretations have been placed upon the design over the years, none conclusive, it seemed reasonable to suggest that the Lid could contain much more information than had hitherto been recognized. Indeed my own interpretation of the carving showed scenes that depicted sunspot activity, as well as how such activity could affect fertility.

This first-level analysis yielded an altogether different interpretation of the meaning of the carving on the Lid than had ever been proposed to date.

First level decoding
This involves interpretation of the design of the carving but involves no decoding.
Interpretation: The carving could be seen to tell of the previous 'four' ages of creation; as did the Aztec sunstone and other meso-american literature, (but raised the question of missing information relating to the 'fifth' age—which seemed not to be depicted, see main text).

The question now was, given that the fifth age of the Jaguar was not represented, was this first interpretation conjecture?

I decided, at least for the time being, to set aside this account and return to the 'official' one which suggested that the centrally reclining figure was the occupant of the tomb falling into some 'after-life' region. But no evidence existed to support this assertion. Likewise the official interpretation suggested that the falling occupant was sitting on top of an 'Earth monster' but what is an Earth monster?

One by one, I eliminated each of the postulates given in the orthodox interpretation—all except one that is. At the foot of the reclining figure, so the archaeologists maintained, were pictured a few 'maize seeds'. Examining these I agreed that there were certainly a few 'marks', and giving the benefit of the doubt decided that this observation must therefore be given a fair hearing.

I had read earlier, during my investigations into Mayan mythology, that the home of 'maize' was the home of women who died in childbirth; the Paradise known as 'Cincalco' which lay to the West. Given that the seeds were positioned at the feet of the reclining figure, and to the left hand side (the West), could the reclining figure actually represent a female giving birth, with legs open?

Indeed, there were four other known mythological Paradises for the Maya; Tonatiuhcan lay to the East and was the home of the Sun-God Tonatiuh. This was the home of those who died in battle and sacrifice. Tonatiuh had already been recognized in the first interpretation of the 'four previous ages'. Could Tonatiuh have a dual role as an indicator of the paradise Tonatiuhcan?

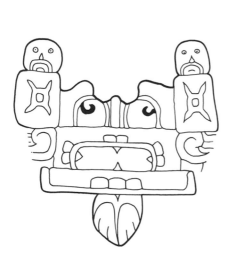

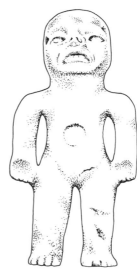

Figure A74(i)   Tonatiuh, on the Lid, flanked by two solar babies

Figure A74(ii)   Solar baby carving, Teotihuacan c. 80AD

Examining Tonatiuh on the Lid design I noticed that either side of him were positioned two 'solar babies', with sad looking mouths and the solar symbol on their stomachs. A well known carving of these solar babies had been unearthed in Teotihuacan, and supported this assertion.

Moreover, a Paradise was known to exist which was the destination of babies who died at birth. This was 'Tomoanchan', suggesting that the reclining figure above was indeed depicting a female giving birth. In Tomoanchan grew the 'Suckling Tree' which was said to have 400,000 nipples. Dead babies from Tomoanchan were said to suckle the nipples of the tree and hence gain enough strength to reincarnate on Earth. With this in mind the central cross, carrying the marker pegs, might be seen as representing the suckling tree with nipples.

Only two Paradises were left to be found: the first, Tlalocan, was easily located in the south as the home of Tlaloc, the rain god. He had already been recognized along with Tonatiuh in the 'four previous ages'. Here he was said to live with his wife Chalchiutlicue, goddess of water. The only missing Paradise was, it seemed, Omeocan, the home of the first divine couple Ometeotl (the Mayan equivalent of the Adam and Eve of the gods, from whom all the other gods were born). Could yet another interpretation, of the centrally reclining figure, represent one half of the divine couple—Eve, for example?

Once again, a rational interpretation of the meaning of the information on the Lid appeared to fall short because yet another piece was missing—Adam.

I catalogued this interpretation of the Four Paradises alongside that of The Four Previous Ages, and began searching again for yet another possible interpretation of the carving.

I now compared this more recent interpretation, with its preoccupation with childbirth and fertility, with my own research into sunspots and infertility, to produce yet another rational interpretation. Could the central cross represent the sun, with its four magnetic fields? The cross could indeed be seen covered in 'loops' and pegs. Could the 'loops' represent sunspots and perhaps the pegs numbers of sunspots, because each peg itself was accompanied by one half of a loop?

The cross is a symbol of the sun. The loops represent magnetic loops from sunspots (black spots that can be seen on the Sun's surface). The 'pegs' and half-loops that drape over the top of the cross represent the nine full sunspot cycles and two half sunspot cycles that take place during one half of a grand sunspot period. A full period takes 1,366,560 days.

Story of destruction that the Maya believed

After 1,366,560 days the sunspot cycle will end. Fertility will decline. Babies will be born dead. Because the sun's magnetic field changes the Earth's magnetic field changes. The world ends because of earthquakes, floods, fires and hurricanes.

Here we see a woman in a hot tub of water opening her legs to the sun to increase fertility (*see* Plate A3). The dead babies can be seen descending into Tomoanchan. The Sun-God Tonatiuh is seen eating the people. He has only a few teeth left indicating he has 'finished eating the population'. It is the end of the era. A new era will now begin.

On the face of it, it seemed that this story of 'Cosmogonic Destruction' was a plausible interpretation. However, there was one problem—my research had shown that after 20 sunspot cycles the sun's magnetic field reversed, resulting in a drop in fertility and a possible pole shift. But here I could count only ten marker pegs (nine full plus two halves). Half of the pegs were missing.

It seemed that every time I came up with a rational interpretation it failed due to 'missing information'.

Summary of interpretation of first-level decoding

At the end of the 'first level' of decoding the following loose ends are apparent: this interpretation is calling for more information in regard to (i) the fifth age of creation (ii) the missing partner of Ometeotl and (iii) a quantitative solar activity indicator.

Without these the 'interpretation' may not necessarily be efficacious, and may only be a question of opinion, or conjecture. This meant that more information must be 'concealed' within the carving; but, at this stage, close examination of the carving did not yield any more clues. Up to this point, research into the area circumscribing the central design of the carving had been neglected. This comprises a pattern of 'codes' that run around the outer top surface of the Lid.

Second-level decoding

It seems extraordinary that no-one appears to have questioned this deficiency before my own examination of the Lid. Why were the corners missing? Why carve such an exquisite masterpiece and then vandalize the corners? After all, to expend such effort as is required to construct a temple-pyramid on top of a once beloved leader, knowing that the corners of the Lid buried beneath, covering the tomb of the Priest-King, had been damaged, defies belief. But, neither could the corners have been 'damaged' accidentally, with such symmetrical parity.

Figure A75   The first thing to notice is that two of the corners of the Lid are missing.

The inference is that the corners had been removed deliberately by those who carved the Lid, and moreover, that they had been removed for a very important reason. Could this important reason in some way lead to a 'decoding mechanism' that might accommodate the missing pieces of the puzzle encountered on the first-level decoding 'interpretations' discussed above?

(i)   Priority was now given to 'finding' the missing pieces and repairing the much beloved Lid. To understand the next step we need to understand just how the mind of the Maya operated. The Maya believed that each part of the microcosm was only one piece of the larger macrocosmic universe. Each individual was likewise a self-same piece of creation. This interpretation extended to the 'self' and in so doing each individual was seen as a tiny piece of oneness which begat the perception that 'I am you', and 'you are me'. This was further epitomized with their pantheon of gods representing the opposing forces of nature; both the nature of the physical Earth and the nature of man along the spectrum of duality of opposing forces, such as day and night and birth and death. Night would become day, as surely as the day must become night. Good would in time become bad, (through excess) as surely as bad would become good (following aversion to pain and suffering).

This understanding of the psyche of the Maya provided the next key of the decoding process. If I am you and you are me, and if night becomes day and day becomes night, perhaps the missing corners are not actually missing? And, of course, if the corners are not actually missing, they must still, therefore, be there.

(ii) The 'missing corners' had taken with them the overlaid corner patterns. One missing corner pattern was easy to extrapolate for two reasons. Firstly, it consisted of a series of juxtaposed dots and circles, the inference of the completed pattern could be easily conjectured and, secondly, an identical pattern appeared in another border box (the central border box) a few boxes away from the missing code.

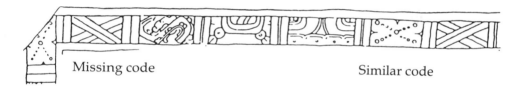

Missing code   Similar code

Figure A76

It is a simple matter to repair half of a missing cross, for example a mirror held at the axis of the cross, would complete the missing half. And so it was with the Lid of Palenque. But the mirror could not be held close enough to the damaged dots to complete the pattern. The only way the pattern could be completed was to make a photocopy transparency (acetate) of the Lid and place the acetate on top of the missing corner. The complete pattern was thus restored. The missing corner was re-paired. The investigation had produced an acetate copy of the original Lid design and moreover, the missing corner could only be reinstated by *overlaying* the acetate on top of the original. The second step in the decoding process had been successfully accomplished.

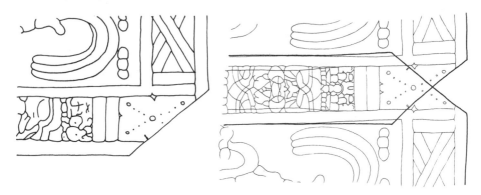

Missing corner showing part of
coded pattern, a cross made from
dots— but half of the pattern was
missing

Using an acetate copy of the
carving, I was able to restore
the pattern

Figure A77

Third level decoding

Although one corner had been found, the other missing corner did not
repair itself until the acetate and original were slightly withdrawn apart
until the second missing corner code completed itself. When this was
done the code 'loops' completed their mirror images. This done, small
pictures could be seen descending down the border. The three steps
involved in decoding the border codes are shown in Plate A5.

The next step was a systematic search for more composite border code
pictures. A total of 26 was found along the four sides. A sample of some
of the other discovered composite border codes of the Lid can be seen in
Plate 22a.

These 'story indicators' tell us that each of these stories may also be
found on the inner carving, when the decoding process is used. However, although the same story appears, it is depicted differently.

Fourth level decoding

It became clear that the Lid design contained more concealed information, because the anomalies uncovered in level 1 had still not been
resolved, suggesting that the decoding was not yet complete. The border
was again studied to find any other 'defects' which might have been
repaired.

The next defect noted was that of an unusual mark or shape, attached
to the nose of a border code character cameo. Clearly this was not usual.

A1 The east wing of the Nunnery showing the six formations of serpent bars above the doorway.

A2 Hartung counted 584 crosses within the serpent bars.

A3 The Paradises

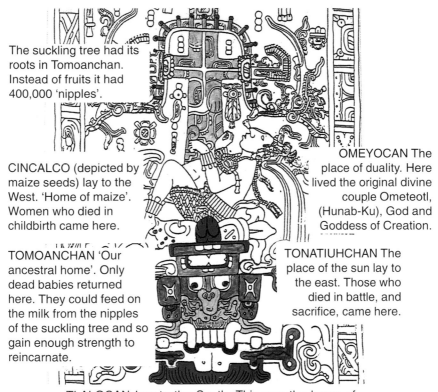

The suckling tree had its roots in Tomoanchan. Instead of fruits it had 400,000 'nipples'.

CINCALCO (depicted by maize seeds) lay to the West. 'Home of maize'. Women who died in childbirth came here.

TOMOANCHAN 'Our ancestral home'. Only dead babies returned here. They could feed on the milk from the nipples of the suckling tree and so gain enough strength to reincarnate.

OMEYOCAN The place of duality. Here lived the original divine couple Ometeotl, (Hunab-Ku), God and Goddess of Creation.

TONATIUHCHAN The place of the sun lay to the east. Those who died in battle, and sacrifice, came here.

TLALOCAN Lay to the South. This was the home of Tlaloc (Chaac) God of Rain. Here he lived with his wife Chalchiuihtlicue, Goddess of Water. This was a place filled with flowers, fresh streams and bird song. The birds sang loudly, to keep Tlaloc awake, so that he would not forget to send rain, to make the land fertile.

The dragon heads on either side of the cross represent fertility. The beaded dragon tails represent the rattle of the rattle snake and represent death. The left tail of the cross belongs to the head on the right and the right tail of the cross belongs to the dragon head on the left.

A4 The cause of Cosmogonic Destruction

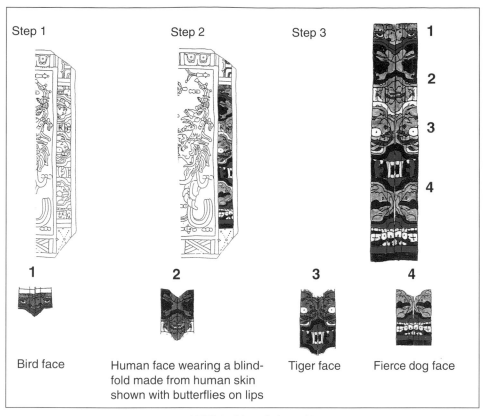

Step 1 Step 2 Step 3

1 2 3 4

Bird face

Human face wearing a blind-fold made from human skin shown with butterflies on lips

Tiger face

Fierce dog face

A5 Third level decoding

A6 The approaching bat (scenes 1 and 2). *We can see the appearance of a tiny bat in the lower centre of the Plate. The bat is then seen more closely with claws open ready to land, or 'strike' its victim.*

A7 The approaching bat (scene 3). *The landing bat (arrival of death)*

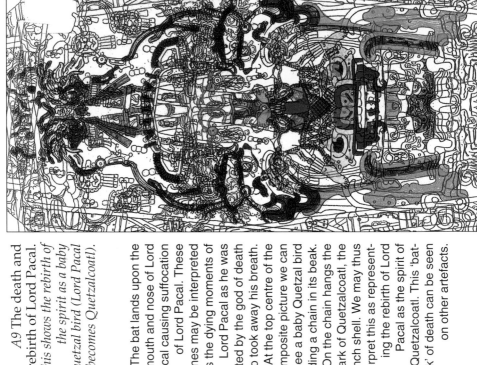

A9 The death and rebirth of Lord Pacal. This shows the rebirth of the spirit as a baby Quetzal bird (Lord Pacal becomes Quetzalcoatl).

The bat lands upon the mouth and nose of Lord Pacal causing suffocation of Lord Pacal. These scenes may be interpreted as the dying moments of Lord Pacal as he was visited by the god of death who took away his breath.

At the top centre of the composite picture we can see a baby Quetzal bird holding a chain in its beak. On the chain hangs the mark of Quetzalcoatl, the Conch shell. We may thus interpret this as representing the rebirth of Lord Pacal as the spirit of Quetzalcoatl. This 'bat-mark' of death can be seen on other artefacts.

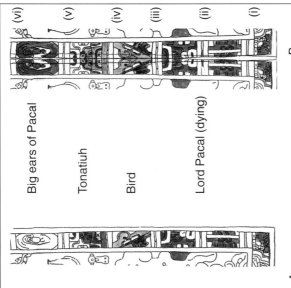

(vi)

(v) Big ears of Pacal

(iv) Tonatiuh

(iii) Bird

(ii)

(i) Lord Pacal (dying)

B

A

B(i), (ii) and (iii) together depict a cartoon icon with folded hands upon the chest, bare feet, closed eyes and 'big ears'. B(iv) shows an icon of a bird with open wings. B(v) shows an icon resembling Tonatiuh, the Sun-God, with the circle of the sun on his forehead. Finally, above this, are shown shapes resembling two human ears.

A8 Additional border composite

Figure A78

Of course I could repair the defect with a touch of white paint—but this would be going against all the rules because I had not been instructed to use any paint. But I had been given an acetate. I had also been instructed that the acetate may be placed on top of the original and that 'mirror images' were within the rules of the game. Placing the cameo head together with its mirror image, the incongruous shape was erased from the design. The composite picture showed only two cameo heads with their foreheads and nose-tips touching.

Figure A79

The defect had once again been repaired. But what had I learned on this step? Nothing, so far. But looking to the central character of the Lid, I noted the same defect to the nose. The light had dawned, the instruction contained here was 'place the shape on the nose of the central character of the Lid together with the mirror image of the shape on the nose of central character of the acetate'.

Figure A80

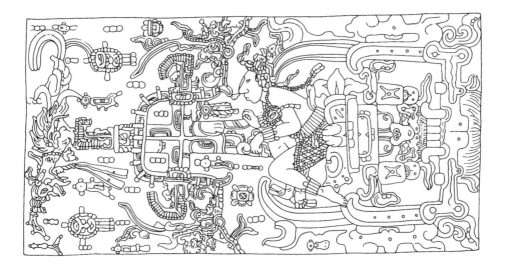

Figure A81

The inner carving central character carries a defect mark on the nose ridge. The instruction contained in the border code requests removal of the defect by placing an acetate on top of the defect.

The inner carving
This done, a bat, the god of death for the Maya, could be clearly seen flying toward the viewer at the top of the composite acetate arrangement and away from the viewer in the lower half of the composite picture. (*See* Plate 23.)

The Bat-God represented death to many cultures, from the Olmec onwards. The 25 piece jade figure (*see* Figure 82) was found in a tomb in Monte Alban. It dates from around 700 AD.

Fifth level decoding
I remembered that a bat had been detected in level 2 decoding, in the composite border codes, and it became apparent that the composite border codes listed the hidden pictures that could be found in the inner Lid design. I had found 26 composite border codes, one of which was the bat. The border code bat had now been reconciled with its counterpart on

the inner Lid. 25 composite border codes thus remained to be reconciled with their corresponding inner Lid pictures. The search was on.

The next border code to be reconciled was that of another pair of profile heads facing each other. The instruction here being, place the acetates so that the faces of the two main characters face each other. This done, it became apparent that I had found one of the missing pieces to the puzzle in level 1. I had found the missing partner of the first creative couple, who lived in the Paradise of Ometeotl, which I not been able to find during my interpretation of the Paradises. This orientation of the Creative Couple amounted to three scenes in the Maya story of Creation (the equivalent to Adam and Eve), and this story led to the discovery that the acetate could be moved (actioned) thus enabling moving pictures to be generated, in addition to the static composite picture of the Bat-God.

In addition, 23 central composite stories were quickly revealed, and in turn paired and reconciled with their corresponding border code indicators. One of the most interesting, and complex, is that of Lord Pacal dying.

The approaching bat
A series of 3 scenes depicting an approaching bat had been detected in the inner lid whilst searching for inner lid composite pictures. (*See* Plates A6 and A7.)

Although the scenes of 'the approaching bat' had been recognized, an 'additional' border code matching these scenes had not thus far been detected, which was curious, and raised the possibility that these scenes may form only a part of a larger story not yet detected. Indeed, a series of border codes did remain that had not been reconciled with inner Lid pictures, and these are pictured in Plate A8.

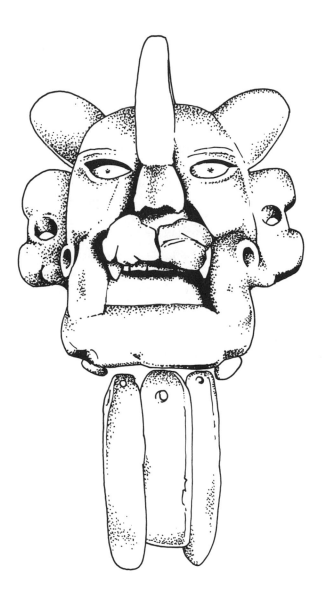

Figure A82   The Bat-God

Pausing, briefly, we note that two stucco heads were found on the floor of the tomb of Lord Pacal. Moreover, we note differences between the two heads. Figure A83 shows Pacal as a younger man with a short hairstyle and only one ear. Figure A84 shows Lord Pacal with a rising hair style, and, more correctly, with two ears. These are additional clues to help find the complex story of Lord Pacal dying; bringing the clues together the interpretation becomes:

B i–B iii:	To see the man in the tomb (the dead man)
B iv:	Look for a bird on the head
B v:	The bird is the Sun-God (Tonatiuh, or Quetzalcoatl)
B vi and stucco heads:	First reposition the ears in the border code (either side of the head) and, examining the hair, see the emergence of a bird

Following these instructions, the inner lid acetates were positioned in the place where the two ears rested either side of the composite (where human ears are normally expected to be found). Next, watching the hairstyle, the acetates were rotated until a small bird appeared at the top, dead centre of the composite where the hair could be seen in Figure A84. In its beak the bird carries a chain. Upon the chain hangs the conch shell—the mark of Quetzalcoatl, the feathered snake. (The shell represented the wind, and the bird that ruled the wind.) Quetzalcoatl was the highest god of the Maya.

Carefully colouring in the area beneath the bird we see the emergence of the face of the man in the tomb, Lord Pacal. Covering his mouth rests the landed bat from 'the approaching bat' series. The bat obscures the lower part of Pacal's face.

This complex composite therefore reads 'The god of death (the bat) landed upon Lord Pacal and took away his breath. He was re-born as a baby Quetzal bird. He began a new life as Quetzalcoatl, the highest of gods', *see* Plate A9.

The Jaguar
Another composite picture depicted a jaguar. This was said to represent the fifth age of creation (*see* Plate 24). By placing the five dot central border code marker on top of itself the 'fifth sun' composite picture of 'the jaguar' could be seen, reconciling the missing fifth sun component of data from the first level decoding process featured in the 'Four Previous Ages'. The jaguar was the fifth and present sun of creation.

Figure A83   Young Pacal with low cut hairstyle and missing ear

Figure A84   Pacal, with high hairstyle and two ears

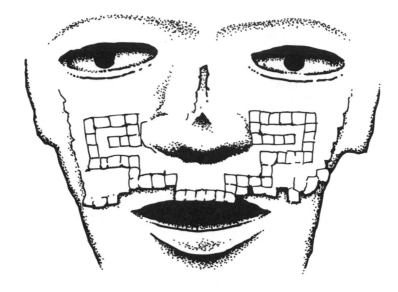

Figure A85   Skull inlaid with turquoise showing bat-mark of death inlaid with sea-shell. Teotihuacan.

Another central composite showed that '20 suns' (20 × 68,328 = 1,366,560 days) was the duration of the fertility/destruction cycle on Earth; thus clearing up all of the questions raised in level 1 interpretation. Moreover, it meant that the Maya were acutely aware of the sunspot cycle. But out of these four layers of decoding one loose end remained: of the 26 border codes, only 25 had been reconciled, one was missing. And this is the way the story remained, for ten more months.

It was the day after I had returned from the publishers. I had sat down again in an effort to tie up the remaining loose end that had been nagging away within me for almost a year. Placing the main centre (used in Lord Pacal dying) again on top of itself, I began to slowly rotate the two acetates. Of course I had done this before and had located 25 stories on the inner Lid, using this and other centres of rotation. But this time instead of looking at the inner Lid, searching for a hidden inner Lid story, I again examined the border codes. As they *rotated* I began to see correspondence with the *border codes* as the acetates rotated and intermeshed.

At each node of border code correspondence a story could be picked out on the inner Lid. I had discovered another 'layer' of border codes—

each of which required the decoding of a corresponding inner Lid story—only this time it was more difficult. Each border code node contained at least two scenes on top of each other, some visible only when the pair of acetates were jointly rotated through 180 degrees.

Although a further 22 scenes were detected from the rotational composite border code nodes of symmetry, a scene was also detected that corresponded with the missing level 4 decoded border code, thus reconciling the level 4 loose end; the missing (26th) border code story. It became clear that the Maya had used this 'rogue' (26th) code as a pointer to the existence of a second layer in the decoding mechanism.

In time these new stories were arranged into a second volume *The Amazing Lid of Palenque Volume 2*. Volume 2 was to contain the main 'spiritual' message of the Maya. It tells of the meaning of life and of the 'after life', of purgatory and purification, and of the cycles of destruction on Earth.

In the early days I had decoded the borders, but they had just been the 'index', or list of contents, to a book. Then I had successfully decoded the book itself. But then the 'book' turned out to be just a programme (in the sense that when you visit the Theatre the 'programme' lists the actors and the plot). Finally I had come to realize that Volume 1 simply contained a list of the cast that appear in Volume 2. Volume 2 was the 'performance' of the Maya. An incredible journey into the mind of man; an incredible journey of discovery. And, because of the layers involved in the structure and logic of the decoding mechanism, each of the actors appears up to six times in various costumes lending legitimacy to the decoding process. With such inbuilt redundancy there can be no ambiguity as to the intent of the Maya to transfer specific information.

But, of course, the two volumes contain 37 full-colour acetates and more than 100 colour pages. And to *see* the stories the acetates must be removed and placed on top of the pictures—a publisher's nightmare. However, despite all the obstacles, nine copies have been hand produced, each costing £625 ($997) per copy. These have been placed in the British Museum in London, the libraries of the Universities of Oxford and Cambridge, The National Library of Scotland, Trinity College Dublin, and the National Library of Wales. CD ROM publishers are keen on publishing the books, for computer users, and negotiations are now underway. This will hopefully reduce the price to £20 ($32) or so.

Since decoding the carving on the Lid of Palenque, I have found and decoded other Maya carvings using the same technique. These are the Mosaic Mask of Palenque, the Mural of Bonampak (Temple of the Frescoes Room 1), Lintel 25 Yaxchillan (British Museum, London) and

Lintel 53 Yaxchillan (British Museum, London). All of these have been published either in limited editions or are in the process of being published in a series specifically about Maya 'transformers'; these are artefacts that contain much more information than their face value suggests.

It should be noted that without the decoding of the Lid of Palenque the tremendous gains and discoveries in other related areas could never have been made. The decoding of Maya numbers, for example, could never have been achieved without first finding the 'missing' key Maya number to insert into the Maya cycle sequence (*see* section on Maya numbers). The 'key' corners of the Lid were removed so that the carving would one day be decoded and the 'key' number 260 was deliberately missing from dates in the inscriptions for the same reason. Without this link there could be no logical connection between the breaking of either the carving code or the numbering system. Similarly, no proof would exist to show that the Maya understood the duration of the sunspot cycle, the link between solar radiation and fertility, or catastrophe cycles, if neither the Lid nor the Maya numbers had been deciphered.

The Popol Vuh

> . . . The Popol Vuh, (the sacred book), as it is called, cannot be seen anymore . . . The original book, written long ago existed, but its sight is hidden from the searcher and the thinker . . .

Thus begins the Popol Vuh, the long lost 'sacred book', or 'bible', of the Quiche Maya of Guatemala which is without doubt the most revered and distinguished example of native American literature to have survived the centuries.

It is not known who wrote, or compiled, the original version which is referred to as 'lost'. An account of that original seems first to have been written in roman characters in the middle of the sixteenth century, shortly after the Spanish Conquest, by a Quiche Indian who had learned to read and write in roman characters.

The manuscript which contains an account of the cosmogony, mythology, traditions and history of the Quiche tribe of the Maya, was found in 1645 hidden in a church by Father Francisco Ximenex, a parish priest of the village of Santo Tomas Chichicastenango, in the mountains of Guatemala, (about 200 miles up river from the site of Palenque in today's modern Mexico), who transcribed the document from the Quiche tongue into Spanish.

In the introduction of the English translation, by Goetz and Morley, the authors state that 'it seems doubtful that the ancient Quiche book could have been a document of set form and permanent literary composition'. Father Ximenex says, 'the truth is such a book (from which the Quiche translation was made) never appeared or has been seen, and thus it is not known if this way of writing was by paintings, as those of Mexico, or by knotting strings, as the Peruvians did . . . or some other method'.

But, the Popol Vuh was the book of prophecies and the oracle of the kings and lords, it goes on to say . . . 'and the Kings knew if there would be war, and everything was clear before their eyes; they saw if there would be death and hunger, if there would be strife'. Hence, the Popol Vuh was the book of the past, the present, and the future.

Like the original Popol Vuh, the Lid of Palenque was hidden from the searcher, beneath the Temple of Inscriptions. Likewise it was hidden from the thinker, it required decoding before it could be understood. Similarly it contains prophecies that tell, for example, of the migration of the Mexicas (the story of Quilatzli—the Green Heron, for example) to the valley of Mexico, as well as the gods of war that the Aztec would adopt in due course. These depictions, prophecies and predictions were possible because those who 'wrote' the Lid of Palenque were 'gods'; the first of creation. This too is mentioned in the Popol Vuh, . . . 'they were endowed with intelligence; they saw, and could see instantly far, they succeeded in seeing, they succeeded in knowing all that there is in the World. When they looked, instantly they saw all around them and they contemplated in turn the arch of heaven and the round face of the Earth. The things hidden (in the distance) they saw all, without first having to move; at once they saw the World, and so too, from where they were they saw it. Great was their wisdom'.

The intellectual accomplishment of the Maya

Just how the Maya acquired their high degree of knowledge, or their highly developed spatial abilities is not yet known. That they did is exemplified by their achievements in astronomy, counting systems, architecture and carvings. More specifically, whether this superior knowledge was common to all Maya of the classic period or just one, or a few ruling elite priestly members, is not known. Many observers have suggested that evidence for a hierarchical structure in Maya society existed, and that it was indeed only a few priestly scholars who were involved with, or capable of involvement with, the esoteric teachings.

But again, just how they achieved the spatial abilities to encode the Lid of Palenque is not known. But we can see, using modern technology in the form of acetate overlays as a substitute for their spatial powers,

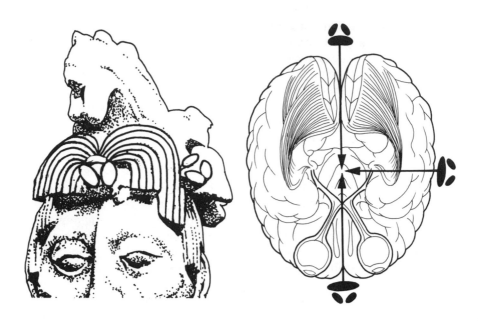

Figure A86   *Figure A87*

that they did. In the main body of the text we noted that the Maya subscribed to cranial deformation, or forehead flattening. Orthodox anthropology has suggested that this was a mere fashionable whim, but it may have enabled the brain to function much more effectively.

In the Appendix on solar radiation and hormones we noted that modulating magnetic fields do affect the endocrine system, and in so doing can affect the body's bio-rhythmic and fertility functioning.

Returning to the head of Lord Pacal found upon the floor of the Tomb at Palenque; we can observe some unusual 'objects' resembling three-petalled flowers, strategically placed upon the head. From the forehead 'flower' a fountain-like pattern of lines resembling magnetic lines of force, emerges to cover the forehead and temple lobe areas.

Examining all three 'flowers' together (on the three-dimensional head model) and assessing the common locus, we note that all three occupy the same axis and are positioned to impinge upon the central pineal/hypothalamus region of the brain, suggesting that these 'flower' shaped objects could be magnetic in nature. Could this have enabled the left and right hemispheres of the brain to function and communicate more effectively, thus increasing the operating efficiency of the brain, precluding the need for acetate overlays? Could this concentrated field accommodate the storage of information in one neuro-hemisphere, the storage of the mirror image in the other hemisphere, and the processing power to overlay the contents of one hemisphere upon the other, rather like a computer programme which stores data in separate memories for independent processing? And just how did the Maya move blocks of stone, some as heavy as 30 tons, without the use of beasts of burden, or the wheel?

To answer these questions we need to understand the nature of technological advancement, because, like footprints in the sand each new wave of technology 'erases itself'. Take the abacus counting machine as an example. The logarithmic table (use of exponents) 'erased' the abacus. The logarithmic table, in its turn was 'erased' by the slide-rule. The slide-rule was erased by the electronic calculator, and so on. Soon the telegraph (telephone) pole will be erased, completely, by the geostationary satellite, in space.

To future generations, following a catastrophe on the scale of the great flood, this might suggest that we, today, were a very 'low-tec' people 'who didn't even use the telephone'. But of course this is not true. And we must therefore look again at how the Maya 'appeared' to be. If they did not use the wheel it would seem more likely that they were far more advanced than modern humans, not less, and had no need for the wheel during their stage of development. It is as though, in our arrogance, we imagine the crew of a space ship resorting to bicycles (the wheel) to get from their spaceship to the surface of a planet.

It comes as no surprise, then, that modern archaeology, while concentrating on 99% of the Maya population, perceives a race of savages, whilst at the same time, an alternative view of a highly developed 1% exists to provide a completely different view upon closer examination. In other words, 'everybody is right'.

Whatever it is that we cannot understand about the Maya, and other Earth mysteries, rest assured that it is because we have not yet reached their stage of development.

Glossary

Acotzintli: (Aztec) Wild fruit eaten during the second age according to the *Vatico-Latin Codex*.

Ahau Can: (Mayan) Great Lordly serpent.

Apachiohualiztli: (Aztec) The Flood.

Aztec: Last ruling tribe of Mexico before the coming of the Spanish.

Baktun: (Mayan) Time period equal to 144,000 days.

Cabrillas: (Spanish) Literally 'little goats', name for the Pleiades star-cluster.

Camazotz: (Mayan) Bat who snatches off the head of Hunahpu in the *Popul Vuh*.

Canamayte: (hybrid) Square pattern on the back of *crotalus* rattlesnake.

Caracol: (Spanish) Literally 'snail', circular observatory at Chichen Itza.

Ceiba: (Mayan) Large tree symbolic of the Tree of Life and the Milky Way.

Chaac: (Mayan) Rain god.

Chac Chel: (Mayan) Ancient goddess of water.

Chacmool (or Chac-Mool): Mysterious type of statue found in Yucatan.

Chalchiuhtlicue: (Aztec) Goddess of water.

Chan Bahlum: (Mayan) Snake jaguar, son of Pacal of Palenque.

Chanes: (Mayan) Name for priests initiated into the serpent cult.

Chilam Balam: Mayan savant said to have predicted the coming of the Spanish.

Coatlicue: (Aztec) Earth goddess of hideous appearance.

Codex: (Latin) Manuscript, either bark book or early Spanish parchment.

Cortesianus: Part of the *Madrid Codex*.

Coyolxauhqui: Aztec goddess who may represent the Milky Way.

Crotalus durissus durissus: Type of rattlesnake endemic to Mayan lands.

Cu: Figure of a god or shrine, possibly the same as Chacmool.

Ehecatl: (Aztec) God of wind, aspect of Quetzalcoatl, the second age in the *Vatico-Latin Codex*.

Gavilla: (Spanish) 'Sheaf', group of 52 years, making an Aztec 'century'.

Hunaphu: (Mayan) One of the hero twins in the *Popul Vuh*.

Itzamna (Zamna): Head of the Mayan pantheon, bringer of civilization.

Itzas: (Mayan) Warlike late-comers to Chichen Itza.

Katun: (Mayan) Period of time equal to 7,200 days.

Kin: (Mayan) Day.

Kukulcan (Cuculcan): (Mayan) 'Feathered serpent', equivalent of Quetzalcoatl.

Matlactili: (Aztec) First sun (age) according to the *Vatico-Latin Codex*.

Mixtecs: One tribe inhabiting the Oaxaca Valley.

Nachan-Can: (Mayan) Believed by many to be the original name of Palenque.

Nahui Atl: (Aztec) *Chimalpopoca Codex* fourth age.

Nahui Ehecatl: (Aztec) *Chimalpopoca Codex* second age.

Nahui Ocelotl: (Aztec) *Chimalpopoca Codex* first age.

Nahui Ollin: (Aztec) *Chimalpopoca Codex* fifth age.

Nahui Quihahuitl: (Aztec) *Chimalpopoca Codex* third age.

Nanahuatzin: (Aztec) Aged god who sacrificed himself to become the present sun.

Olmecs: (Aztec) Literally 'Rubber People', proto-Mayans of the Gulf of Mexico.

Pacal: 'Hand-shield', Palenque lord buried under the Pyramid of Inscriptions.

Polcan: (Mayan) 'Snake-head'.

Popol Vuh: Quiché Mayan Creation epic.

Quetzalcoatl: (Aztec) 'Feathered serpent', initiator of civilization, a title.

Quiché: Linguistic and highland tribal branch of the Mayan people.

Tecuciztecatl: (Aztec) Arrogant god who became the moon.

Tenoch: Aztec king who led his people from the north to Lake Texcoco.

Teotihuacan: Fabled city of pyramids 40 kilometres north of Mexico City.

Tezcatlipoca: (Aztec) 'Smoking mirror', militaristic rival of Quetzalcoatl.

Tlaloc: (Aztec) Rain god, equivalent of Mayan Chaac.

Tleyquiyahuillo: (Aztec) Third age according to the *Vatico-Latin Codex*.

Toltec: Warlike people ruling much of Mexico before the Aztecs.

Tonalamatl: (Aztec) Period of 260 days, equivalent of the Mayan *tzolkin*.

Tonatiuh: (Aztec) Sun god.

Troano: Part of the *Madrid Codex*.

Tun: (Mayan) Period of 360 days.

Tzabcan: (Mayan) 'Rattlesnake'.

Tzincoacoc: (Aztec) Type of fruit eaten during the third age.

Tzolkin: (Mayan) Period of 260 days, equivalent to the Aztec *tonalamatl*.

Tzonchichiltic: (Aztec) 'Red Hair', name of the third age in the *Vatico-Latin Codex*.

Tzontlilac: (Aztec) 'Black Hair', name of the fourth age in the *Vatico-Latin Codex*.

Uinal: (Mayan) Period of 20 days.

Votan: Fabled bringer of civilization; may have been Carthaginian.

Xbalanque: (Mayan) One of the hero twins in the *Popul Vuh*.

Xiuhmolpilli: (Aztec) Fire festival at end of 52-year period.

Zamna (Zamana): Head of the Mayan pantheon, bringer of civilization.

Zapotecs: Oaxaca tribe who took over Monte Alban from the Olmecs.

Bibliography

Adamson D, *The Ruins of Time*, BCA (G Allen & Unwin), 1975

Annequin G, Baudry J, de Gans R, Verbeek Y, *Discovering of Famous Archaeological Sites*, Ferni, 1978

Baudez C, Picasso S, *Lost Cities of the Maya*, Thames & Hudson, 1992

Benson-Gyles A, Sayer C, *Of Gods & Men*, BBC TV, 1980

Bernal Dr I, *Official Guide, Oaxaca Valley*, Inah-Salvat, 1985

Bolio J D, *The Rattlesnake School*, Maya Area,

Bolio J D, *Why the Rattlesnake in Mayan Civilization*, Maya Area, 1988

Bolio J D, *The Geometry of the Maya*, Maya Area, 1987

Cayce E E, *Edgar Cayce on Atlantis*, Warner, 1968

Childress D H, *Lost Cities of North & Central America*, Adventures Unlimited, 1992

Calleja R, Signoret H S, Ahumada A T, *Official Guide, Palenque*, Inah-Salvat, 1990

Clark B F C, *The Genetic Code*, Edward Arnold, 1977

Coe M D, *The Maya*, Thames & Hudson, 1994

Coe M D, *Breaking the Maya Code*, Penguin Books, 1994

Cotterell M M, *Astrogenetics*, Brooks Hill Robinson & Co, 1988

Cotterell M M, *The Amazing Lid of Palenque*, Vol 1, Brooks Hill Perry & Co, 1994

Cotterell M M, *The Amazing Lid of Palenque*, Vol 2, Brooks Hill Perry & Co, 1994

Cotterell M M, *The Mosaic Mask of Palenque*, Brooks Hill Perry & Co, 1995

Cotterell M M, *The Mural of Bonampak*, Brooks Hill Perry & Co, 1995

Darlington C D, *Genetics and Man*, Allen & Unwin, 1966

Donnelly I, *Atlantis the Ante-Diluvian World*, Sidgwick & Jackson, 1950

Evans J, *Mind, Body & Electromagnetism*, Element, 1986

Eysenck H J, Nias D K, *Astrology, Science or Superstition*,

Fell B, *America B.C.*, Pocket Books, 1976

Fernandez A, *Pre-Hispanic Gods of Mexico*, Panorama, 1987

Fullard H (Ed), *Universal Atlas*, Philips, 1976

Gates W, *An Outline Dictionary of Maya Glyphs*, Dover, 1978

Gendrop P, *A Guide to Architecture in Ancient Mexico*, Editorial Minutiae Mexicana, 1991

Hadingham E, *Early Man and the Cosmos*, Wm Heinemann, 1983
Harrison B, *Mysterious Regions*, Aldus Books, 1979
Hapgood C, *Earth's Shifting Crust*, Philadelphia/Chilton, 1958
Heyerdahl T, *The Ra Expeditions*, George Allen & Unwin, 1971
Hitching F, *The World Atlas of Mysteries*, Wm Collins & Son, 1978
Ivanoff P, *Monuments of Civilisation Maya*, Cassell, 1978
Kemp R, *Cell Division & Heredity*, Edward Arnold, 1970
Lamb HH, *Climate, Past Present and Future*, Methuen & Co, 1977
Lancaster Brown P, *Astronomy in Colour*, Cox & Wyman Ltd, 1979
Landa D de, *Rélacion de las cosas de Yucatan*, trans. W Gates, Dover, 1978
Lawrence C, *Cellular Radiobiology*, Edward Arnold, 1971
Mayo J, *Astrology*, Penguin, 1995
McElhinny M W, *Palaeomagnetism and Plate Tectonics*, Cambridge, 1973
Mitton S (Ed), *Cambridge Encyclopaedia of Astronomy*, Jonathan Cape, 1977
Moore P, Hunt G, Nicolson I, Cattermole P, *The Atlas of the Solar System*, Mitchell Beazley, 1984
Moore P, *The Guinness Book of Astronomy*, Guinness, 1979
Morley S G, *An Introduction to Maya Hieroglyphs*, Dover Press, 1975
Muck O, *The Secret of Atlantis*, Collins, 1976
Munoz J, *The Valley of Oaxaca*, Salvat, 1992
Nicolson I, *Gravity, Black Holes and the Universe*, David & Charles, 1980
Nicolson I, *The Sun*, Mitchell Beazley International, 1981
Pearson R, *Climate and Evolution*, Academic Press, 1978
Plato, *The Timaeus*, Penguin Books, 1965
Price R H, Glickstein M, Bailey R H, *Principles of Psychology*, CBS College, 1982
Repetto Tio B, Cardenas R M, Suaste B Q, Negron T G, *Official Guide North of Yucatan*, Inah-Salvat, 1988
Rubio A B, *Official Guide, Uxmal*, Inah-Salvat, 1985
Santillana G de, Dechend H von, *Hamlet's Mill*, Gambit, 1969
Sten M, *Codices of Mexico*, Panorama, 1987
Stephens J L, *Incidents of Travel in Yucatan* (2 Vols.), Dover, 1963
Taube K, *Aztec & Maya Myths*, British Museum Press, 1993
Tedlock D (trans.), *Popol Vuh*, Touchstone, 1985
Tomkins P, *Mysteries of the Mexican Pyramids*, Harper & Row, 1976
Velikovsky I, *Earth in Upheaval*, NY Pocket Books, 1977
Velikovsky I, *Worlds in Collision*, BCA, 1973
Ward R, *The Living Clocks*, Collins, 1972
Westwood J (Ed), *The Atlas of Mysterious Places*, BCA, 1987
White J, *Pole Shift*, ARE Press, 1993
Wilson C (Ed), *The Book of Time*, Westbridge Books, 1980

INDEX

INDEX